Concise Medical Textbooks
Sociology as Applied to Medicine

Concise Medical Textbooks

Sociology as Applied to Medicine

The Sociology Teachers Group from London Medical Schools

edited by
Donald L. Patrick, PhD, MSPH
Senior Lecturer, St Thomas's Hospital Medical School
and
Graham Scambler, BSc, PhD
Lecturer, Middlesex Hospital Medical School

with a foreword by
Professor Margot Jefferys, BScEcon
Bedford College, London

Baillière Tindall

London Philadelphia Toronto
Mexico City Rio de Janeiro Sydney Tokyo Hong Kong

Baillière Tindall   24–28 Oval Road
W. B. Saunders   London NW1 7DX

The Curtis Centre
Independence Square West
Philadelphia, PA 19106–3399, USA

1 Goldthorne Avenue
Toronto, Ontario M8Z 5T9, Canada

Harcourt Brace Jovanovich Group (Australia)
Pty Limited, 32–52 Smidmore Street
Marrickville, NSW 2204, Australia

Harcourt Brace Jovanovich (Japan) Inc.
Ichibancho Central Building, 22–1 Ichibancho
Chiyoda-ku, Tokyo 102, Japan

First published 1982
Second edition 1986
Reprinted 1987 and 1988

Typeset by Scribe Design, Gillingham, Kent
Printed and bound in Great Britain by The Alden Press, Oxford

British Library Cataloguing in Publication Data

Sociology as applied to medicine—2nd ed.
    —(Concise medical textbooks)
    1. Social medicine
    I. Patrick, Donald L.   II. Scrambler,
    Graham
    306′.46   RA418

ISBN 0-7020-1164-9

Contributors

Sociology Teachers Group from London Medical Schools

David Blane, MB, BS, MSc
Lecturer, Charing Cross Hospital Medical School

Ray M. Fitzpatrick, BA, MSc
Lecturer, Bedford College and Middlesex Hospital Medical School

Sheila M. Hillier, BSc, MSc
Lecturer, St Bartholomew's and London Hospital Medical Schools

David Locker, BDS, PhD
Visiting Assistant Professor, Faculty of Health Sciences, University of Ottawa; formerly Lecturer, St Thomas's Hospital Medical School

Myfanwy Morgan, BA, MA
Lecturer, St Thomas's Hospital Medical School

Donald L. Patrick, PhD, MSPH
Associate Professor, School of Medicine, University of North Carolina; formerly Senior Lecturer, St Thomas's Hospital Medical School

Graham Scambler, BSc, PhD
Lecturer, Middlesex Hospital Medical School

Ellie Scrivens, BA, PhD
Honorary Lecturer and Research Fellow, University of Bath; formerly Lecturer, St Thomas's Hospital Medical School

Contents

Part IV Deviance and social control 173

Part V Organization of health services 193

Part VI Measurement and evaluation in health 223

Foreword

Students of medicine and of other related disciplines may be forgiven for feeling that their schools and colleges insist that they learn more and more about an increasing number of aspects of the human condition in health and illness. There was a halcyon time, not so long ago, when the pre-clinical curriculum consisted of one course in human anatomy and another in physiology; the clinical phase involved merely learning the skills needed to recognize the signs and symptoms of a wide but ultimately limited range of diseases. Moreover, there was little institutional pressure on students to study since they were free to repeat examinations until they passed them.

The picture is very different today. Knowledge of the molecular structure of living beings and the factors which determine natural and pathological growth and decay has expanded exponentially in the last fifty years and continues to do so. Students are expected to know a good deal about the theories and research methods of the scientific disciplines, the 'ologies', which have led to this increased knowledge, as well as about the implications of their findings for medical practice. More and more disciplines claiming relevance to medical knowledge and practice jostle each other for a place in the pre-clinical curriculum; new clinical specialties want medical students to be exposed at some time during their clinical studies to what they have to offer. All make claims to the indispensable nature of their own contribution to the curriculum. Meanwhile, medical students are no longer free to work at their own pace. Examinations weed out those who cannot satisfy their teachers after a maximum of two failures. The pressures are those of the institution. Students of other health professions, such as nursing, dentistry, pharmacy and optometry, are exposed to broadly comparable pressures in the process of qualifying as practitioners.

Sociology is one of the disciplines which has recently claimed the attention of the medical and other related health professions and their students. Its formal introduction into the curriculum as a basic medical science, which by the 1980s had taken place in most of the medical schools of the United Kingdom, was a radical innovation. Compared with most of the other new subjects it involves a break away from the traditional preparation for medicine based exclusively on the detailed study of parts of the biological organism which we call the human body. Its focus is not on the human individual *per se*: it is on the two-way relationships between the individual and society. Sociology as applied to medicine is concerned specifically with those aspects of the relationship which influence the experiences of health and illness in individuals and the response to them of others — relatives, doctors, nurses, administrators and governments.

Not surprisingly, not all those already involved in medical education welcomed the advent of sociological teaching. Some of the staff involved in teaching the traditional laboratory-based or clinical subjects saw in it an intrusion of a largely unknown and untested quantity competing for the students' limited span of attention time. They were unfamiliar with its methods or potential and sceptical about its contribution to the making of a good practitioner. Some students, expecting the medical curriculum to resemble in essence the pre-medical natural science courses they had taken prior to entry, also needed to be persuaded that sociology was relevant to their preparation as future doctors, especially when they felt themselves to be under pressure to absorb all that the teachers of subjects which were more thoroughly examined put before them.

Such early doubts have not entirely disappeared, but they have substantially diminished. Indeed, the General Medical Council's recommendations for medical education in the 1980s are even more insistent than earlier recommendations on the necessity for broadening the students' basic understanding of the social context of health and illness and of the social determinants of medical practice and health service provision. This then is the major task and challenge for those responsible for the teaching of sociology as applied to medicine, and the contributors to this book are to be congratulated for providing a concise introduction to the subject.

In this book, which will form an admirable basic text upon

which teachers and students can build, the contributors have shown how some of the theories, concepts and methods developed by sociologists can illuminate aspects of human experience in health and illness. They look at how such socially determined factors as marital status, social class and family composition influence the pattern of morbidity and mortality. They show that medical perceptions of what constitutes mental or physical illness are not necessarily shared by the populations served and that the absence of shared perceptions may frustrate much medical effort. They look at the variety of ways in which old age, death and ethnicity are regarded and treated and the dilemmas which such variety can pose for practitioners. They explore the social origins of contemporary systems of health care in order to obtain greater understanding of their present problems. They examine too the various interpretations which can be placed upon the collective and individual behaviour of members of the medical profession, and on the expansion of medical concern and metaphors into many aspects of social life. This list does not exhaust their concerns and there are many other developments in the sociology of health and illness which cannot be covered in a volume of this size.

It seems to me impossible to argue that acquaintance with such findings and with the methods and conceptual frames of the discipline on which they are based is not an essential ingredient in the preparation of the doctor for medical practice whether it be in general practice, an age-band or body system specialty, or community medicine. He or she needs it at the very least for protection against the very real hazard of frustration and unhappiness when it proves difficult to implement medical measures: but above all it is needed if the medical and other health-related professions are to make their greatest potential contribution to the welfare of the populations they are privileged to serve.

August 1981   MARGOT JEFFERYS

Preface

This book arose from lengthy discussions among teachers of sociology as applied to medicine in five London medical schools about the needs of students in the health professions for a concise guide to the major topics and issues in the sociology of health and illness. More and more medical, nursing, social work and other students of health are taking courses in sociology or behavioural sciences which vary widely in length and content. In many of these courses students find it necessary to grasp sociological concepts and research findings quickly while taking many other courses in a busy curriculum. Some courses cover a few areas; others are more comprehensive.

The Sociology Teachers Group decided to write a concise introduction to a large number of topics from which teachers and students could choose according to interests and time. A larger number of topics were proposed than could be included in a text of this length. The topics finally selected are the main ones taught by members of the group and are thought to be the most important for health students. They are grouped into six sections which represent major subdivisions in the field. Each chapter covers the main concepts, issues and research studies for one topic, although some material is treated in several chapters from different points of view. Tables are as important as text, since the limits of space required economic presentation of material.

The chapters do not stand alone. Although many of the major issues are covered, it was impossible in some cases to present all the competing evidence and points of view. Where considerable controversy exists, however, alternative theories or explanations are presented, even though they are not always resolved for the student. The chapters should be viewed primarily as guides for students to think through the issues for themselves. By offering an accessible summary of basic themes it is hoped that teachers will be able to use the limited time available to them to fill in the gaps and explore problems in more depth than is usually possible. For students who wish to do further study, there is a list of recommended reading which, in the group's view, should be made generally available to health students.

This volume has been a collective effort. The Teachers Group initially discussed the topics to be covered, the desirable content and the problems of presenting material concisely for each topic. Members volunteered to draft particular chapters and submitted them to the group for revision. After a complete draft was prepared, the Group selected two editors who revised each chapter and returned it to the principal author for completion. The Group met regularly during the course of preparing the book to discuss problems and progress.

This collective procedure had both strengths and weaknesses. On the one hand, the special expertise of individual authors in a particular area was beneficial in selecting and preparing material. On the other, all eight authors brought different philosophical and theoretical perspectives to the selection and presentation of ideas and research studies. Consequently, it was difficult to achieve a uniformity of style and treatment. The editors have attempted to strike a balance between the wishes of individual authors and the need for consistency and integration.

The Teachers Group would like to thank Professor Margot Jefferys for her encouragement and very helpful comments on each chapter and the colleagues and students who gave us the challenge and will judge the reward.

October 1981   SOCIOLOGY TEACHERS GROUP from
LONDON MEDICAL SCHOOLS

Part I
Health and Illness as Social Concepts

Social Concepts of Disease and Illness

Ray M. Fitzpatrick

Perhaps no other topic is discussed more often in everyday conversation than that of health and illness. This is hardly surprising, since so much of people's lives depends on their state of physical, mental and social well-being. In their discussions people use terms such as 'health' and 'illness' to describe and analyse their own and other people's conditions without reflecting on their meaning. Yet if any of us were pressed to give an exact definition of what we meant by such terms, some of the complexities and ambiguities that lie behind their familiar usage would become apparent. One might resort to synonyms and suggest that 'illness' is an absence of 'health' and *vice versa*. One might try to clarify matters by concrete examples: 'illness' is having a cold, pains in the joint, angina or symptoms like that. More ambitiously, one could attempt to summarize what such examples have in common and argue that illness is any departure from normal physical or mental feelings.

All these suggestions give some indication of the sense of such terms, but it is apparent that none offers a precise definition. One American study explored some of these issues of definition by presenting some examples of individuals with various health problems and asking a sample of people whether or not they thought these individuals were ill and, if so, what the illnesses were (Apple 1960). The author found that two factors seemed most likely to lead to judgements of illness: whether the symptoms were of recent onset and whether they interfered with the performance of normal activities. Other social analysts have also suggested that changes in feeling state, whether from pain or from weakness, were salient features of ideas people have about illness. It can be seen from this brief discussion that the meaning of illness is not clear-cut because of the immense diversity of meanings and actions that occur in response to similar experiences of symptoms.

Social determination of the meaning of illness and disease

One of the major propositions in medical sociology is that people's definitions and values concerning health and illness are socially determined; that is, that they arise from experience of membership in different groups. To take some examples that are discussed in more detail in later chapters, age, sex, family circumstances, ethnic background and social class all influence attitudes, values and beliefs about illness. For example, older people are less likely than younger people to report acute episodes of illness and are more likely to assess their health as good in comparison to others of their own age. Such views and behaviour reflect socially acquired beliefs about what is to be expected of old age, so that symptoms which would be seen as distressing or unusual in young people are regarded as normal. Similarly, working-class patients make less use than middle-class patients of preventive medical services, such as well-baby clinics or screening for cervical cancer, and this can be partly explained in terms of attitudes and values with regard to what the individual can do about his or her own health. Ethnic minorities may draw on beliefs from their own culture which attach quite different significance to particular signs and symptoms from those of the majority. These examples illustrate the principle that every individual draws on those meanings that are socially available to him to interpret his experience of illness. Thus, whilst an important implication of illness appears to be departure from 'normal', 'standard' or 'average', the meaning of normality with regard to bodily experience varies immensely between individuals and between social groups.

At this point one might conclude that laymen are unavoidably uncertain about matters of *illness* because they do not have enough knowledge of *disease*. Illness refers to the subjective interpretation of problems which are perceived to be health-related. Disease, on the other hand, conventionally refers to a medical conception of pathological abnormality diagnosed by means of signs and symptoms. It is sometimes assumed that disease, unlike illness, is founded on immutable fact. The concept of disease, however, is also socially determined; the remainder of this section is devoted to illustrating this.

Consider the question, how much disease is there in the country? In seeking to answer this question use might be made of an authoritative list of medically recognized diseases, such as the International Classification of Diseases (ICD). General practitioners might be asked to record all the consultations in their surgeries in terms of this system of classification. In fact, this 'simple' procedure is close to that system currently used by representatives from the Royal College of General Practitioners to collect statistics for the Office of Population Censuses and Surveys on sickness reported to general practices in England and Wales. The ICD attempts to be comprehensive and diseases are divided into 17 chapter headings according to the different body systems, as shown in Table 1. Each chapter heading is divided into subheadings for specific conditions.

It is apparent that a number of different kinds of disease are included in the classification. One group of diseases is composed of different instances of organic pathological processes related to localized sites of the body, of which examples are 'malignant neoplasm of the larynx' and 'acute renal failure'. A second group is formed by diseases identified by signs and symptoms which are linked to a particular identifiable cause, as with 'viral hepatitis' and 'asbestosis'. The third kind of disease is mainly identified either by a single symptom, for example 'excessive vomiting in pregnancy', or by a syndrome of symptoms, for example 'migraine'. As this and other classifications reflect, the basic disease entities of medicine are quite heterogeneous in form and knowledge about them varies in character.

One problem, returning to the question posed above, is simply that an accurate picture of disease could not be drawn using data derived from general practitioner consultations. This is because doctors only see the tip of an 'iceberg' of disease: so many health problems are simply not taken to the doctor (see Chapter 4). This problem could in principle be dealt with by a survey of the total population (see Chapter 19). Some further problems of defining illness and disease can be more fully illustrated using specific examples.

Tension headache

In the ICD the chapter 'mental disorders' includes, under 'physiological malfunction arising from mental disorder', 'tension headache', which is in fact one of the most commonly

Table 1.   *International classification of diseases*

Categories of disease	Examples
1. Infections and parasitic diseases	Malaria, viral hepatitis
2. Neoplasms	Malignant neoplasm of larynx, Hodgkin's disease
3. Endocrine, nutritional and metabolic diseases and immunity disorders	Diabetes mellitus, gout
4. Diseases of blood and blood-forming organs	Iron-deficiency anaemia, diseases of white blood cells
5. Mental disorders	Alcohol-dependence syndrome, physiological malfunction arising from mental disorders
6. Diseases of the nervous system and sense organs	Epilepsy, migraine
7. Diseases of the circulatory system	Essential hypertension, acute myocardial infarction
8. Diseases of the respiratory system	Acute sinusitis, asbestosis
9. Diseases of the digestive system	Acute appendicitis, gastritis
10. Diseases of the genitourinary system	Acute renal failure, infertility (female)
11. Complications of pregnancy, childbirth and the puerperium	Excessive vomiting in pregnancy, postpartum haemorrhage
12. Diseases of the skin and subcutaneous tissue	Contact dermatitis, psoriasis
13. Diseases of the musculoskeletal system and connective tissue	Rheumatoid arthritis, flat foot
14. Congenital anomalies	Spina bifida, cleft palate
15. Certain conditions originating in the perinatal period	Slow fetal growth, birth trauma

Table 1. International classification of diseases (continued)

Categories of disease	Examples
16. Symptoms, signs and ill-defined conditions	Symptoms involving hand and neck, sudden death cause unknown
17. Injury and poisoning	Fracture of carpal bone, poisoning by psychotropic drugs

Source: *International Classification of Diseases. Manual of the International Statistical Classification of Diseases, Injuries, and Causes of Death* (1977) Ninth revision. Geneva: WHO.

presented symptoms in general practice. In hospital medicine, tension headache is rarely seen except as a result of referrals from general practitioners when the specialist may be asked to exclude the possibility of more serious organic pathology. Tension headache appears to carry no life-threatening implications and to lead to no structural deterioration in the body. Consequently it does not fall within the working definition of disease of some hospital doctors. In general practice, tension headache may be presented as a health problem or as a symptom of other problems in life. Diagnosis and treatment in general practice cannot be bound by academic distinctions between organic disease and social problems: it has to deal with whole persons rather than cases of discrete disease. This is well conveyed in a comment by Menninger in talking about changing concepts of disease: 'What is the diagnosis in a patient who has coronary symptoms whenever he takes his wife to a party, or in a woman who has migraines on the weekends that her son is home from college? What kind of arthritis is it that becomes activated with each quarterly meeting of the board of directors?' (Menninger 1948).

Essential hypertension

Another item in the ICD raises difficulties of a different kind with the concept of disease. Under diseases of the 'circulatory system' is included 'essential hypertension'; that is, high blood pressure not due to any specific organic disorder. Many of the patients recorded as hypertensive are asymptomatic; that is, they do not experience anything that makes them aware of their raised blood pressure and they are therefore, in this particular sense of the word, not 'ill'. High blood pressure has become a concern of medicine partly because of evidence that it is a risk factor in coronary heart disease. Thus, those who believe that medicine should be more concerned than it is at present with prevention advocate screening people who are particularly at risk of developing heart disease. Many cases of symptomless hypertension are thus identified not as a result of the patients presenting with a complaint, but because their high blood pressure is detected by routine screening, which is being increasingly carried out by general practitioners on patients in particular age groups. Thus, part of the concept of disease in examples like essential hypertension is the idea of 'risk' or 'statistical disadvantage'.

There are other difficulties with conditions such as hypertension. Many people argue that cases of essential hypertension do not consistute a distinct group but are one end of a single continuous distribution of blood pressure levels. Thus, although there is evidence to suggest that risks of cardiovascular disease are greater for those with high blood pressure, the level at which this risk becomes significant is not clear; nor is the degree of increase in risk for any given increase in blood pressure level well defined. Therefore definitions of normal and abnormal blood pressure are in some senses arbitrary. Some would wish to define hypertension as commencing at a level at which the majority of the adult population would be included, thus making disease the 'normal' state of affairs.

A second problem is that of actually measuring blood pressure to identify 'disease', since readings are known to vary from one occasion to the next and to be influenced by factors such as the anxiety of being in a doctor's surgery.

A third problem that is only beginning to be recognized is that identifying and treating patients as hypertensive can itself be responsible for creating more 'disease' (i.e. iatrogenic disease). For example, the side-effects of drugs that are used to reduce blood pressure in the elderly, such as methyldopa and frusemide, may present more problems than leaving the hypertension untreated. Not uncommon, therefore, are cases where the elderly patient has no 'illness' in the sense of bodily or mental discomfort until hypertension is identified and treated, after which he experiences disturbing symptoms such as fainting (Jackson et al. 1976). In addition, there is evidence that absentee rates are nearly doubled among workers who have been informed that they have raised blood pressure, suggesting that anxiety and worry are having a serious impact on their lives (Haynes et al. 1978). Thus the level at which blood pressure is to be defined as disease involves conflicting considerations.

Alcoholism

Alcoholism is a good example of a problem which has been dramatically re-defined. The majority of people today, if asked whether it is a disease, reply that it is. In the Victorian era it was regarded as a moral weakness. It is now medically classified as a disease, specific medical treatments are available and there are a number of competing physiological and sociopsychological theories of addiction to alcohol. If alcoholism is to be regarded as a disease, it needs to be distinguished from less damaging forms of drinking. This creates difficulties. Is its differential diagnosis to be based on the amount of alcohol an individual drinks? Probably most people would argue that essential to a definition is a more important consideration, namely whether drinking causes difficulties for the individual at home or work. Also important are judgements as to whether heavy drinking is 'out of control'. However, if one accepts such arguments, social criteria are being brought into the definition of disease, which considerably extend the term beyond its orthodox medical usage. However, two studies by Robinson (1976) and Strong (1980) of the views of doctors suggest that what troubles them most is whether they can help the alcoholic. Although few doctors seem to blame the alcoholic in a moral sense, they nevertheless feel irritated about their involvement in a problem where patients often deny their illness and are poorly motivated to cooperate in treatment. Doctors feel there are few effective medical remedies available for what they see as a complex social problem.

It is also apparent that in practice doctors generally become involved in cases where the alocholic has created unbearable strains in the family or has developed other, better understood, medical problems such as cirrhosis. Medical involvement, in other words, tends to come at a later stage than for other diseases. Attitudes towards alcoholism of groups such as Alcoholics Anonymous have led to the increasingly widespread perception of alcoholism as a disease. It may be difficult, however, to put the disease concept into operation at a practical level. One writer summarizes the situation as follows: 'The promulgation of disease concepts of alcoholism have been brought about essentially as a means of getting a better deal for the "alcoholic" rather than as a logical consequence of scholarly work and scientific discoveries' (Room 1972).

There are several general points to draw from these examples. First, disease can be seen as a matter of perspective and, moreover, of a socially determined perspective. This may be difficult to grasp if one is used to thinking about disease as 'entities in the body'. In fact the meaning and significance of bodily pathology vary according to one's perspective. Consider again the example of how the different work experiences of the general practitioner, and hospital doctor can lead to different perspectives on the significance of 'headache'. In the example of hypertension the preventive perspective leads to a wholly different conception of disease from that held by many laymen and, indeed, by many doctors. In prevention, the problem becomes the set of conditions prior to organic pathology and not the pathological 'end product' itself.

The second important point to recognize is that perspectives in health care change and that these changes are not so much a function of 'progress' as a reflection of complex social changes. For example, it is possible to detect in medicine a greater concern and interest in the appropriate management of minor illnesses, such as tension headache, than was the case 20 years ago. This may reflect changes in the kinds of problems presented to health services. It may also be partly due to developments such as the establishment of a Royal College of General Practitioners in 1952. This body has attempted to promote ideas and forms of practice more appropriate to the health problems encountered in primary medical care. Another example of such change would be the impact Alcoholics Anonymous has had in changing beliefs about the nature and meaning of heavy drinking. Thus, perceptions of disease and illness are socially influenced over time and reflect the changing values of different groups in society.

Illness beliefs in other cultures

By looking at societies very different from our own we can see more clearly that modern western beliefs about disease constitute but one of a variety of different systems that man has produced to make sense of sufferings, and many alternative systems survive today relatively uninfluenced by western technological medicine. Ayurvedic medicine, for example, is a folk system which has thrived in India since circa A.D. 400. It is based on theories regarding the importance of balance between 'humours' (*dosha*) for good health; imbalances are treated by a wide range of foods and herbs. Many Latin–American peasant communities retain beliefs that derive, through the Spanish Conquistadores, from Arabic and Greek medicine and in which theories of natural balance between metaphorically hot and cold substances explain illness and provide the principles for treatment.

The study of such systems not only draws attention to the immense variety of ways in which disease may be defined, but may also bring more clearly into focus the wider functions that medicine fulfils beyond providing explanations for the immediate causes of disease.

Anthropologists often describe non-western systems as 'personalistic', since non-western explanations of the causes of illness commonly focus on the strains and tensions in relations in the community, such as jealousies, rivalry and so on. A second common feature of particular interest to anthropologists is a concern in non-western medicines to explain the misfortune of illness rather than to uncover its physical cause. It is apparent that many non-western health care systems function mainly to make the sufferer's misfortune understandable and acceptable by dealing with the question 'Why am *I* ill *now*?' rather than, as in western systems, by explaining the impersonal mechanisms of illness. Often, however, both explanations may occur together, so that when someone falls ill, for example, the illness may be attributed initially to a germ or virus, but ultimately to bad relations with a neighbour.

One well known study by Evans-Pritchard (1937) is of an African community, the Azande, whose beliefs about illness combine both characteristic features of non-western medicine; that is, they are personalistic and offer a philosophy of misfortune (Evans-Pritchard 1937). When a Zande becomes ill or has an accident he may ascribe his misfortune to witchcraft. If he suspects witchcraft, he will consult an oracle which he invokes by means of an appropriate ritual and which will indicate whether his suspicion is correct or not. If he is told that it is correct, the appropriate treatment may be seen as asking or compelling the witch to withdraw his evil magic. These sound strange ways of explaining illness, but the fact is that for the Azande they work. When the oracle does not provide an appropriate answer, it is the particular oracle or ritual employed on that occasion which is thought to be at fault, not the whole system of beliefs about witchcraft. Since accusations of witchcraft are made only against neighbours and peers, there is little likelihood of absurd or 'unreasonable' results being obtained from the oracles. Thus the logic of the system is maintained and in any specific episode always 'makes sense'.

Social anthropologists point out that our system of beliefs in western medical science has many similarities. We maintain beliefs in drugs, 'wonder cures' and the progress of science even if a particular prescription or visit to a doctor seems ineffective for a particular illness. The wider set of cultural beliefs is not upset by occasional 'failures'. It has also been argued that cultures like the Azande may actually be more effective in some respects than our own, because they offer a meaning for misfortune. Western society, with its emphasis on science and technological intervention, often fails to address itself to the more personal dimensions of suffering. For example, when parents discover that they have a child who is handicapped, they may be concerned that they are in some way responsible, a level of causality that may never be dealt with in their exchanges with doctors and other helping agents.

Illness beliefs in historical contexts

Historical changes in medicine also unsettle assumptions about the nature of disease and illness. Beliefs and values have undergone radical transformations over time.

Medicine in eighteenth-century Europe was based on a large number of rival systems or schools of thought about disease. Schools had their roots in Greek humoral pathology, but each one offered a different theoretical explanation for disease. The task of medicine was not to identify localized lesions but to explain illness in terms that embraced the total mental and physical disposition of the patient. The doctor had to explain how his general theory of illness was relevant to each particular patient's problem by taking account of how the specific temperament, social background and psychological characteristics of the patient shaped and modified the general illness process. Doctors did not belong to a single profession but were rivals competing for employment, which usually took the form of service to powerful, aristocratic patrons. There was no medical scientific *élite* in a position to develop a body of knowledge available to the whole profession. Success in medicine could be achieved only by a combination of elegant social manners, a familiarity with classical texts and an ability to relate general principles from this reading to the unique circumstances and complaints of each patient. Treatment had to be blood-curdling to convince the patient of the efforts that the doctor was making. This medical system may be described as 'person-orientated' because the doctors were very much bound to make their diagnosis fit the emotional and theoretical perspective of powerful clients (Jewson 1976).

Since the last half of the eighteenth century, however, hospitals have grown in number and importance and a new approach to disease has developed. During the nineteenth century medicine increasingly focussed on specific anatomical lesions that could be correlated with felt symptoms of illness. The feelings and sensations of the patient, which had been central to interpretation in 'person-orientated' medicine, were now secondary to the signs of internal pathology. It was social change that made this new 'hospital medicine' possible. The poor used the eighteenth-century hospitals and were treated mainly out of charitable funds. This placed them in a subordinate position and the hospital doctor had for the first time in history large numbers of passive, compliant patients. In these circumstances doctors were able to develop anatomical knowledge, which hitherto had not been possible.

A third era of medicine, sometimes termed 'laboratory medicine', appeared at the beginning of the twentieth century. The natural sciences became more central to developments in medical knowledge, particularly with regard to cellular processes, and physicians made much greater use of laboratory tests in diagnosis. Laboratory medicine further reinforced the autonomy and power of the medical profession. One result was that an alternative career structure to clinical practice became available in scientific research.

Thus each successive set of medical ideas was influenced by the kind of society in which it functioned. This is no less true of the present time, in which respect, sometimes amounting to awe, towards science and technology is a basic value in society. Medicine is frequently criticized for the degree to which it reflects this reverence toward science, particularly when over-dependence on technology in health care results in the basic concerns of the patient being lost from sight. Historical and cross-cultural studies are a reminder that meeting patients' fundamental concerns with regard to illness is a universal function of medical systems, regardless of their level of technical sophistication.

It may be that ideas about disease are beginning to change again (see Chapters 2 and 3). Many of the major chronic and degenerative health problems such as heart disease and cancer are now best understood as the results of multiple long-term pathogenic influences on the individual. Disease is thus seen as the end state of a combination of environmental and behavioural factors, interacting with genetic predispositions, which place the individual, statistically, at greater risk, whether through long-term consumption of an inappropriate diet, chronic exposure to chemical pathogens at work, 'stress' or whatever. This is the meaning of the 'multifactorial' approach to disease, which requires much more complex kinds of explanations than were considered necessary when, following the discovery of the role of micro-organisms in various infectious diseases, single causes sufficed. Not only are diseases now more identified with multiple causal factors which are distant in terms of time from the end result, but, more importantly, this shift in ideas about disease processes suggests that health care provision ought to be directed more towards intervention in the state of affairs prior to the ultimate manifestation of disease, by influencing the risk factors that lead to pathological outcomes.

References

APPLE, D. (1960) How laymen define illness. *J. Hlth soc. Behav.*, **1**, 219–25.
EVANS-PRITCHARD, E. E. (1937) *Witchcraft, Oracles and Magic Among the Azande*. Oxford: Clarendon Press.

HAYNES, R. B., SACKETT, D. L., TAYLOR, D. W., GIBSON, E. S. & JOHNSON, A. L. (1978) Absenteeism from work after the detection and labelling of hypertensives. *New Engl. J. Med.*, **299**, 741.

JACKSON, G., PIERSCIANAUSKI, T. A., MAHON, W. & CONDON, J. (1976) Inappropriate antihypertensive therapy in the elderly. *Lancet*, **2**, 1317–18.

JEWSON, N. (1976) The disappearance of the sick man from medical cosmology. *Sociology*, **10**, 225–44.

MENNIGER, K. Changing concepts of disease. *Ann. intern. Med.*, **29**, 318–25.

ROBINSON, D. (1976) *From Drinking to Alcoholism: A Sociological Commentary*. London: John Wiley.

ROOM, R. (1972) Comment on the alcohologist's addiction. *Q. Jl. Stud. Alcohol.*, **33**, 1049.

ROYAL COLLEGE OF GENERAL PRACTITIONERS, OFFICE OF POPULATION CENSUSES AND SURVEYS, DEPARTMENT OF HEALTH AND SOCIAL SECURITY (1979) *Morbidity Statistics from General Practice, 1971–2*. London: HMSO.

STRONG, P. (1980) Doctors and dirty work. *Sociol. Hlth Illness*, **2**, 24–47.

2

Society and Changing Patterns of Disease

Ray M. Fitzpatrick

One of the most important recent developments in ideas about health care and illness has been the widespread recognition that social and economic conditions have a major effect upon patterns of disease and on death rates. A wide range of sources — historical, medical and sociological — have provided the evidence for such influences. This chapter considers how we can trace lines of influence from society and the economy to patterns of disease.

The starting point of this analysis is the dramatic variation to be found in death rates both in the past and at present. For example, the death rate per annum has virtually halved in England and Wales over the last 150 years: in 1851 it was 22.7 per 1000 population and by 1978 it had fallen to 11.9. Another way to express the difference over this period is to talk in terms of the average number of years an individual could expect to live at birth, life expectancy. Whereas a man and woman in 1840 could on average expect to live to 40 and 43 respectively, by 1978 life expectancy had risen to 70 and 76. Such differences in overall mortality rates, however, disguise a more complex picture if we look at particular age groups. The higher death rates of the mid-nineteenth century were much more severe in particular age groups, especially in infancy and childhood. Thus, future life expectancy for those who have reached the age of 45 has improved slightly over the last 100 years but not nearly as dramatically as has the life expectancy of a child at birth.

The higher death rates and lower life expectancies are of course not simply an historical phenomenon. Many third world countries at present have crude death rates much higher than those of England; for example, tropical Africa (Zaire, Central African Republic, 22 per 1000) and middle south Asia (India, Pakistan and Bangladesh, 17 per 1000). Third world countries with higher death rates resemble nineteenth-century England and Wales in that infant and child mortality are one of the main reasons for lower life expectancy.

Variation in disease patterns in human society

The diseases that man has encountered have not remained the same over time. Man's history might be viewed as a progressive victory over disease, but this is an oversimplification. Whilst some diseases are less important as causes of illness or death than in the past, others have become more important. Complex social and biological processes have altered the balance between man and disease. A number of authorities (Powles 1973; McKeown 1980) now agree that man has passed through three characteristic disease patterns in historical sequence.

Pre-agricultural disease patterns

Before about 10 000 B.C., indeed for most of man's evolution as a distinct species, man lived as a hunter–gatherer, that is without any form of settled agriculture for subsistence. Although conclusions based on such early evidence are somewhat speculative, anthropologists and epidemiologists have argued that the infectious diseases which were later to become major causes of illness and death were relatively uncommon at this stage of social evolution. Furthermore, diseases which are sometimes described as diseases of civilization, such as heart disease and cancer, were less common than at the present time (Powles 1973). It is likely that mortality in adults arose from environmental and safety hazards, for example hunting accidents and exposure.

Diseases in agricultural society

Knowledge of the diseases which plagued agricultural societies is more certain. These were predominantly the infectious

Table 2.   Standardized death rates (per million) for selected conditions: England and Wales

	1848–54	1971
Tuberculosis	2901	13
Bronchitis, pneumonia, influenza	2309	603
Cholera	1819	33
Prematurity, immaturity and other diseases of infancy	1221	192
Scarlet fever and diphtheria	1016	0
Cardiovascular disease	698	1776
Cancer	307	1169

Adapted from McKeown (1979).

diseases, which for the purposes of discussion can be divided into the following:

1. Air-borne diseases such as tuberculosis.
2. Water-borne diseases such as cholera.
3. Food-borne diseases such as dysentery.
4. Vector-borne (i.e. carried by rats or mosquitoes) diseases such as plague and malaria.

In England and Wales, and in Europe generally, the plague was a particularly important cause of death and at its most virulent, in the Black Death of 1348, it killed one-quarter of the English population. It last occurred on any large scale in England and Wales in 1665 and it disappeared from Europe shortly after. The plague was spread by the fleas carried by black rats. The disappearance of the plague was due to the replacement of the black rat by the brown rat which was much less prone to infest human habitations.

Malaria was never as great a health problem in England and Wales as it has been in the tropics where conditions are ideal for the natural life-cycle of both vector and parasite. By the mid-nineteenth century when reliable vital statistics were available in England and Wales, and the country's economy was moving from agricultural to industrial, the major causes of death were as indicated in Table 2.

The modern industrial era of disease

By the mid-twentieth century, infectious diseases had become relatively unimportant causes of death in England and Wales and in the western world in general, although some infectious diseases such as influenza remained common causes of death, particularly in the elderly. Table 2 shows, however, that the infectious diseases have been replaced as major causes of death by the so-called degenerative diseases, cancer and cardiovascular disease.

This dramatic increase in importance of the chronic degenerative diseases is characteristic of almost all countries that have undergone industrialization, although the exceptions and the variations in rates from one country to another provide important and intriguing problems for the medical and social scientist. Japan, for example, has a much lower incidence of heart disease than comparable industrialized societies. On the other hand, the level of stomach cancer is considerably higher in Japan compared with, for example, the USA.

Explaining changes in disease prevalence

It would be all too easy to regard changes in disease patterns as the inevitable consequence of medical and technical progress without further explanation. Close examination of the major influences on disease patterns, however, uncovers a complex picture which is increasingly recognized as important for the understanding of diseases in the contemporary world. The study of how disease patterns have changed indicates the pervasive influence of social and economic factors on disease prevalence.

Three main factors seem important in the changes in disease patterns that followed the transition from nomadic hunting and gathering to agricultural life. Firstly, the development of cereals such as wheat allowed agricultural societies to feed more mouths and hence support higher population densities. Evidence from epidemiological studies, however, shows that many infectious organisms thrive when human populations grow above certain densities. Secondly, agricultural work necessitated permanent settlement, whereas hunter–gatherers periodically moved settlement in search of fresh food sources. However, in the absence of sanitation and awareness of its importance,

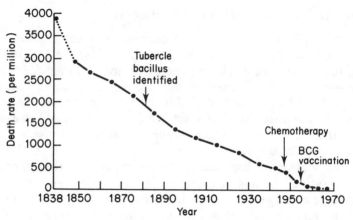

Fig. 1   Pulmonary tuberculosis: annual death rates for England and Wales, 1838–1970. (*From McKeown 1979*)

permanent settlement often led to the contamination of water supplies by waste products which increased the risks of infection from a number of organisms. Thirdly, the development of cereals as the major source of food, whilst supporting greater numbers of people, paradoxically narrowed the range and quality of diet, a factor which crucially reduced resistance to infection.

More careful examination is needed to explain the remarkable changes in death rates and the decline in significance of mortality from infectious disease that occurred with the transition from agricultural to industrial economies. The nineteenth and twentieth centuries' victory over death and disease still represents the most dramatic improvement in health in the history of man. Death rates for the various infectious diseases did not decline simultaneously. Tuberculosis, the most common cause of death in the nineteenth century began to decline in the first half of that century, as indicated in Fig. 1. There are a limited number of possible explanations for such a marked decline in mortality from an infectious organism. It is possible that a change occurred in the virulence of the organism itself or that the genetic immunity of the population improved. Both these possibilities are generally discounted. There is no theoretical reason why the organisms responsible for tuberculosis and a number of other infectious diseases should fortuitously change in their virulence at approximately the same time; nor could genetic immunity improve in such a short time. The most convincing explanation for the decline in mortality from tuberculosis and, later in the century, from air-borne diseases such as pneumonia, is that an increased resistance to infection resulted from improvement in nutritional intake as agricultural techniques improved and transportation of produce became faster and more efficient.

In many third world countries today, diseases such as measles or tuberculosis have a much higher fatality, especially amongst the very young in the population whose resistance is reduced by malnutrition. McKeown cites the conclusion of the World Health Organization report that one-half to three-quarters of all statistically recorded deaths of infants and young children are attributed to a combination of malnutrition and infection (McKeown 1980).

The incidence of illness and mortality from water-borne diseases such as cholera declined somewhat later in the century, largely as the result of concerted efforts by the public health movement to prevent the contamination of drinking water supplies by sewage: gastroenteric infectious diseases came under control by the beginning of the twentieth century, resulting in a dramatic impact on infant mortality. The sterilization and more hygienic transportation of milk in particular, and improved food hygiene in general, constitute another form of environmental change that produced the decline in infectious disease mortality.

Thus, most of the decline in death rates achieved in this country and in the western world generally by the Second World War can be attributed to environmental factors such as improvements in food and hygiene which were the products of economic development. Other social changes, such as the decline in the birth rate, reduced the demand for food and housing resources. Improved housing and better personal hygiene also played their role in reducing mortality rates.

The historical role of medicine

To this point nothing has been said about the role that medical intervention has played in the relationship between man and disease. At first glance, this might seem an important omission,

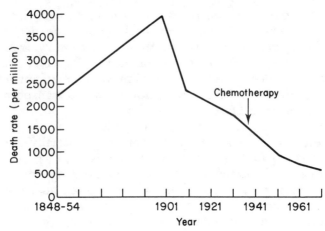

Fig. 2   Bronchitis, pneumonia and influenza: death rates for England and Wales, 1848–1971. (*From McKeown 1979*)

given that medical knowledge was accumulating throughout the period and that hospitals had grown in number since the latter part of the eighteenth century. The evidence that McKeown and others have gathered, however, suggests that very little of the decline in mortality rates can be attributed to improvements in medical care. For example, when Florence Nightingale began to reform the hygienic conditions in hospitals, it was widely thought that hospitals constituted a risk to health; in other words, one stood a high risk of cross-infection, contracting a disease from other patients, since wards were unsegregated as well as unhygienic. Similarly, in spite of the advances in surgery made possible by the development of anaesthetics, there is little evidence that surgical procedures made any impact on life expectancy in the nineteenth century (McKeown & Brown 1969). As for drugs, prior to the twentieth century, a large armoury of medicines appears to have been available to the Victorian doctor. However, only a few such as digitalis, mercury and cinchona, used in the treatment of heart disease, syphilis and malaria respectively, would be recognized by modern standards as having specific efficiency and, in any case, dosages were unlikely to have been appropriate. The first drugs which can be shown to have influenced mortality rates did not appear until the end of the 1930s. The antibiotics used in the treatment of a wide range of bacterial infections were developed in the 1930s and 1940s. Prophylactic immunization against such diseases as whooping cough and polio date from the 1950s. In the case of these medical breakthroughs, however, it is easy to overstate the contribution that they made to mortality rates. The decline in mortality for most infectious diseases took place *before* the introduction of antibiotics. For tuberculosis the period of decline can be seen in Fig. 1, while the mortality rates for bronchitis, pneumonia and influenza are shown in Fig. 2. Moreover, it is difficult to distinguish between the improvements in disease mortality that can be attributed to the introduction of treatment or immunization and those due to the continuing influence of improving social and economic conditions. Most likely, the immunization programmes for diphtheria and polio brought about the greatest improvement which can be attributed to specific medical intervention.

Disease rates and social factors in modern society

The association between diseases and social and economic circumstances is not a purely historical phenomenon. In many parts of the third world life expectancy at birth is much lower than in Europe or North America. Many aspects of the environment in the third world provide much more favourable conditions for the spread of infectious diseases than those that prevailed in historical Europe. For example, tropical ecology is particularly favourable for such vectors of disease as the mosquito (malaria) and tsetse fly (sleeping sickness). Nevertheless it is the extremely low standard of living *above all else* that produces high mortality rates in countries such as Bangladesh and Ethiopia.

In countries like Britain, the social and environmental factors that are responsible for many kinds of commonly occurring disease are somewhat different and may require different explanation. The association between standard of living and the risk of disease, however, is still apparent in the social class differences in illness and mortality rates discussed in Chapter 9. It is evident that environmental factors, whether in the home or at work, continue to play an important role in influencing the risks of illness and mortality.

Whilst environmental conditions associated with poverty increase the risk of disease, many kinds of disease are now associated with behaviour which may have little or nothing to do with poverty. Increasingly, the mass media are focussing attention on the role that overeating or inappropriate diet, smoking and excessive alcohol consumption have in a wide variety of disorders such as heart disease, diabetes, lung cancer and cirrhosis of the liver.

The association between smoking and lung cancer has been established beyond all reasonable doubt. It is important to recognize, however, that contemporary health risks associated with behaviour are just as certainly a function of current social conditions as were the infectious health risks associated with the social conditions of the nineteenth century. This is an essential point to grasp, since it is all too easy to view behaviour such as smoking simply as reflecting an individual's decisions and preferences. To focus on an individual smoker would not only lead to erroneous and over-simplified explanations of the causes of his behaviour, but more importantly it might lead to misguided or naive attempts to change his behaviour.

At present while 29% of men and women in social class I are smokers, 57% of men and 48% of women in social class V still smoke (see Chapter 9 for definition of the five social classes). It is widely assumed that advertising and marketing strategies, governmental health warnings and taxation on tobacco all have a direct influence on attitudes and behaviour. If effective health policies are to be devised, however, evidence on the social factors which influence smoking is required. There may be little point, for example, in increasing expenditure on mass health education programmes to alter behaviour associated with health risks in the particularly vulnerable groups who do not respond to such influences.

A realistic analysis of smoking in modern society would have to include a number of complex political and economic as well as health issues. For example, an increase in taxation on cigarettes might make their cost prohibitive to many. However, one consequence for the Treasury would be a decline in an important source of revenue. Similarly, whilst the National Health Service might cost less if smoking were reduced, much more money would be needed for the pensions of the increased numbers surviving into old age. Again, reduction in the tobacco industry, although reducing the number of days of sickness absence in industry in general, could result in heavy unemployment in cities that depend heavily on the tobacco industry itself.

The example of smoking illustrates that disease is as much a reflection of the economy today as it has been in the past. Diet is another example. It has been estimated by Lock and Smith (1976) that 56% of women and 52% of men in Britain over the age of 40 are at least 15% overweight. The mortality risks of men who are 10% overweight are one-fifth higher than average, especially in mortality associated with diabetes and vascular disease. Clearly, overeating may be a major health risk. Burkitt (1973) and others have argued that inappropriate diet is also a problem. He argues that diverticular disease, cancer of the bowel, diabetes and indeed various venous diseases such as varicose veins and deep vein thrombosis may all be linked to lack of fibre. Populations which have diets with high fibre content seem relatively free of many such diseases. In Britain the daily fibre intake from bread has been reduced to about one-tenth of its level in 1850, whereas we have almost doubled our consumption of sugar and other refined carbohydrates. Again the statistics of change do not reveal the causal links. Changes in diet have reflected changes in the food-producing industries which are now concentrated in a small number of multi-national companies more concerned with producing standardized and well-accepted, easily transported commodities: nutritional values have taken second place to the expansion of profits.

It may seem that such an analysis of the relationship of social and economic factors is unhelpful and depressing because it points to features of our economic system that are central, firmly established and difficult to change. If this is the case, then another parallel is suggested with the nineteenth-century problems of environmental disease. The changes in sanitation, urban planning and building that were required to transform the pattern of infectious diseases in Victorian times were similarly regarded as unrealistic and resisted for long periods by politicians and business interests, but the reforms were slowly adopted and growing awareness of the relationship between commercially-promoted behaviours such as smoking and unhealthy eating in our own time should help to speed the process of securing reforms.

The economy and health policy in modern society

Some of the most recent research on the relationship between the economy and health suggests that even in modern societies, economic factors play the predominant role in determining patterns of illness and that the role of health services is negligible by comparison. Brenner (1977) has argued that most of the variation in annual overall mortality rates for the USA can be statistically explained in terms of changes in the annual level of employment, provided that a time lag of five years is allowed for unemployment to have its effect on health. This impact is produced in two ways: firstly unemployment reduces family income and therefore material standard of living and secondly the individual loses a sense of meaning and purpose found at work, experiences increased fears about the future and tension at home and is thereby more vulnerable to ill health. From USA data Brenner concluded that a 1% increase in unemployment, if sustained for five years, was statistically responsible for nearly 37 000 extra deaths. Similar results have been found for analyses of England and Wales and Sweden (Brenner 1979).

This work has been challenged by Eyer (1977) who argues that the influence on health of experiences such as unemployment generally occurs within a much shorter time than the five-year lag that Brenner allows. If this is the case, the association between unemployment and mortality is considerably reduced. Instead, Eyer argues that death rates *increase* at the time of business booms when employment rates are high. The association between employment and mortality, he explains in terms of four connected social factors that attend business cycles:

1. Economic booms increase workers' migration which weakens social networks that normally protect individuals against disease.
2. 'Stress' through overwork in times of business peaks increases ill health.
3. The unhealthy consumption of alcohol and tobacco increases.
4. Conversely, during low periods of the economy social networks are strong and act to protect individuals.

The issues raised by these two contrasting approaches are complex and far from resolution but both at least agree in placing the main responsibility for health and illness on economic policy rather than on the health services. This controversial position is partly shared by more radical writers who are more concerned to analyse directly the contribution of modern medicine to health. Perhaps the best known is Illich (1977) who argues that medicine has played a very small role in improving health and that its contribution has actually been negative, insofar as it has:

1. Raised public expectations of 'wonder cures' which in reality are ineffective.
2. Extended too far the kinds of problem that are thought to be medical.
3. Been responsible for large amounts of iatrogenic (medically-produced) illness.
4. Decreased the ability of individuals to cope with their own illness by fostering a debilitating dependency on the expert (see Chapter 14).

Illich's own solution is firstly to break down medicine's monopoly in health care, so that there is a 'free market' in which anyone can practice healing, and secondly to reverse the social trend towards dependency by restoring the value of personal responsibility.

This approach, which is attractive to many advocates of 'alternative medicine' and self-help groups, is rejected as mistaken and utopian by writers such as Navarro (1975) because it wrongly blames the medical profession and a 'gullible' public for aspects of ill health which are best understood as products of a *capitalist economy*. It is this which directly creates much illness, maintains an unequal distribution of illness and encourages a very inappropriate health care system for treating illness once it has occurred. Hence Navarro advocates radical political changes in society as the only solution to the kinds of problems that have been identified in this chapter.

Other writers such as McKeown and Powles place more emphasis on the need to reform health care rather than concerning themselves with wider issues of social change. Firstly, they argue, since much disease is environmentally caused and preventable, medicine should give more attention in teaching, research and practice to the prevention of disease rather than dealing with it after it has occurred. Not only has prevention had a significant impact in the past, it would appear a simple, more humane and sound means of reducing disease in the present.

Secondly, these analysts also maintain that health care resources and energy have become too concentrated on high technology and hospital-based acute medicine at the expense of preventive and community resources. In the light of the evidence reviewed above, it seems that there is an unwarranted faith in technological medicine. With the possible exception of antibiotics and immunizing drugs few improvements in health can be attributed to break-throughs in laboratory medicine. Cochrane (1972) argues that all too few medical procedures have been submitted to rigorous evaluation of their effectiveness (see Chapter 19).

Thirdly, it is argued that another shift in the emphasis of medicine is needed, that from cure to care. Since medicine can claim few cures to be effective, it must confront the task of caring for the sick with greater zeal and effectiveness. Caring necessitates concern with the quality of life of the ill and reduction in any handicap or disadvantage consequent to disease. Financial and other resources, reflecting medical values, are at present, however, spent more on efforts in acute medicine than in the psychiatric or geriatric units. Medical education perpetuates such values because it is conducted predominantly in acute hospitals where consultants maintain traditional values in their teaching.

Clearly these arguments are controversial and have not gone unchallenged. Lever (1977) has argued that inferences about current health planning based on historical patterns are hazardous. To prove that environmental factors were the most important determinants of mortality in the past does not necessarily prove that environmental measures will produce such beneficial effects in the present. Given limited funds for health services, a major shift towards environmental and preventive health care would be a major gamble. Whatever the merits of such points, it has to be acknowledged that at present insufficient resources have been committed to such preventive services as health education and occupational medicine, compared with expenditure on hospital technology, to allow any serious examination of their potential role.

At present there remains much work to be done regarding the

influences that social and economic factors exert on health. At the same time controversial debates clearly continue unresolved about the priorities in effort and expenditure that are most appropriate to modern patterns of illness.

References

BRENNER, M. (1977) Health costs and benefits of economic policy. *Int. J. Hlth Serv.*, **7**, 581–623.

BRENNER, M. (1979) Mortality and the national economy. *Lancet*, **2**, 568–73.

BURKITT, D. (1973) Some diseases characteristic of modern Western civilization. *Br. med. J.*, **1**, 274–8.

COCHRANE, A. (1972) *Effectiveness and Efficiency: Random Reflections on the Health Service.* London: Nuffield Provincial Hospitals Trust.

EYER, J. (1977) Does unemployment cause the death rate peak in each business cycle? A multifactorial model of death rate change. *Int. J. Hlth Serv.*, **7**, 625–62.

ILLICH, I. (1977) *Limits to Medicine. Medical Nemesis: The Expropriation of Health.* Harmondsworth: Penguin.

LEVER, A. (1977) Medicine under challenge. *Lancet*, **1**, 353–5.

LOCK, S. & SMITH, T. (1976) *The Medical Risks of Life.* Harmondsworth: Penguin.

McKEOWN, T. (1980) *The Role of Medicine: Dream, Mirage or Nemesis*, 2nd ed. Oxford: Blackwell Scientific.

McKEOWN, T. & BROWN, R. (1969) Medical evidence related to English population changes in the eighteenth century. In: *Population in Industrialisation*, ed. M. Drake. London: Methuen.

NAVARRO, V. (1975) The industrialization of fetishism or the fetishism of industrialization: a critique of Ivan Illich. *Int. J. Hlth Serv.*, **5**, 351–71.

POWLES, J. (1973) On the limitations of modern medicine. *Sci. Med. Man*, **1**, 1–30.

3

Social Causes of Disease

Ray M. Fitzpatrick

One of the most commonly considered causes of disease in popular medical literature and in lay discussion is 'stress', whether it is the stress of city life, of work or of life in general. Popular use of the term suggests a notion that social and psychological factors can substantially influence an individual's health. In recent years the medical and social sciences have examined the role that psychosocial factors can play in causing or influencing disease, and this chapter reviews some of the ideas and evidence that has accumulated.

The concept of psychosomatic disease

As a result of the scientific revolution in nineteenth-century medicine that is associated with names such as Pasteur, the causes of disease were increasingly sought in specific agents like 'germs' and in cellular and subcellular pathological processes. The attraction of seeking specific causes for each disease led to the comparative neglect of more holistic explanations, namely explanations which took into account the quality of an individual's relationships with others and the meaning he attached to his experience. One result was that by the twentieth century the natural sciences tended to ignore explanations of diseases that involved social or psychological terms like 'stress' on the grounds that they were unscientific and outmoded.

The first attempt to offer a systematic alternative to the cellular and mechanistic 'germ theories' came from research influenced by Freudian psychoanalysis. It was argued that certain diseases could be explained in terms of the body's response to internal psychological conflict. Diseases such as peptic ulcer, dermatitis and asthma were thought of as the body's expression or manifestation of unconscious psychological tensions that the individual could not deal with in any other way. These ideas may seem strange today but their influence has survived in two respects. Firstly, there is still a tendency amongst both laymen and some doctors to think that only a few diseases are potentially caused by psychological factors, while the majority have more specific organic explanations which can be discovered given sufficient effort. Another consequence of early work was that the term 'psychosomatic illness' passed into every-day use, although it acquired a meaning never intended by the original researchers, that is that individuals with psychosomatic diseases are 'not really ill'.

Two important developments have occurred since the early work on psychosomatic disease. Firstly, it is now clear that the term created a false assumption that there are two distinct classes of disease: those which are influenced by psychological factors and those which are not. In fact psychological stress may produce vulnerability to a wide range of diseases, from the common cold to cancer, from arthritis to myocardial infarction (Levine & Scotch 1970). The second development has been that a wider range of factors has been investigated in terms of their contribution to the causation of disease. Research has increasingly considered the influence of external social events and circumstances on levels of health in populations, rather than depending solely on exploring the subjective conflicts and impulses of individuals that used to be the main source of explanation in psychosomatic research.

Social stress and health

Social change

Research has been undertaken which attempts to identify the nature and impact of a wide range of social experiences that might be responsible for an increased likelihood of illness or death. One such experience that might influence health is rapid or dramatic social change. Several studies have attempted to explore this possibility. Cassel and Tyroler (1961) studied two groups of rural origin who were working in a factory in the USA. The first was composed of individuals who were the first of their family to engage in industrial work and the second was composed of children of previous workers in this same factory. They lived in the same area and did the same work for the same pay. The hypothesis was that the second group, by virtue of their families' previous experience, would be better prepared for the expectations and demands of industrial living than the first, and therefore less vulnerable to the stress of transition, and would exhibit fewer signs of ill health. As predicted, the first group had more symptoms and a higher rate of absenteeism through sickness. Other studies suggest that migrants to cultures very different from their own are often at risk of either physical illness (Groen 1971) or suicide (Sainsbury 1969).

Bereavement

One of the most devastating forms of stress that is often presented to doctors is bereavement. Studies have shown that individuals who have recently lost a close relative have a much increased risk of sickness or mortality themselves as a result. Parkes et al. (1969), in a study of widowers aged 55 and over, found an increased mortality, largely from cardiovascular disease, for six months following their bereavement. Rees and Lutkins (1967) surveyed the bereaved in a semi-rural general practice in Wales and found much higher rates of mortality compared with a non-bereaved comparison group. Men seemed more vulnerable than women to mortality following the loss of a close relative. The evidence is clear enough but inevitably the psychological and physiological processes that can bring about such pathological responses are complex. Parkes (1971) suggests that the pathological effects of bereavement are mainly due to the loss of meaning and severe disruption to assumptions about the world that are created by the death of a close relative or spouse; they combine to undermine basic coping abilities in the individual, including resistance to illness.

Work

Most people think of work as a major potential source of stress. However, even a brief review of the growing literature on the relationship between stress at work and illness indicates the complexities inherent in this area. Both studies of an experimental kind conducted in the laboratory and field studies of responses to work indicate that actual bodily changes can occur in response to work experiences that can, on common-sense grounds, be seen as stressful. For example, Timio and Gentili (1976) found that manual workers in the confectionery industry, when moved from normal wage payment to 'piecework' ('payment by result'), increased their catecholamine outputs; catecholamine is a hormone that is a commonly used marker of stress and may be implicated in the onset of coronary heart disease. In other words, a more pressurized form of reward was translated by the workers into physical symptoms. Rose et al. (1979) found that air-traffic controllers' blood pressure was markedly raised when on duty compared to off-duty periods, reflecting their experience of heavy and constant vigilance and responsibility. However, it has been difficult to demonstrate long-term, rather than acute, stress-induced responses to work situations. For example, Rose and his colleagues found no psychiatric illness three years later that could be attributed to the stress-induced response they had initially measured.

The disease most commonly associated in popular mythology with stress at work is cardiovascular disease. Few studies, however, have convincingly demonstrated relationships between specific aspects of the work environment, stress and heart disease. Hinkle (1974) reports one study of a large sample of employees of the Bell Telephone Company which attempted to measure stress in terms of the number of job changes, such as demotion, promotion and transfer, that were recorded in employees' records, and to relate these to the onset of any form of heart disease. He did not find, however, that the very successful employees who gained the highest promotion or took on more demanding responsibilities had higher rates of heart disease than comparison groups. Indeed, neither the number of job changes, nor changes involving the transfer of families to new locations, correlated statistically with episodes of heart disease.

No account of this field would be complete without mention of the now famous work by Friedman and Rosenman (1974), who have argued that those with a particular behaviour pattern (Type A behaviour) are especially prone to heart disease. Type A behaviour is characterized by extreme competitiveness, aggressiveness, impatience and a sense of pressure of time and responsibility. A number of studies have now been carried out which have assessed samples of men in terms of the presence (Type A) or absence (Type B) of such behaviour: these have generally suggested that Type A men have twice the risk of heart disease. Such results suggest that only particular individuals are likely to respond to stress at work and this may go some way towards explaining the negative findings of Hinkle. The research on Type A behaviour must not, however, be interpreted as providing evidence of a simple relation between responsibility at work and heart disease. The figure of deaths from heart disease in England indicates higher rates in social classes IV and V than in social classes I and II, and a recent study of British civil servants found lower rates of heart disease in the higher grades of employment, even when a range of risk factors like smoking were taken into account (Marmot et al. 1978). At present it is apparent that a wide range of social, environmental and genetic factors contribute to the causation of heart disease, but it is not yet possible to be precise about their relative contributions.

Research on the impact of retirement from work suggests that it is not itself a major cause of stress-induced disease, especially when it is not accompanied by a dramatic drop in income. Involuntary job loss through redundancy was considered in a study by Kasl and Cobb (1970), who assessed the health of workers at two industrial plants before and after closure. They found considerably increased levels of illness and perceived stress in the period prior to closure as the workers anticipated the event, but there was less clear evidence of increased illness following closure, although some mortality risk factors such as blood pressure and serum cholesterol were found to be raised. More work is required on the relationship between work, stress and health to clarify the issues raised by these findings.

The role of life events

An alternative approach to looking at the impact of a single type of experience such as retirement, transition to industrial employment or job loss has been to estimate the amount of stress brought about by a full range of experience in an individual's life

Table 3. *Some examples of values of life events in the social readjustment rating scale*

Death of spouse	100
Divorce	73
Marriage	50
Major change in responsibilities at work	29
Changes in residence	20
Vacation	13

Adapted from Holmes and Rahe (1967).

and the extent to which this stress is associated with subsequent illness. Holmes and Rahe (1967), assuming that it is change in personal circumstances that underlies stress, attempted to express in quantitative terms the amount of stress involved in a range of specified *life events*. They asked a large sample of people to 'score' each of a list of 42 life events according to the amount of '*readjustment*' entailed by the events. Marriage, with a score of 50, was given as a reference or anchoring point for rating the other 41 events. Pleasant as well as unpleasant events were included in the list since both involved change. The authors found a high degree of consensus amongst respondents as to the relative impact of the life events. From the respondents' scores they produced a social readjustment rating scale (SRRS), which gave numerical expression to the 'stressfulness' of the events, some examples of which are given in Table 3. The total range was fixed as 0 to 100. With this rating scale subjects could be asked about their lives over a given period and assigned a social readjustment score on the basis of the life events they experienced; for example, an individual who had taken two vacations and been divorced in a period of one year would be scored 99.

The SRRS has been used on a number of populations to see how social readjustment might relate to illness. In one prospective study of a sample of doctors, respondents were asked about life events at the outset and their health records obtained nine months later. When the researchers divided the respondents into 'high-', 'medium-', and 'low-risk' groups on the basis of SRRS scores, they found that 49%, 25% and 9% respectively reported illness subsequently. They had conducted studies of naval personnel and found a linear relationship between life change and subsequent illness (Holmes & Masuda 1974). Their instrument has also been used to investigate myocardial infarction and some of the results indicate a raised score for patients with infarcts compared with control groups and also correlations between SRRS scores and catecholamine output (Theorrell 1974).

Research is beginning to indicate the complexity of intervening processes involved in the association between life events and physical illness. For example, Bradley (1979) found that life events were related to disturbance of control of symptoms in patients managing diabetes with insulin. She suggests that hormonal changes, induced by stress, upset the physiological balance maintained by insulin. Murphy and Brown (1980) found, in a sample of London women, an association between severe life events and a range of physical illnesses, for example duodenal ulcer and urticaria. Their results suggested, however, that the development of psychiatric disturbance following the event was essential for the subsequent development of physical illness. Indeed, for their sample, psychiatric illness without a life event was enough to lead to organic illness.

Life events and psychiatric illness

The role of life events has been found to be of particular importance in explaining psychiatric illness. One recent study by Brown and Harris (1978) attempted to investigate the role of life events in clinical depression. They begin by clarifying the characteristics of life events that might produce a response of illness. The SRRS had often found modest or no correlations with subsequent illness, and Brown and Harris argued that this was mainly due to a lack of sensitivity in their method of scoring stress in terms of 'readjustment'. To take an example, the SRRS gave all changes in residence the same score. Brown and Harris argue, however, that the 'stressfulness' of a change in residence depends on the complete context in which it takes place. It will be less serious if a husband is present to assist rather than in gaol. Thus the researcher must take account of the meaning and context of life events.

Brown and Harris explored these issues in a random sample of women, of whom 16% were found to be clinically depressed. Only life events which were rated on the basis of the context as having *long-term threatening implications* were found to be significantly related to depression. Such events generally involved a major potential or actual loss to the person, for example discovering a life-threatening illness in someone close, finding out about a husband's unfaithfulness or experiencing redundancy at work. If events, however disruptive and painful, had only short-term implications (lasting less than a week) for a woman's life, they were not associated with depression. Another social factor which was found to be much more common in the lives of the depressed compared with normal women were serious chronic difficulties such as housing or financial problems that had lasted for at least two years.

Brown and Harris also found, as have most other surveys of mental illness, higher rates of depression in working-class than in middle-class women, a difference which was *not* due to working-class women having more life events and chronic difficulties. A different kind of social effect seemed to explain the class differences. They found that four factors in the women's lives — absence of a close intimate relationship, having three or more children under 15 at home, loss of mother before the age of 11 and having no employment outside the home — operated to make women much more vulnerable to depression *if* they experienced a severe life event. These vulnerability factors did not produce a greater likelihood of depression by themselves; but if they were not present, a woman tended not to react to a life event by developing depression. The chances of illness following a life event increased the more vulnerability factors there were present; most interesting of all, most of the social class difference in experience of depression was explained by taking account of the first three vulnerability factors. Brown and Harris speculate about the underlying mechanisms that are operating in their vulnerability model. They believe that the four vulnerability factors have common, profound effects in reducing women's sense of confidence and their ability to cope with the world. Such negative self-evaluations are exacerbated by the feelings of hopelessness experienced after a severe life event and thus lead on to depression.

The social system and susceptibility to disease

The concept of vulnerability is an important addition to ideas about how social factors may be involved in disease. It suggests that social circumstances may function either to protect individuals or to make them more vulnerable when they are coping with noxious agents, whether physical or psychosocial. In this sense, in addition to their role as stressors, social factors have to be thought of as influencing overall susceptibility to disease. A growing amount of evidence points to a variety of social factors as contributing to general susceptibility. For example, the married have lower mortality rates than do the unmarried, widowed and divorced (Gove 1973). The differences in mortality rates between married and unmarried statuses are greater for men than for women and are greater in mortality from, to take examples, suicide, accidents and alcoholism. Marriage, it is argued, offers a sense of meaning and importance, particularly to men, which is psychologically protective. An alternative explanation, of course, would be simply that fitter individuals are 'selected' into marriage. If this were the case one would expect the differences in mortality between the single and married to be greater in the later years, after virtually everyone who is going to marry has married, and smaller in the earlier years, when the single category still has a sizeable proportion of fit individuals who will eventually marry. In fact, mortality statistics suggest greater differences during earlier years and therefore tend to support the hypothesis of marriage itself being protective.

Sociologists have for a long time argued that integration into a community may be generally protective of an individual's health. In America, for example, religious groups which have stronger social networks, such as Seventh Day Adventists and Mormons, have comparatively low death rates; indeed one study by Berkman and Syme (1979) reported that groups with weaker social networks (measured by items such as the extent of church membership) experienced, over a nine-year follow-up period, more than twice the mortality rates of groups assessed as having strong social networks. Similarly, an Australian study by Henderson et al. (1978) argued that nearly half the variance found in neurosis in a student population could be explained by an index of social integration and attachment to the community.

One way of thinking about such results is to see the social network as 'mediating' between the individual and pathogenic agents.

In this chapter some indication has been given of the immense variety of ways in which the social environment may directly impinge on the health of an individual. Research has been conducted in this field only for a relatively short period of time and, inevitably, there are enormous methodological difficulties in demonstrating the effects of 'real life' stresses compared with the experimentally induced stress of the psychologist's laboratory. However, no artificial experiment has ever shown, nor, on ethical grounds, should ever be used to show, that psychosocial stimuli can actually induce illness; it is to the exciting new field investigations of real populations, for all their difficulties, that we must turn if we are to understand better the social determinants of ill health.

References

BERKMAN, L. F. & SYME, S. L. (1979) Social networks, host resistance and mortality: a nine year follow-up study of Alameda County residents. *Am. J. Epidem.*, **109**, 186–204.

BRADLEY, C. (1979) Life events and the control of diabetes mellitus. *J. psychosom. Res.*, **23**, 159–62.

BROWN, G. & HARRIS, T. (1978) *Social Origins of Depression.* London: Tavistock.

CASSEL, J. & TYROLER, H. (1961) Epidemiological studies of culture change. *Int. Arch. environ. Hlth.*, **3**, 31–9.

FRIEDMAN, M. & ROSENMAN, R. (1974) *Type A Behaviour and Your Heart.* New York: Knopf.

GOVE, W. (1973) Sex, marital status and mortality. *Am. J. of Sociol.*, **79**, 45–67.

GROEN, J. (1971) Social change and psychosomatic disease. In: *Society, Stress and Disease*, ed. L. Levi. London: Oxford University Press.

HENDERSON, S., BYRNE, D., DUNCAN-JONES, P., ADCOCK, S., SCOTT, R. &

HINKLE, L. (1974) The effect of exposure to culture change, social change and changes in interpersonal relationships on health. In: *Stressful Life Events: Their Nature and Effects*, ed. B. S. Dohrenwend & B. P. Dohrenwend. New York: John Wiley.

HOLMES, T. & MASUDA, M. (1974) Life change and illness susceptibility. In: *Stressful Life Events: Their Nature and Effects*, ed. B. S. Dohrenwend & B. P. Dohrenwend. New York: John Wiley.

HOLMES, T. & RAHE, R. (1967) The social readjustment rating scale. *J. psychosom. Res.*, **11**, 213–18.

KASL, S. & COBB, S. (1970) Blood pressure changes in men undergoing job loss: a preliminary report. *Psychosom. Med.*, **32**, 19–38.

LEVINE, S. & SCOTCH, N. (1970) *Social Stress.* Chicago: Aldine.

MARMOT, M., ROSE, G., SHIPLEY, M. & HAMILTON, P. (1978) Employment grade and coronary heart disease in British civil servants. *J. Epidem. commun. Hlth.*, **32**, 244–9.

MURPHY, E. & BROWN, G. (1980) Life events, psychiatric disturbance and physical illness. *Br. J. Psychiat.*, **136**, 326–38.

PARKES, C. (1971) Psycho-social transitions: a field for study. *Soc. Sci. Med.*, **5**, 101–15.

PARKES, C., BENJAMIN, B. & FITZGERALD, R. (1969) Broken heart: a statistical survey of increased mortality among widowers. *Br. med. J.*, **1**, 740–4.

REES, W. & LUTKINS, S. (1967) Mortality of bereavement. *Br. med. J.*, **4**, 13–16.

ROSE, R., HURST, M. & HERD, J. (1979) Cardiovascular and endocrine responses to work and the risk for psychiatric symptomatology among air traffic controllers. In: *Stress and Mental Disorder*, ed. J. Barrett. New York: Raven.

SAINSBURY, P. (1969) Social and community psychiatry. *Am. J. Psychiat.*, **125**, 1226–31.

THEORELL, T. (1974) Life events before and after the onset of a premature myocardial infarction. In: *Stressful Life Events: Their Nature and Effects*, ed. B. S. Dohrenwend & B. P. Dorenwend. New York: John Wiley.

TIMIO, M. & GENTILI, S. (1976) Andrenosympathetic overactivity under conditions of work stress. *Br. J. prev. soc. Med.*, **30**, 262–5.

Part II
Social Factors in Medical Practice

4

Illness Behaviour

Graham Scambler

One popular assumption is that people who experience distressing symptoms of illness almost invariably consult a doctor. In this chapter this assumption is challenged and the role played by various social factors in influencing (a) how people come to define themselves as 'ill' and (b) the decision whether or not to seek medical help, is discussed. Self care is considered, both as a complement to and, perhaps more significantly, as a substitute for professional medical care.

The clinical iceberg

In statistical terms it is normal to feel unwell. The authors of two surveys found that over 90% of those in their samples experienced one or more symptoms in the two weeks prior to interview (Wadsworth et al. 1971; Dunnell & Cartwright 1972). It is equally clear, however, that only a minority of symptoms are reported to a doctor. The findings of Wadsworth and colleagues are typical of retrospective studies in this area. As Table 4 shows, they found that only one in five of those in their sample who experienced symptoms in the two weeks before interview saw a doctor. In a prospective study by Morrell and others, a sample of women aged 20–44 kept health diaries in which they recorded all the symptoms they experienced over a 28-day period (Banks et al 1975). Note was also made of the number of times they visited the doctor in the course of a year. From these two sets of data it was calculated that only one in 37 symptom episodes led to a patient-initiated consultation with the general practitioner. The authors were also able to estimate

Table 4.   *Two-week incidence of symptoms and subsequent behaviour
in a random sample of 1000 adults living in London*

Individuals with no symptoms	49
Individuals with symptoms taking no action	188
Individuals with symptoms taking non-medical action	562
General practitioner patients	168
Hospital out-patients	28
Hospital in-patients	5
Total	1000

Adapted from Wadsworth et al. (1971).

the likelihood of particular symptoms being taken to a doctor
(Table 5).

It might be thought that, although many mild symptoms may
remain unseen by general practitioners most, if not all, moderate
or severe symptoms are likely to receive fairly prompt attention.
In fact, other studies have shown that this is not the case. These
studies indicate that, regardless of what symptoms are
considered and regardless of how serious the underlying
conditions, there exists a real and significant *clinical iceberg*. As
Table 6 reveals, the medical services treat only the tip of the sum
total of ill health. The existence of a clinical iceberg has
important implications.

The problem of unmet need

Most obviously there is the disconcerting problem of unmet
need: many people, adults and children alike, are enduring
avoidable pain, discomfort and handicap. Put another way,
there is a gap between the need for and the demand for health
care. It must be remembered, however, first that any substantial
increase in the existing level of demand would swamp the
primary care services; and second that many general
practitioners contend that there is currently a widespread
tendency for people to consult for trivial, unnecessary or
inappropriate reasons: in one study it was reported that a fifth of
the general practitioners questioned felt that half or more of

Table 5.   *Likelihood of symptoms leading to a consultation among a random sample of 516 women living in London*

Symptom	No. of episodes in 28-day diary period	Estimated no. of episodes in a year	No. of patient-initiated consul-tations in a year	Ratio of symptom episodes to consul-tations
Changes in energy	140	1825	4	456:1
Headaches	282	3676	20	184:1
Disturbance of gastric function	67	873	8	109:1
Backache	84	1095	21	52:1
Pain in lower limb	34	443	9	49:1
Emotional/psychological	89	1160	25	46:1
Abdominal pain	62	808	28	29:1
Disturbance of menstruation	32	417	21	20:1
Sore throat	46	600	33	18:1
Pain in chest	15	196	14	14:1

Adapted from Banks et al. (1975).

their surgery consultations fell into this category (Dunnell & Cartwright 1972). Basic to all these issues, of course, is the question of how to define 'need'.

The problem of the 'representativeness' of diagnosed cases

A more subtle implication concerns the fact that much of medical science, policy and practice rests on the assumption that known or diagnosed cases of 'x' or 'y' are 'representative' of the total number of (diagnosed *and undiagnosed*) cases of 'x' and 'y' in the community. It may be, however, that medical perceptions of the nature and impact of certain diseases, let alone of their prevalence and incidence, are distorted because, as a result of

Table 6.   *The clinical iceberg: England and Wales 1962*

	No. of recognized sufferers ('000)	Estimated total no. of cases ('000)	Cases in which no treatment was being sought ('000)
Hypertension[a]			
males 45 +	170	620	450
females 45 +	500	2720	2220
Urinary infections,[b]			
females 15 +	420	830	410
Glaucoma,[c] aged 45 +	60	340	280
Epilepsy	160	280	120
Rheumatoid arthritis,[d]			
aged 15 +	230	520	290
Psychiatric disorders[e]			
males 15 +	560	1200	640
females 15 +	1290	2120	830
Diabetes mellitus[f]	290	600	310
Bronchitis[g]			
males 45–64	500	980	480
females 45–64	390	500	110

    Adapted from Office of Health Economics (1964).
[a] Casual diastolic BP 100 mm Hg and over.
[b] Significant bacteriuria.
[c] Early chronic glaucoma.
[d] 'Definite' and 'probable' rheumatoid arthritis.
[e] 'Conspicuous psychiatric morbidity'.
[f] Glycosuria and 'diabetic' blood sugar curve.
[g] Signs and symptoms of bronchitis.

various social and psychological factors, only 'untypical' cases are presented for diagnosis and treatment. For a long time it was thought that Buerger's disease (a narrowing of the arteries and veins, especially in the legs) was particularly prevalent among East European Jewish men, mostly because Buerger's contacts with patients were largely restricted to Mount Sinai Hospital in New York City, which served predominantly Jewish patients.

In the case of 'high blood pressure', it was discovered with some surprise that a considerable proportion of the general population outside the consulting room manifest the signs without any apparent complaint or ill effect (Freidson 1970). For these reasons it is important that more is known about the social and psychological factors that help determine whether or not people consult their doctors.

Understanding illness behaviour

Many studies have documented the socio-demographic characteristics of users and non-users of medical services. It is known, for example, that women consult more than men, children and the elderly more than young adults and the middle-aged; social class, ethnic origin, marital status and family size are other factors which have been shown to be related to utilization (see Chapters 9, 10 and 11 respectively). These studies tell us *who* does and does not make use of the services, rather than *why*. To begin to answer the more complex question of *why* people seek or decline to seek professional help is to begin to theorize about *illness behaviour*.

It is crucial to recognize that whether or not people consult their doctors does not depend only upon the presence of disease but also upon how they, or other people, respond to its symptoms. Mechanic and Volkart (1961) define 'illness behaviour' as 'the way in which symptoms are perceived, evaluated and acted upon by a person who recognizes some pain, discomfort or other sign of organic malfunction'. Numerous factors have been shown to influence illness behaviour and the most important of these can be described under the following headings.

Cultural variation

The significance of cultural factors in determining how symptoms are interpreted has been well documented, perhaps most convincingly in studies of ethnicity and the experience and reporting of pain. In a pioneering study conducted in New York, Zborowski (1952) found that patients of Old-American or Irish origin displayed a stoical, matter-of-fact attitude towards pain and, if it was intense, a tendency to withdraw from the company of others. In contrast, patients of Italian or Jewish background were more demanding and dependent and tended to seek, rather than shun, public sympathy. Subsequent research has both corroborated Zborowski's findings and afforded support for the more general view that there is a marked cultural difference in the interpretation of and response to symptoms between so-called Anglo–Saxon and Mediterranean groups. It is tempting to assume that such cultural variation is explicable in terms of socialization alone, namely that differences in illness behaviour merely reflect different culturally-learned styles of coping with the world at large. The authors of a recent study of Anglo–Saxon, Anglo–Greek and Greek groups in Australia, however, have suggested that other factors may also be important: they found, for example, that immigrant status and, relatedly, the stress of adapting to the majority culture played a significant part in accounting for the different patterns of illness behaviour among the Anglo–Saxon and Mediterranean groups (Pilowsky & Spence 1977). In short, cultural patterns may vary depending on the social context.

Dimensions of symptomatology and medical knowledge

Studies have indicated that those symptoms which present in a 'striking' way (e.g. a sharp abdominal pain or a high fever) are more likely to be seen as illness and to receive prompt medical attention than those which present less dramatically (Suchman 1965). Consultation in such circumstances may simply be a function of the pain or discomfort; alternatively, it may be a function of the degree of incapacitation or social disruption engendered by the pain or discomfort (see 'Triggers' below). Many painful or distressing symptoms are not indicative of serious conditions; but, equally, some serious conditions (e.g. some cancers) rarely appear in a striking fashion: their onset may be slow and insidious. The actions of potential patients are thus also dependent on their *knowledge* of diseases and their symptomatology and on their capacity to distinguish between 'threatening' and 'non-threatening' symptoms and between conditions which can and cannot be effectively treated. Table 7 compares doctors' and laymen's views on self-treatment in certain hypothetical circumstances. It should, however, be interpreted with caution: people do not in the event always behave in the way they predict they would.

Table 7.   *Comparison of doctors' and laymen's views of self-treatment*

Symptom	Proportion of doctors who thought the symptoms suit- able for self- treatment	Proportion of laymen who thought they would treat the symptoms themselves
Constant feeling of depression for about three weeks	9%	26%
Difficulty in sleeping for about a week	58%	45%
Heavy cold with a temperature and running nose	86%	70%
Headache more than once a week for a month	17%	40%
Very sore throat for three days but no other symptom	27%	55%
Boil that fails to clear up in a week	12%	22%

Adapted from Dunnell and Cartwright (1972). Number of doctors sampled, 307; number of laymen sampled, 1412.

'Triggers'

While many of the symptoms people experience are recognized as indicating disease processes, it is not necessarily the case that treatment is sought. What, when and if action to resolve any problem is undertaken often depends upon a number of other factors. Zola (1973) has looked at the *timing* of decisions to seek medical care. He found that most people tolerated their symptoms for quite a time before they went to a doctor and that the symptoms themselves were often not sufficient to precipitate a consultation: something else had to happen to bring this about. He identified five types of 'trigger':

1. The occurrence of an interpersonal crisis (e.g. a death in the family).
2. Perceived interference with social or personal relations.
3. 'Sanctioning': pressure from others to consult.

4. Perceived interference with vocational or physical activity.
5. A kind of 'temporalizing of symptomatology': the setting of a deadline (e.g. 'If I feel the same way on Monday ...'; 'If I have another turn ...').

The decision to seek medical care is, then, very much bound up with an individual's personal and social circumstances. Zola also found that, when doctors paid insufficient attention to the specific trigger which prompted an individual or which an individual used as an excuse to seek help, there was a greater chance that the patient would eventually break off treatment.

The relativity of 'good health' as a goal

Doctors and other health care personnel tend to assume that a rational person will report any symptoms which are causing him distress or anxiety; in other words, they assume that the maintenance or restoration of 'good health' is a natural first priority. Good health, however, is one goal among others: it is not always supreme. At any given time a person may deem obtaining treatment, which may perhaps involve hospitalization, to be less important or urgent than, for example, looking after young children at home, preparing for an examination, being at work or going on holiday. It is misleading and simplistic to dismiss such a person as irrational.

Lay referral

It is comparatively rare for someone to decide in favour of or against a visit to the surgery without first discussing his symptoms with others. Suchman (1965) found that three-quarters of those participating in his study discussed their symptoms with some other person, usually a relative, before seeking professional help. Freidson (1970) has claimed that just as the doctor has his professional referral system, so the potential patient has his 'lay referral system': 'the whole process of seeking help involves a network of potential consultants from the intimate confines of the nuclear family through successively more select, distant and authoritative laymen until the "professional" is reached'. Freidson has himself produced a 'model' in terms of (a) the degree of congruence between the subculture of the potential patient and that of doctors and (*b*) the relative number of lay consultants interposed between the initial perception of symptoms and the decision whether or not to go to the doctor. Thus, for example, a situation in which the potential patient participates in a subculture which *differs* from that of doctors and in which there is an *extended* lay referral system would lead to the 'lowest' rate of utilization of medical services. In line with this example, one Scottish study reported that a high degree of interaction with interlocking kinship and friendship networks might well have 'inhibited' women in social class V from using antenatal care services (McKinlay 1973).

Access to health care facilities

Ease of access to health care facilities has obvious implications for usage. Tudor Hart (1971) has argued that what he terms an *inverse care law* applies in Britain; that is, the provision of health care is inversely related to the need for it (i.e. poor facilities in depressed regions characterized by high morbidity and good, or better, facilities in affluent regions characterized by low morbidity). He relates this to the survival of the market economy: the more prosperous areas attract the most resources, including skilled manpower, in both primary and secondary care. Empirical support for this 'law' has accumulated steadily. To cite a single study, West and Lowe (1976) analysed data on the need for and provision of child health services for each of the 15 pre-1974 hospital board regions of England and Wales and found, for example, that regional provision of general practitioners and health visitors was negatively correlated with a number of indicators of need, including stillbirth rate, level of infant mortality and birthrate to teenage mothers. More specifically, it has been found that as distance between home and general practice increases the likelihood of consultation diminishes; this is particularly true for elderly or disabled people, who are relatively immobile (Parkin 1979).

Self care

Evidence quoted in the first part of this chapter showed that only a small minority of all symptoms are presented to a doctor. This suggests that self care, and especially *self-medication*, may be of considerable importance. Wadsworth et al. (1971) found that self-treatment with non-prescribed medicines and home remedies is indeed extremely common. Jefferys et al. (1960) produced evidence from their investigation of working-class families in 1954 that self care was used in addition to rather than as a substitute for doctor's care. In their more recent study of a national population sample, however, Dunnell and Cartwright (1972) found lower consultation rates among people who reported self-medication. It seems likely that the opposing findings of these two studies reflect real changes in patient behaviour over a span of two decades, as well as differences in behaviour among social classes.

Dunnell and Cartwright found that in a two-week period the ratio of non-prescribed to prescribed medicines taken by adults was approximately two to one; 67% of their sample had taken one or more non-prescribed medicines during this period. Moreover, only one in ten of the non-prescribed medicines consumed had been first suggested by a doctor; most were recommended by members of lay referral systems. The data suggested that adults tended to use self-medication as an alternative to medical consultation. Anderson et al. (1977) provide support for this finding, but add that while self-medication seems to be more popular among non-users than among users of the primary care services, non-users are also less inclined than users to obtain medical help for potentially serious symptoms. Dunnell and Cartwright found that for children self- or parent-medication seemed to be used more as a supplement to medical consultation. Table 8 shows the variation in medicine-taking by age for both adults and children.

Apart from simply ignoring symptoms, alternatives to consulting a doctor or self-medicating include reliance on *alternative medicine* (e.g. faith healing, homeopathy, herbalism, acupuncture and so on): it is thought that approximately 20 000 people in Britain are now practising 'medicine' without any official qualification or approval, about a quarter of them deriving a full-time living from their various therapies. Of particular interest, however, is the rapid growth of *self-help groups*. Some groups, like Alcoholics Anonymous, have been established for a long time and are well known; but there are many newer, less well-known groups — for schizophrenics, people with skin diseases, the depressed, people with hypertension, people with cancer, parents of handicapped

Table 8.   Variation in medicine-taking by age in a two-week period

Proportion of adults who had taken	Age group							All adults
	21–24	25–34	35–44	45–54	55–64	65–74	75 +	
Any medicine	75%	80%	80%	78%	80%	82%	92%	80%
Prescribed medicine	33%	40%	36%	32%	43%	49%	71%	41%
Non-prescribed medicine	67%	69%	71%	67%	64%	65%	71%	67%
Average number of medicines taken	2.1	2.0	2.1	2.1	2.2	2.7	3.2	2.2
No. of adults (= 100%)	81	230	289	269	258	194	87	1412

Proportion of children who had taken	Age group				All children
	Under 2	2–4	5–9	10–14	
Any medicine	78%	65%	49%	46%	55%
Prescribed medicine	35%	21%	16%	16%	20%
Non-prescribed medicine	74%	55%	43%	37%	48%
Average number of medicines taken	2.0	1.3	0.9	0.8	1.1
No. of children (= 100%)	68	113	169	169	519

From Dunnell and Cartwright (1972).

children and so on. Some of these were the brainchildren of health workers who are still active within them, but many operate quite independently of the formal health services: in fact, the impetus for the formation of a number of groups has so often been the lack of adequate understanding, care, treatment or support from the various health professions. Some commentators regard self-help groups as a poor substitute for people who are starved of 'real' services. Others, like Robinson (1980), argue that 'it is the professional health services which should be seen as the stop-gaps, filling in where basic mutual self-help needs specific technical, organizational or expert assistance'; they contend that self-help should be regarded as one of the basic components of primary health care.

In conclusion, it ought to be noted that some social scientists have attempted to incorporate all the factors known to influence illness behaviour into over-arching theories. As yet, no general theory has been very convincing. Moreover, it is difficult to see why it should be possible to generate an all-embracing theory which is at the same time informative and appropriate to *all* potential patients. A better policy would be to concentrate on how the various kinds of factors combine or interact to shape the illness behaviour of people with specific types of symptoms in specific types of personal, social and material circumstances. The need, then, is for highly focussed research and for a healthy scepticism concerning premature and over-ambitious generalizations.

References

ANDERSON, J., BUCK, C., DANAHER, K. & FRY, J. (1977) Users and non-users of doctors — implications for self-care. *J. R. Coll. gen. Practnrs*, **27**, 155–9.

BANKS, M., BERESFORD, S., MORRELL, D., WALLER, J. & WATKINS, C. (1975) Factors influencing demand for primary medical care in women aged 20–44 years: a preliminary report. *Int. J. Epidem.*, **4**, 189–95.

DUNNELL, K. & CARTWRIGHT, A. (1972) *Medicine-Takers, Prescribers and Hoarders*. London: Routledge and Kegan Paul.

FREIDSON, E. (1970) *Profession of Medicine*. New York: Dodds, Mead & Co.

JEFFERYS, M., BROTHERSTON, J. & CARTWRIGHT, A. (1960) Consumption of medicines on a working-class housing estate: *Br. J. prev. soc. Med.*, **14**, 64–76.

McKINLAY, J. (1973) Social networks, lay consultation and help-seeking behaviour. *Soc. Forces*, **53**, 255–92.

MECHANIC, D. & VOLKART, E. (1961) Stress, illness behaviour and the sick role. *Am. Soc. Rev.*, **5**, 51–8.

OFFICE OF HEALTH ECONOMICS (1964) *New Frontiers in Health*. London: HMSO.

PARKIN, D. (1979) Distance as an influence on demand in general practice. *Epidem. commun. Hlth*, **33**, 96–9.

PILOWSKY, I. & SPENCE, N. (1977) Ethnicity and illness behaviour. *Psychol. Med.*, **7**, 447–52.

ROBINSON, D. (1980) The self-help component of primary care. *Soc. Sci. Med.*, **14A**, 415–21.

SUCHMAN, E. (1965) Stages of illness and medical care. *J. Hlth soc. Behav.*, **6**, 114–28.

TUDOR HART, J. (1971) The inverse care law. *Lancet*, **1**, 405–12.

WADSWORTH, M., BUTTERFIELD, W. & BLANEY, R. (1971) *Health and Sickness: The Choice of Treatment.* London: Tavistock.

WEST, R. & LOWE, C. (1976) Regional variation in need for and provision and use of child health services in England and Wales. *Br. med. J.,* **2**, 843–6.

ZBOROWSKI, M. (1952) Cultural components in response to pain; *J. soc. Issues,* **8**, 16–30.

ZOLA, I. (1973) Pathways to the doctor: from person to patient. *Soc. Sci. Med.,* **7**, 677–89.

5

The Doctor–Patient Relationship

Myfanwy Morgan

There is a growing recognition that the interaction between doctor and patient during the consultation can have a considerable influence on the patient's well-being. That this is so is perhaps best illustrated by reference to the placebo effect. It has been estimated that as much as one-third of the success of any drug or procedure may be attributable to this effect (Beecher 1955). Indeed, the placebo effect makes the assessment of a new drug difficult, because even if the drug is completely inert it may still seem effective. To get a true picture, therefore, it is necessary to compare the new drug either with a previously used drug or with a placebo given to a similar group of patients. Whether the effectiveness of a placebo is attributed to the doctor's ability to inspire confidence and reduce anxiety, or to the faith and hope experienced by the patient on entry into a general practitioner's surgery or a hospital clinic, it is the social relationship between doctor and patient that engenders this powerful therapeutic effect.

Another way of showing the importance of the relationship between doctor and patient is to consider its influence on the communication of information. Information communicated by the patient usually plays a vital role in diagnosis and treatment decisions. It has been found however, that patients often fail to disclose their problems and anxieties, important reasons for this being their perception of the doctor's manner as abrupt and dismissive and their general awe of doctors (Fitton & Acheson 1979).

Features of the doctor–patient relationship

Sociologists have examined the doctor–patient relationship from a number of viewpoints, two of which have been especially prominent. Some sociologists, like Parsons (1951), have emphasized the shared understandings between doctor and patient, who are each seen as acting out roles or socially prescribed patterns of behaviour. Others, like Freidson (1970), have focussed on the potential conflict in this relationship and to the means employed by both doctors and patients to achieve their own goals. These two approaches, while emphasizing different aspects of the doctor–patient relationship, each contribute to an understanding of the nature of the social encounter between doctor and patient and form the basis of the following discussion.

Reciprocal roles of doctor and patient

The roles of doctor and patient, like other roles, such as those of husband, father or teacher, are associated with certain expectations, which consist of both rights and obligations. The particular rights and obligations associated with the roles of doctor and patient were described by Parsons (1951) as part of his comprehensive theoretical analysis of modern industrial society. Parsons viewed the role of the sick person or patient as essentially a temporary and undesirable one, imposing an obligation on those who enter it to return to a state of health as quickly as possible. To this end, sick people are accorded certain privileges; they are allowed, and may even be required, to give up some of their normal activities and responsibilities, and are regarded as being in need of care. However, these privileges are conditional on the obligation of the sick person wanting to get well, seeking professional medical advice, and most importantly for the doctor–patient relationship, cooperating with the doctor (Table 9). As Parsons points out, the specific expectations of the sick person, such as the number and type of activities the ill person is expected to give up, will be influenced by the nature and severity of the condition. It is also recognized that not all illness requires people to relinquish their normal social roles and occupy the status 'sick'. For example, much minor illness can be

Table 9.   Parsons' analysis of the roles of patients and doctors

Patient: sick role	Doctor: professional role
Obligations and Privileges	*Expected to*
1. Must want to get well as quickly as possible	1. Apply a high degree of skill and knowledge to the problems of illness
2. Should seek professional medical advice and cooperate with the doctor	2. Act for welfare of patient and community rather than for own self-interest, desire for money, advancement, etc.
3. Allowed (and may be expected) to shed some normal activities and responsibilities (e.g. employment, household tasks)	3. Be objective and emotionally detached (i.e. should not judge patients' behaviour in terms of personal value system or become emotionally involved with them)
Regarded as being in need of care and unable to get better by his or her own decision and will	4. Be guided by rules of professional practice
	Rights
	1. Granted right to examine patients physically and to enquire into intimate areas of physical and personal life
	2. Granted considerable autonomy in professional practice
	3. Occupies position of authority in relation to the patient

After Parsons (1951).

coped with without recourse to the doctor and does not require any changes to a person's every-day life; in the case of chronic illness people may need to consult the doctor regularly but are often expected to take up the other rights and obligations of the sick role only if they experience a change in their usual state of health. However, Parson's concept of the sick role is important in drawing attention to the general expectations of those who occupy the role of patient and to their relationship with the doctor.

Parsons viewed the role of the doctor as complementary to the role of the patient; whereas the patient is expected to cooperate fully with the doctor, doctors are expected to apply their specialist knowledge and skills for the benefit of the patient. In order to carry out the tasks of diagnosis and treatment, doctors often need to know intimacies about the patient which are not usually known between strangers. It may, for example, be necessary to carry out intimate physical examinations and to ask for information about the patient's personal affairs. The potential tensions arising from the personal nature of medical practice are, however, reduced by the obligation on the doctor to remain objective and emotionally detached, and to use this privileged position for the benefit of the patient and not for personal advantage.

The socially prescribed rights and obligations of doctor and patient are important in reducing the potential conflict and tension in the medical consultation but this may not be entirely eliminated (see p. 62). In addition, both doctors and sick people may experience uncertainty in their roles. Many potential patients, for example, are uncertain as to whether or not to consult the doctor, owing to their difficulty in assessing the nature or seriousness of their symptoms. Doctors may, in turn, experience uncertainty in their diagnosis or treatment decisions. This may arise from their incomplete or imperfect mastery of current medical knowledge, or from the limitations of medical knowledge itself, while in some instances doctors may find it difficult to distinguish between these two sources of uncertainty. When doctors are faced with uncertainty in diagnosis, the general tendency is to continue to suspect illness, the assumption being that it is better to continue to search for disease than to risk overlooking it. However, this assumption in favour of disease may have serious negative consequences for patients if they have to undergo unnecessary investigation or treatment.

Types of doctor–patient relationship

Parsons depicted the doctor–patient relationship in broad terms as an asymmetrical relationship in which the doctor occupies a dominant position by virtue of his or her specialized knowledge and skill and the high status accorded to the medical profession. Szasz and Hollender (1956) subsequently identified three basic types of doctor–patient relationship, which they labelled 'activity–passivity', 'guidance–cooperation' and 'mutual participation'. Their model is summarized in Table 10.

The relationship characterized as 'guidance–cooperation' is probably the most common, especially in general practice consultations. However, the relationship of 'mutual participation' is becoming increasingly prevalent, for this approach is regarded as essential for the management of chronic illness in which the treatment programme is carried out by the patient with only occasional instruction by the doctor. For example, in the case of diabetes mellitus patients rely episodically on the doctor's expertise, but have to make their own judgements as to food intake, to monitor their own blood sugar level and to alter the dose of insulin or tablets when necessary.

Szasz and Hollender believe that the particular type of relationship which characterizes a medical consultation may be different at different stages of the patient's treatment and will depend on both the condition of the patient and the therapy the doctor considers appropriate. However, it has been suggested that Szasz and Hollenders' analysis depicts the type of relationship the doctor would like to achieve in treating particular conditions, rather than the inevitable outcome of these conditions, because in practice the nature of the encounter is often subject to negotiation between doctor and patient. It has also been pointed out that Szasz and Hollender might have added a fourth type of relationship, in which the patient guides and the doctor cooperates. This could be said to occur when the doctor fulfils a patients' expectations and demands for a prescription, referral, and so on.

Conflict and control in the doctor–patient relationship

So far the relationship between doctor and patient has been viewed as reciprocal and based on shared understandings. However, although the shared expectations of doctor and patient provide a general framework for the medical consultation, other writers have drawn attention to the potential conflict in the relationship arising from the differing interests, expectations and knowledge of the lay person and professional.

Table 10. Szasz and Hollender's three basic models of the doctor–patient relationship

Model	Physician's role	Patient's role	Clinical application	Proto-type
Activity–passivity	Does something to patient	Recipient (unable to respond)	Anaesthesia, coma, acute trauma, delusion etc.	Parent–infant
Guidance–cooperation	Tells patient what to do	Cooperator (obeys)	Acute infections, diseases etc.	Parent–child (adolescent)
Mutual participation	Helps patient to help himself	Participant in 'partnership'	Most chronic illness, psychoanalysis etc.	Adult–adult

After Szasz and Hollender (1956).

For example, Freidson (1970) states, 'It is my thesis that the separate worlds of experience and reference of the layman and the professional worker are always in potential conflict with one another.' He believes that the doctor–patient relationship should thus be viewed in terms of a 'clash of perspectives'.

One important source of conflict lies in the differing interests and priorities of doctor and patient. Whereas the individual patient is concerned only with his or her particular condition and treatment, the doctor has to balance the competing needs of large numbers of patients. The individual patient's desire for a longer consultation with the doctor to discuss his or her problems more fully, or to remain in hospital for a few extra days before having to cope at home, has, for example, to be balanced by the doctor against the needs of other patients in the waiting room or other patients requiring hospital admission. Doctors may also experience conflicts between their obligations to help individual patients and their duties as agents of the state. For example, when does a general practitioner decide not to give a certificate which will entitle the patient to a financial benefit and absence from work?

Conflict and tension in the doctor–patient relationship also arise from the recognition that in every age there are a number of worthless treatments and that doctors may make errors in their diagnosis or treatment decisions. Patients, rather than accepting the expertise of the doctor, may therefore try to evaluate and influence the medical process, while doctors may be reluctant to relinquish control of the consultation and their position as medical expert. Doctors and patients may also differ in their evaluations of the seriousness of a condition as a result of differences both in their medical knowledge and in their personal experience of illness. This is illustrated by a study in which both general practitioners and their patients were asked to assess the seriousness of presented conditions in both a medical and social sense (Fitton & Acheson 1979). Judging by the doctors' assessments, some patients underestimated the medical seriousness of their condition and others overestimated it. On the other hand, doctors often did not appreciate the effect of the condition on the patients' every-day life; 67% of the conditions were assessed by patients as serious in terms of their every-day life compared with only 53% by the doctors.

A further source of conflict stems from the doctors' contradictory expectations of patient behaviour. Doctors frequently complain about patients who consult with 'trivia' and characterize the ideal patient as someone who is able to assess his or her own health with sufficient expertise to know which conditions should be presented and when they should be presented for medical attention. Indeed, much health education is directed toward this end of increasing the population's knowledge of health matters to enable the layperson to arrive at reasonably well founded decisions in this sphere. However, this role prescription for potential patients contrasts with the expectation that the patient who consults the doctor will exhibit a deferential manner and accept unquestioningly the doctor's diagnosis and suggested course of action. Patients are therefore placed in what has been referred to as a *double-bind* situation. This is used not in the technical sense in which it is employed in relation to mental illness, but in the every-day sense to describe a situation in which a person is subject to conflicting sets of expectations (Bloor & Horobin 1974).

Conflict between doctor and patient rarely becomes overt. However, both doctors and patients may employ strategies to try to influence the course and outcome of the consultation. These strategies may be grouped into four broad categories:

1. *Persuasion.* Patients may try to persuade the doctor that a particular type of treatment is appropriate by presenting information in a form which they believe is likely to lead the doctor to their desired course of action. For example, a study of parents and specialists in ENT clinics showed that parents commonly mentioned the general practitioner's diagnosis, and the general practitioner's feelings that tonsillectomy might be necessary, rather than directly stating their opinion that their child's tonsils should be removed (Bloor 1977); the assumption was that the consultant was more likely to be impressed by the general practitioner's opinion than by that of the patient. Doctors, rather than accepting patients' requested or suggested course of action, may try to convince patients that their approach is best by overwhelming patients with evidence in the form of laboratory tests, or their own previous experience in treating patients with similar types of conditions, in support of their chosen course of action. This may be accompanied by a warning of the likely consequences of neglecting their advice.

2. *Bargaining.* This refers to the process whereby doctors and patients reach a compromise. Roth (1963) describes the

bargaining between patients with tuberculosis and their doctors over the length of their treatment programme. He attributed the patients' success in shortening their medical 'timetable' largely to the medical uncertainty concerning the likely course of their condition.

3. *Functional uncertainty.* Even when doctors are themselves certain about the course of a disease or outcome of therapy, they may deliberately prolong patients' uncertainty. This 'functional uncertainty' serves managerial ends, such as saving staff time and avoiding the emotional scenes with the patients and their families which sometimes follow the disclosure of information (Davis 1960). Prolonged uncertainty also enables doctors to maintain their power over patients, for the less uncertain patients become about the nature of the illness and the effects of treatment, the less willing they may be to leave decision-making to the doctor.

4. *Non-verbal behaviour.* It has been calculated that in a normal two-person conversation the verbal component carries less than 35% of the social meaning of the situation and more than 65% is carried by the non-verbal component (Pietroni 1976). Non-verbal cues in the consultation, as in other forms of social interaction, are important in establishing a rapport between doctor and patient and in influencing the amount of information exchanged. For example, continued rifling through notes, twiddling with pens and failure to look directly at the patient may be viewed as a sign of disinterest and result in patients failing to disclose their problems. The relative positions of doctor and patient in the consulting room may also influence the nature of the relationship. This is illustrated by a simple experiment carried out by a cardiologist in which he removed the desk from his clinic on alternate days. He found that when he removed his desk 50% of the patients sat back in their chair in an at-ease position, whereas only 10% did so when he was sitting behind his desk (Pietroni 1976). Another example of the influence of the physical organization of the consultation is provided by Bloor (1977) in his study of ENT clinics. Bloor describes a consultation in which the doctor examined a child who was accompanied by his mother. In carrying out the examination the doctor placed himself between the child and the mother and kept his back to the mother throughout, thus making it difficult for her to speak to him. Carrying out certain diagnostic tests which require the doctor's attention and

concentration is also in itself an effective way of silencing a patient. Non-verbal techniques may be used not only to control the consultation but also to serve as a signal that the consultation has ended, as for example when doctors rise to their feet, write out a prescription or hold open the door.

Doctors generally occupy the dominant position in the consultation owing to their professional status and specialist knowledge and greater experience in managing the medical encounter. It is thus the doctor who generally controls the dialogue and creates entry and exit cues for the patient and decides when the consultation has come to an end. The patient's ability to influence the consultation depends on such factors as his level of medical knowledge about his illness problem, whether or not he is experiencing great pain and discomfort and his general ability to express his feelings, as well as on the doctor's willingness to release control and recognize the patient's role in the medical process. This may in turn be influenced by the nature of the medical system in which the consultation takes place. Doctors may accommodate more readily, for example, to patients' expectations in a fee-for-service system than when they are salaried employees. Hospital doctors who see patients on referral from colleagues may also be more able to resist patients' demands than general practitioners whose incomes depend directly on attracting and retaining the loyalty of patients.

The social functions of prescribing

Prescribing is a common feature of general practice consultations; on average between 65 and 70% of such consultations now end with a prescription, although there is a wide variation between individual general practitioners (Howie 1977). The large volume of prescribing can be explained in part by the high proportion of chronic conditions presented to the doctor. In many cases, however, prescriptions appear to be given for minor illness for which they are unlikely to have any intrinsic therapeutic value. One reason for the tendency to prescribe may be the influence of drug advertising and promotion on doctors' behaviour. However, prescribing also fulfils important social functions in the consultation. For example, doctors may prescribe in order to satisfy what they perceive, sometimes incorrectly, to be patient expectations. Issuing a prescription also helps doctors to cope with problems of uncertainty, by allowing them to engage in positive action and thereby to convey to the patient that they are in control of the situation. Prescribing can also serve to communicate the doctors' concern for their patients and may make for a shorter consultation than the only available alternatives, for example a willingness to listen to the patient.

Marsh (1977) reported the result of an experiment designed to reduce the volume of prescribing for minor illness in his general practice unit. The doctors stopped the receptionists issuing repeat prescriptions and deliberately assumed the traditional role of teacher. They discussed the nature of minor illness with patients and where appropriate explained that the condition for which they sought a prescription was self-limiting and would not respond faster to drugs; at the same time they taught patients about a variety of home remedies for symptomatic relief. The result was that the number of items prescribed per month in the study practice decreased by 19% compared with 4% in other practices in the locality.

The issuing of a prescription at one consultation may have implications extending beyond that particular consultation. This is because when the doctor prescribes for a patient the implicit message is that the consultation was appropriate and that the problem was appropriate for medical treatment. The doctor's action in a particular consultation is thus likely to affect the patient's future expectations and behaviour.

The outcome of the consultation

Doctors are often unaware of whether or not patients are satisfied with a consultation. This is because, whatever their views, patients tend to retain a deferential attitude in the medical encounter, reflecting the general expectations of the patient role. When the doctor dismisses a problem as unimportant or ignores a symptom presented by the patient, the patient's lack of persistence may therefore not necessarily indicate that he or she perceives the problem as unimportant, while patients rarely tell the doctor if they disagree with their advice or have no intention of following it. As Cartwright and

Anderson (1981) point out, it is much easier to communicate a positive than a negative desire and so doctors may be unaware when patients do not want a prescription, referral and so on, but will generally realize it when they do.

For patients, a medical consultation forms part of a continuing process of coping with illness. Before the consultation patients often 'rehearse' what appear to be important facts about their condition so as to ensure as far as they can that their needs are stated. They also tend to evaluate the process and outcome of the consultation, in terms both of their own aims and expectations in seeing the doctor and of the advice and assessments of relatives and friends.

One important source of dissatisfaction is the doctor's failure to uncover the problem which gave rise to the consultation. This may be due to the limited time available for the consultation (an average of six minutes for a general practitioner consultation), but it may also reflect the patient's difficulty in expressing fears or describing symptoms or the doctor's lack of receptivity to distress signals. The psychodynamic literature suggests that, for a variety of deep-seated reasons, patients may mask the 'real' problem which brings them to the consultation and that the task of the doctor is to 'get behind' what patients say to find out what they 'really' mean (Balint 1975).

Changes in medical practice

A number of changes are taking place in the medical field which may have implications for the doctor–patient relationship. One such change relates to the perception of the general practitioner's role. A national survey conducted in 1977 by Cartwright and Anderson (1981) found that only 67% of doctors and 30% of patients thought it was appropriate for people to seek help from their general practitioner for problems in their family lives, compared with 87% of doctors and 40% of patients in a similar survey in 1964 (Cartwright 1967). It is not easy to interpret this finding. However, it is possible that the setting up of social services departments may have given both doctors and patients the idea that social workers would be available for this aspect of their care, while doctors may be becoming increasingly concerned about their ability to help with such problems. The appropriate role of the general practitioner, in relation to social and quasi-medical problems such as attempted suicide, alcoholism and aggressive behaviour, is subject to debate. Patients' reasons for consulting the doctor about such problems include the ease of access to the doctor's surgery, the confidentiality of the doctor–patient relationship and fear of the stigma often associated in people's minds with the use of other types of services. However, doctors can generally only help people cope with such problems, often through drug therapy, rather than bring about changes in a person's domestic or work situation which gives rise to the problems. What is widely accepted, however, is that doctors do have an important role in providing social care, particularly for those with chronic illness and disabilities. The doctor may also often need to take account of the patient's domestic and work situation in making decisions about, for example, hospital admission or fitness to return to work.

Two changes are taking place which are likely to reduce the personal nature of the relationship between doctor and patient. One change is the steady decline in home visiting. Cartwright and Anderson (1981) found in their 1977 survey that 91% of patients had received no home visit or only one during the previous 12 months, compared with 85% in 1964. The number of home visits patients had received in the last year was also found to be closely related to patients' satisfaction with their care, to their definition of the doctor as friendly rather than business-like and to their assessment of whether or not they would consult their doctor about a personal problem that worried them. Another significant and continuing change is in the size of general practices. In England and Wales the proportion of single-handed practices has declined from 25% in 1964 to 17% in 1976, while the number of group practices with four or more partners and health centres has increased. This in turn has been associated with an increase in the employment of nurses and other health workers on these premises. As a result, patients attending a general practice are less likely to see their 'own' doctor and are more likely to see a nurse as well as, or even instead of, a general practitioner.

A further change with implications for the doctor–patient relationship is the increasingly critical attitude being adopted by patients towards their medical care. This is probably partly due to the current emphasis on individual responsibility for health and the increasing awareness and education of the public in medical and health matters, together with the trend in many spheres of life for authority to be questioned more openly. Patients may increasingly ask for explanations of the doctor's actions and treatment and insist on a negotiating stance with the doctor, rather than fulfil the role of the dependent unquestioning patient.

This examination of the social nature of the doctor–patient relationship has shown that, although the interaction between doctor and patient often appears to be unproblematic, it may conceal underlying tensions and conflicts. Similarly, what may appear to be an ideal consultation from the doctor's perspective may not accord with the patient's appraisal. In view of the apparent influence of the relationship between doctor and patient on both the content and outcome of medical practice it is important that the physician is aware of the social influences on the consultation and in particular of the effects of the doctor's verbal and non-verbal management of the consultation on patient's behaviour and satisfaction with the encounter. To the extent that the relationship between doctor and patient becomes more equal and doctors more readily reveal the limits of medical knowledge this is likely to have the positive effect of making patients' expectations more realistic.

References

BALINT, M. (1975) *The Doctor, His Patient and the Illness.* New York: International Universities Press.

BEECHER, H. (1955) The powerful placebo. *J. Am. med. Ass.*, **159**, 602–6.

BLOOR, M. (1977) Professional autonomy and client exclusion: a study in ENT clinics. In: *Studies in Everyday Medical Life*, ed. M. Wadsworth & D. Robinson. London: Martin Robertson.

BLOOR, M. & HOROBIN, G. (1974) Conflict and conflict resolution in doctor-patient interactions. In: *A Sociology of Medical Practice*, ed. C. Cox & A. Mead. London: Collier Macmillan.

CARTWRIGHT, A. (1967) *Patients and their Doctors: a Study of General Practice.* London: Routledge and Kegan Paul.

CARTWRIGHT, A. & ANDERSON, R. (1981) *General Practice Revisited: A Second Study of Patients and Their Doctors.* London: Tavistock.

DAVIS, F. (1960) Uncertainty in medical diagnosis — clinical and functional. *Am. J. Sociol.*, **66**, 41; 47.

FITTON, F. & ACHESON, H. W. K. (1979) *Doctor/Patient Relationship: A Study in General Practice.* London: HMSO.

FRIEDSON, E. (1970) Dilemmas in the doctor–patient relationship. In: *A Sociology of Medical Practice.* ed. C. Cox & A. Mead. London: Collier Macmillan.

HOWIE, J. G. (1977) Prescribing. *Trends in General Practice,* ed. J. Fry. London: Royal College of General Practitioners.

MARSH, G. N. (1977) 'Curing' minor illness in general practice. *Br. med. J.,* 2, 1267–9.

PARSONS, T. (1951) *The Social System.* Glencoe, Ill.: The Free Press.

PIETRONI, P. (1976) Language and communication in general practice. In: *Communication in the General Practice Surgery,* ed. B. Tanner. London: Hodder and Stoughton.

ROTH, J. (1963) *Timetables.* Indianapolis: Bobbs-Merrill.

SZASZ, T. S. & HOLLENDER, M. H. (1956) A contribution to the philosophy of medicine: the basic models of the doctor–patient relationship. *Archs intern. Med.,* 97, 585–92.

6

Hospitals and Patients

Myfanwy Morgan

Hospitals have developed during this century from their role of providing a refuge for the sick and homeless or for the dying poor to occupy a central place in medical practice (see Chapter 16). Many hospitals also provide education and training for doctors, nurses and other health workers, and many serve as a setting for research. The patient admitted to hospital thus enters a complex institution with a variety of goals and a well developed system of rules and procedures for coordinating the different activities and the large numbers of specialized staff.

The experience of being a patient in hospital necessarily varies according to the patient's medical condition and the environment of the particular hospital. Despite these differences it is possible to identify some common features of patients' experiences *in* hospital and of the effects *of* hospitalization.

Patterns of hospital care

One way of examining the different forms of hospital organization is through the use of an ideal type model. The term 'ideal type' is used to refer to a model which abstracts and presents what are regarded as the fundamental features of a particular social organization or social role and forms an important method of analysing and describing very complex social phenomena. Table 11 presents three such ideal type models: those of custodial, classical and rehabilitative care. These characterizations are useful in drawing attention to differences in the goals and patterns of care which occur

Table 11.   Models of patient care

	Models of patient care		
Dimension	*Custodial*	*Classical*	*Rehabilitation*
(Stated) goal	Comfort	Care	Restoration
Assumptions about disease process	Incurable	Reversible	Mutable
Therapy	Sporadic	Central	Supplementary
Sick role	Permanent	Temporary	Intermittent
Patient motivation	Obedience to institution's rules	Obedience to 'doctors' orders'	Achieve mastery
Resulting institutional model	Total institution	Acute general hospital	Rehabilitation centre

After Coe (1970).

between hospitals, or even between wards within a hospital. However, as with all ideal type models, they abstract what are regarded as the main features of different forms of hospital organization and do not take into account the overlap between the various types of care that often occur in the real world.

Custodial care model

This pattern is characteristic of hospitals (and individual wards) in which the actual, if not the official, objective is to provide care designed to make the patient as comfortable as possible in an enduring situation, for it is assumed that the patient's condition is more or less permanent. The goal of patient management in turn leads to an emphasis on efficiency of organization and conformity with institutional rules.

The custodial care model was common prior to the advent of modern medicine and is still found on many long-stay wards. In its extreme form it approximates the characteristics of the total institution described by Goffman (1961). Goffman defined a total institution as 'a place where a large number of like-situated individuals, cut off from the wider society for an appreciable period of time, together lead an enclosed, formally administered round of life'. Total institutions include such establishments as mental hospitals, old people's homes, prisons and army barracks. These institutions differ in their stated goals and ideology, whether membership is voluntary or involuntary, and in the degree to which actual barriers separate them from the outside world. However, despite these differences, Goffman viewed total institutions as sharing a similar pattern of internal organization characterized by the following features:

1. *Batch living.* This refers to a situation where all the different activities of daily life, such as work, sleeping and leisure activities, are carried out with a large group of others, all of whom are treated alike. This, of course, forms a marked contrast to non-institutional life where work, sleeping and leisure activities are carried out in different places and often with different people. In addition, in total institutions all activities are carried out according to a programme which is imposed on the inmate, rather than being left to individual choice and decision.

2. *Binary management.* This consists of a basic distinction between the staff who are the managers and the patients who are the managed. Goffman described the relationship between staff and patients as being characterized by hostility and there being little communication between the two groups.

3. *Institutional perspective.* The various activities, rules and methods of organization form part of an overall plan which is supposedly designed to fulfil the official aims of the institution. For example, the rules and activities in psychiatric hospitals devoted to custodial care are all designed to contribute to the stated goal of caring for large numbers of people on a long-term basis.

Goffman recognized that these three features of the internal organization of total institutions are not unique to such institutions but believed that total institutions possess each of these characteristics to a greater degree than other types of institutions.

Goffman identified three mechanisms which are employed in such institutions, knowingly or not, to facilitate the uniform management of inmates. One mechanism is *stripping*, which refers to the removal of the physical and psychological reminders of the individual's self-identity and status in the outside world. Stripping can occur in three ways:

1. Through the restriction of personal possessions and the replacement of the individual's own clothing and other items with standard issue.

2. The individual may experience an intrusion into his privacy and be required to make personal information widely available.

3. Submission to various demeaning practices may be required, such as asking for permission to smoke or post letters, being addressed in an unaccustomed manner such as being referred to by surname only, or being forced to engage in behaviour usually confined to children, such as eating of food with a spoon.

A second mechanism is the *control of resources*, which involves the control of information related both to events in the institution and to information concerning the individual. The third mechanism is the *restriction of mobility*, with permission being required to move outside certain confines.

Goffman described the organization of total institutions as presenting conflicts for staff, especially between the goals of efficient management on the one hand and the maintenance of humane standards of care on the other. Potential conflicts between these two legitimate goals may be most acutely felt by the nurses and other staff in hourly contact with patients. It is not altogether surprising that if resources of personnel and time are short, as they often are in long-stay psychiatric or geriatric wards and hospitals, humane treatment may break down, even erupting occasionally in the uncontrolled violent behaviour of staff to patients.

Studies of psychiatric hospitals, children's homes and homes for the elderly have provided empirical evidence of this custodial-management model of care, with its emphasis on conformity with institutional rules and the existence of rigid rules and standardized practices. Although patterns of care which resemble Goffman's total institution can still be found, especially in large institutions, there has been a marked decline in this type of organization since the early 1960s (Scull 1977). This has been associated with an attempt to restructure institutions to provide a rehabilitative rather than a custodial environment, and with a move from institutional to community care. For example, in just 20 years, mental hospitals in the USA have reduced their patient population by two-thirds, and those in Britain by one-third, owing to the substantial decline in patients' length of hospital stay.

The reasons for the decline in the psychiatric hospital population are subject to debate. Some believe that the major factor was the introduction of the phenothiazine drugs during the mid-1950s, which reduced the numbers of patients with aggressive or disruptive behaviour. The role of drug therapy is, however, questioned by those who believe that the major factor was the change in ideas regarding mental illness. They point to several hospitals which initiated the regimen of early discharge before the new drugs were available. Others place considerable emphasis on the importance of humanitarian concerns about the harmful effects of custodial care institutions. The role of humanitarian concerns is, however, questioned by those who view the changes in policy largely as an economic response to the increasing cost of institutional care. For example, Scull (1977) challenges the view that the move from institutional to community care in the 1960s was essentially a beneficient reform arising from progress in understanding the harmful effects of such institutions, or from developments in drug therapy. He argues that the real reason was the government's urgent need to reduce the costs of care and the belief that this could be achieved by reducing the numbers in hospital beds, while this was made possible from the mid-1950s by the growth of financial benefits and community services which enabled such people to exist outside the institution.

Classical care model

This now forms the most prevalent pattern of hospital care. It assumes that patients will be treated primarily for acute conditions and that once diagnosis and treatment have taken place they will either be discharged from hospital to take up their normal social roles or have died. Interaction between patients and staff tends to be episodic and oriented towards the implementation of specific procedures. The patient is expected to be passive and to cooperate with the staff in order to expedite the curative process. Relationships between different categories of staff tend to be hierarchial and authoritarian, the unquestioning obedience of the lower ranks being justified on the grounds of the emergency nature of most medical tasks.

The pattern of care associated with the classical care model bears some resemblance to the total institution, for the general hospital provides, if only temporarily, for all the necessities of life for patients, many activities are carried out to schedule and a gulf exists between staff and patients. However, there is a greater emphasis on individual treatment and care and the opportunities for batch management are limited because a wide variety of illness and stages of treatment are represented on any given ward and many patients are physically too ill to do anything without assistance.

Rehabilitation model

This pattern of care exists mainly where patients have chronic conditions, which, if they respond to treatment at all, do so only over a relatively long period. The emphasis is therefore on the restoration of normal function, adjustment and retraining. The goal of rehabilitation means that patients cannot be regarded as passive recipients of medical care but must be encouraged and motivated to collaborate with the staff in achieving the maximum level of functioning. Such collaboration over a relatively long period serves to reduce the social distance between patients and staff, while the various categories of staff tend to coordinate their activities and work with the medical profession as members of a treatment team.

One study which illustrates the differences between the custodial and rehabilitation models of patient care is Coser's study of Sunnydale Hospital, a community hospital in the USA (Coser 1963). Coser compared the social structure and the attitudes of staff in five buildings which together provide 650 beds for the long-term chronic sick for whom no major improvements were deemed possible, with a sixth building which consisted of a 100-bed rehabilitation centre for patients with poliomyelitis, respiratory, muscular, rheumatic and other diseases who were thought capable of responding to an intensive rehabilitation programme. Coser's findings with regard to staff attitudes and practices in these two settings are summarized in Table 12.

Another study which draws attention to the differences between the custodial and rehabilitation patterns of care is a

Table 12. Staff perceptions and behaviour in two treatment facilities

Staff perceptions and behaviour	Centre (rehabilitation)	Other hospital beds (custodial care)
Staff perceptions of discharge	Gratifying and rewarding	Disruptive of normal routine
Nurses' conception about the ward at its best	Patients out of bed and active	Clean ward (i.e. housekeeping focus)
Staff–patient interaction	High	Low

After Coser (1963).

comparison of residential care for mentally handicapped children provided in hospital wards and in residential homes conducted by King et al. (1973). The hospital wards were found closely to resemble Goffman's total institution, with the children being subject to batch management and having little contact and communication with staff. In contrast, the residential homes were child-oriented and based on a household type of organization: staff of all grades mixed freely with the children, ate their meals with the children and shared in other activities of the unit, and considerable emphasis was placed on the children's individual needs. An important consequence was that the children were significantly more advanced in speech and feeding than those in the institutionally oriented hospital wards. The authors concluded that the differences in the patterns of organization could not be explained by differences in the size of the institutions or in the degree of handicap of the children. Instead they identified the key factors as being the differences in institutional goals and in the freedom accorded to the head of the unit to organize the institution according to the needs of the children, rather than all decisions concerning staff activities, the purchase of new clothes and toys for the children and other matters being decided centrally. They also point to the importance both of the orientation of staff and of their availability in determining the pattern of care, for individualized care is not possible when staff–patient ratios fall below certain levels at peak times.

Staff perceptions and patient care

Staff perceptions and responses to patients within a particular institutional setting are often influenced by social considerations. One way in which social factors affect patient care is through admission and discharge decisions. In making such decisions doctors may have regard not only to the patients' clinical conditions but also to their broader physical and social environments. Thus patients may be admitted or retained in hospital for conditions which would otherwise be treated on an out-patient or primary care basis if they are perceived as lacking family support or having unfavourable housing conditions. Reviews of hospital use have shown that between 3% and 25% of beds are occupied primarily for social reasons, the proportion being greatest in long-stay and geriatric hospitals. The major factor responsible for such use is the lack of, or inability of family members to provide, care at home. This is most common when patients are elderly and single, widowed or divorced. For example, a survey of surgical and orthopaedic beds showed that 16% of the 265 occupied beds were filled by patients who had no medical need to be in an acute ward (Murphy 1977). Of these patients, 67% had previously lived alone, compared with only 24% of the patients who were regarded as having a medical need to be in an acute ward. The term 'blocked bed' is often used by administrators and doctors when patients remain in hospital for a prolonged period (generally 30 days or more) because of their need for care, rather than medical treatment or skilled nursing, and the lack of alternative residential facilities in the community to which they might be transferred. Problems in discharging patients are a cause of considerable concern to staff, especially in the acute sector with its emphasis on active medical intervention. (The adverse consequences of long-term hospitalization for patients are considered later in this chapter.)

Staff perceptions of patients not only influence admission and discharge decisions but may also affect the treatment and care patients received. For example, hospital staff have been shown to evaluate patients in terms of concepts of social worth common in the larger society. One widely held belief in western industrial society is that the young are more valuable than the old, which has been shown to be associated with differences in efforts to resuscitate young and old patients (Sudnow 1967). Another type of evaluation concerns the appropriateness of patients' demands on the hospital service. Patients who present at accident and emergency departments with trivial or self-inflicted conditions, such as those who have attempted suicide or are drunk, are often viewed as placing unnecessary demands on the service and may be 'punished' by being given less sympathetic treatment by staff or by being made to wait for medical attention. Similarly, Lorber (1975) found in a study of patients on surgical wards that those who were perceived as uncooperative, over-emotional or complaining, when such behaviour was regarded as unwarranted by their illness, were labelled as 'problem patients' by staff members who had to bear the brunt of the trouble. Such problem patients in the in-patient setting are frequently dealt with by being given tranquillizers or sedatives and may on occasion be referred to a psychiatrist or discharged earlier from the ward (Lorber 1975).

Psychosocial effects of hospitalization

The admission of a patient to hospital forms a regular and routine experience for the hospital staff. In contrast, hospital admission generally forms an infrequent but major event in the life of the individual patient and many have psychological consequences of both a short- and a long-term nature.

Stress and hospitalization

Patients who enter hospital are generally people with 'something wrong' with them that requires diagnosis, treatment or both. This in itself is often sufficient to arouse anxiety, while for some patients there may be considerable uncertainty about whether they may be really cured, left with a physical disability or faced with an early death. In addition, patients may have worries about how their family will manage without them or whether they will be able to return to their usual job. A further factor contributing to patients' anxiety is the general environment of the hospital, especially if they lack knowledge about the various routines and procedures and the functions of the different categories of staff, as well as the stress produced by other patients' behaviour and the general activities of the ward.

Not surprisingly, studies have shown that a fairly high proportion of hospital patients report feelings of anxiety. For example, a study by Hugh-Jones et al. (1964) of recently admitted patients in a medical ward of a London teaching hospital found that 41% of men and 36% of women were worried about being in hospital. Similarly, Franklin (1974), in a study of 160 male patients in the surgical wards of four hospitals, classified 13% as being 'very worried' on admission to hospital and 36% as 'a little worried'. While anxiety is common among hospital patients, the main cause and level of anxiety may change during a patient's hospital stay. For example, Wilson-Barnett and Carrigy (1978), in a longitudinal study of medical patients, found that patients reported significantly more anxiety on 'special test' days than on others, because of their concern about what would happen and how much discomfort would be experienced. Patients' level of anxiety may in turn affect their experience of pain and requirement for analgesics when undergoing special tests, such as endoscopy, or during the postoperative period (see Chapter 7).

Before discharge patients may experience anxiety about how they will manage when they return home. A study of patients' attitudes to the hospital service carried out for the Royal Commission (1978) showed that 18% of the 800 recently discharged patients interviewed were worried about being able to manage at home. Anxiety about managing at home was particularly common among maternity patients, with 30% experiencing anxiety; however, despite concern about coping after discharge, 95% of them said that once they got home they managed all right.

One group of patients who often exhibit great emotional stress are children. Many young children admitted to hospital show an immediate reaction of acute distress and crying, followed by a period of misery and apathy, and later a period of detachment, while disturbed behaviour may persist for several months after the child returns home. Children shown to be most distressed by hospitalization are those who are generally uncommunicative, isolated, shy, very young or without brothers or sisters. In order to try and reduce the adverse effects of hospitalization on child patients, emphasis is now placed on avoiding hospitalization if possible and encouraging a greater amount of contact between parents and children in hospital (Stacey et al. 1970).

An important factor in patients' anxiety is fear of the unknown which can be reduced by the provision of information.

Patients' uncertainties about what to expect in hospital, such as the general organization and routines, may be dealt with by giving them an explanatory booklet prior to admission. While this is common practice in many hospitals, a recent national survey found that only 59% of discharged patients reported being given such a booklet, although the majority of these people regarded the booklet as very useful (Royal Commission 1978). However, of greater importance, and particularly in relation to medical matters, is the direct communication of information by staff.

Depersonalization

The experience of hospital in-patient care not only gives rise to feelings of fear and anxiety but often produces a sense of depersonalization, or loss of self-identity. Unlike the psychiatric symptom of the same name, this type of depersonalization stems from the loss of the patients' normal social roles and separation from their familiar environment, and is accentuated by the impersonality of the hospital system. The Royal Commission's study showed that just over one-third (36%) of the recently discharged patients interviewed felt they had been treated in hospital as 'just another case' rather than as individuals. Such feelings can be promoted by the management practices of hospitals, in particular by the uniform treatment of large groups of patients. Lack of privacy may also contribute to feelings of depersonalization. The Royal Commission's study showed that 10% of patients reported a lack of privacy in being treated or examined due to their being overheard or seen by other patients, 13% reported a lack of privacy when washing or bathing and 23% felt they did not have enough privacy when having visitors, although this caused least concern. A survey carried out in a London teaching hospital indicated that there was no significant difference in the proportions of patients complaining of a lack of privacy in the large 31-bed wards and the 4-bed wards (Noble & Dixon 1977). This is possibly because, although a small ward reduces the number of patients in an individual's immediate environment, he or she may feel more exposed to the gaze of others and the activities taking place in the ward.

Although the depersonalization of patients can be viewed as a negative consequence of hospital management practices, it is believed by some to have positive functions for both patients and staff. For example, it can be argued that the treatment of patients on an impersonal basis, as 'a case of x', helps to protect nursing and other staff from the strain which arises from close involvement with chronically sick and dying patients and so enables them to cope with situations of inherently great psychological stress. Similarly, nurses on a ward may be asked to do specific tasks for all the patients rather than the total nursing care of a small number on the grounds that it reduces the possibility of close personal attachments, which are seen as dangerous to both nurse and patient. It should be pointed out, however, that such a view is increasingly questioned by current nursing theory which emphasizes the therapeutic value to the patient of a continuing relationship with a nurse able to give emotional support as well as technically competent nursing services.

In some circumstances, it has been argued that depersonalization facilitates the carrying out of medical procedures of a potentially embarrassing nature, as for example when the medical consultation relates to a gynaecological or obstetric problem. Elaborate procedures designed to depersonalize such consultations were described and analysed by Emerson (1970). She showed that, although the use of technical and impersonal language and the matter-of-fact stance adopted by the staff were designed to emphasize the medical context and protect both doctor and patient from a potentially embarrassing encounter with sexual connotations, the depersonalization of patients could constitute an indignity in itself, arousing anxiety and hostility especially if doctors did little to reassure patients or recognize feelings of pain. The goal, as Emerson states, is to '... convey an optimal combination of impersonality and hints of intimacy that simultaneously avoid the insult of sexual familiarity and the insult of unacknowledged identity'.

Institutionalization

Institutionalization refers to the process by which patients in long-stay hospitals and other total institutions acquire the characteristics of apathy, general lack of interest and inability to undertake simple tasks and to make choices and decisions. Institutionalized patients generally fear leaving the institution and having to cope in the outside world. This response to long-term custodial care is often accompanied by particular physical characteristics, such as a slow and shuffling gait, the head bent forward, and mumbled speech (Barton 1959).

The relatively high prevalence of patients exhibiting characteristics of institutionalization in long-stay hospitals and other total institutions is commonly attributed to the effect of the environment of such institutions and particularly to the inmates' loss of autonomy and self-identity and to the passive role expected of them by the staff. Long-stay patients in psychiatric hospitals have been described as suffering from two conditions, the one that brought them into institutional care and a second which is the product of the institution (Barton 1959). However, this view is criticized by those who believe that the behaviour associated with institutionalization can itself be attributed to the disease process.

One study which has examined the effect of the institutional environment on patients is by Wing and Brown (1970) and based on women patients with schizophrenia. These patients had spent between two and six years in one of three mental hospitals, which differed markedly in their social conditions. Poverty of the hospital environment, measured in terms of ward restrictiveness, lack of occupation, lack of personal possessions, lack of contact with the outside world and unfavourable nurse attitudes, was found to be highly correlated with patients' clinical poverty, measured in terms of lack of expressed emotion, poverty of speech and social withdrawal; the hospital with the richest social environment contained patients with the fewest negative symptoms, even though patients did not appear to have differed in the severity of their illness at the time of admission. They also found that attitudes to discharge became progressively more unfavourable with increasing length of stay, regardless of the patients' clinical condition. A follow-up study of the same group of patients showed that improvements in the social environment of the three hospitals during the period 1960–8 was associated with a reduction in the clinical poverty of patients, an improvement in which could not be explained in terms of changes in drug treatment. Such findings thus strongly support the notion that the social environment is the key factor in producing the attitudes and behaviours associated with institutionalization. This points to the possibility of reducing the prevalence of such characteristics througn the current trend towards a more rehabilitative pattern of care, the decreasing length of hospital stay and the increase in patients' contact with the outside world.

Although the organization of patient care is especially critical in institutions where patients are likely to remain for a long period, this chapter has shown how the goals of patient care and the attitudes and practices of hospital staff exert an important effect on the recovery and general well-being of hospital patients. Thus, even in short-stay hospitals it is important to ensure that individual patient's needs, and particularly the need for information, are not overlooked in the concern with organizational efficiency.

References

BARTON, R. (1959) *Institutional Neurosis.* Bristol: John Wright.

COE, R. M. (1970) *Sociology of Medicine.* New York: McGraw Hill.

COSER, R. (1963) Alienation and social structure: a case analysis of a hospital. In: *The Hospital in Modern Society*, ed. E. Freidson. New York: Free Press.

EMERSON, J. P. (1970) Behaviour in private places. In: *Recent Sociology 2*, ed. H. Dreitzel. New York: MacMillan.

FRANKLIN, B. L. (1974) *Patient Anxiety and Admission to Hospital.* London: Royal College of Nursing.

GOFFMAN, E. (1961) *Asylums.* Garden City, NY: Doubleday.

HUGH-JONES, P., TANSER, A. R. & WHITLEY, C. (1964) Patients' views of admission to a London teaching Hospital. *Br. med. J.*, **2**, 660–4.

KING, R. D., RAYNES, N. & TIZARD, J. (1973) *Patterns of Residential Care.* London: Routledge and Kegan Paul.

LORBER, J. (1975) Good patients and problem patients. *J. Hlth soc. Behav.*, **16**, 213–25.

MURPHY, F. W. (1977) Blocked beds. *Br. med. J.*, **1**, 1395–96.

NOBLE, & DIXON, R. (1977) *Ward Evaluation: St. Thomas's Hospital.* Polytechnic of North London: Medical Architecture Research Unit.

ROYAL COMMISSION ON THE NATIONAL HEALTH SERVICE (1978) *Patients' Attitudes to the Hospital Service.* Research paper No. 5, by J. Gregory. London: HMSO.

SCULL, A. (1977) *Decarceration.* New Jersey: Prentice Hall.

STACEY, M., DEARDEN, R., PILL, R. & ROBINSON, D. (1970) *Hospitals, Children and their Families.* London: Routledge and Kegan Paul.

SUDNOW, (1967) *Passing On: The Social Organisation of Dying.* Englewood Cliffs, N.J.: Prentice Hall.

WING, J. K. & BROWN, G. W. (1970) *Institutionalism and Schrizophrenia: A Comparative Study of Three Mental Hospitals, 1960–1968.* Cambridge: Cambridge University Press.

WILSON-BARNETT, J. & CARRIGY, A. (1978) Factors influencing patients' emotional reactions to hospitalization. *J. adv. Nursing*, **3**, 221–9.

7

Death and Dying

Graham Scambler

One American sociologist has drawn a distinction between 'quick' and 'slow' dying and noted that it is only in recent times, with the relatively high incidence of deaths from chronic and degenerative diseases, that the latter has become a common experience (Lofland 1978) (Table 13; and see Chapter 2). Reflecting this distinction, this chapter concentrates, if not exclusively, on 'slow dying' and makes particular use of the literature on deaths from cancer. It deals with the problems of communication about dying between doctors, patients and relatives; various 'stages' of dying; alternative facilities for the care of the terminally ill in Britain; and some of the patterns and problems associated with the treatment of dying persons in hospital settings.

Talking about death

Some commentators have claimed that it is more difficult to talk about death openly and honestly today than it has ever been before. Ariès (1974), for example, has maintained that during the Middle Ages, when expectation of life at birth in Britain was about 30 years, death (from malnutrition and the 'killer diseases') was omnipresent and was perceived somewhat fatalistically as the collective destiny of the species. It was not until the nineteenth century, he argues, that death started to become shameful and ugly, something to be hidden. Gorer (1965) has claimed that even in the late nineteenth century 'death was no mystery, except in the sense that death is always a mystery'. Indeed, the Victorians developed a fascination with

Table 13.   *Conditions facilitating 'quick dying' in the pre-modern era and 'slow dying' in the modern era*

Conditions facilitating quick dying	Conditions facilitating slow dying
Low level of medical technology	High level of medical technology
Late detection of disease- or fatality-producing conditions	Early detection of disease- or fatality-producing conditions
Simple definition of death (e.g. cessation of heart beat)	Complex definition of death (e.g. irreversible cessation of higher brain activity)
High incidence of mortality from acute disease	High incidence of mortality from chronic or degenerative disease
High incidence of fatality-producing injuries	Low incidence of fatality-producing injuries
Customary killing or suicide of, or fatal passivity towards, the person once he or she has entered the 'dying' category	Customary curative and activist orientation toward the dying with a high value placed on the prolongation of life

death and dying and 'funerals were the occasion of the greatest display for working class, middle class and aristocrat'. Both these authors agree, however, that in the twentieth century death has become more and more 'unmentionable'.

While the arguments of Ariès, and to a lesser extent Gorer, can be criticized as too general or simplistic, it remains true that in modern Britain death is something of a taboo subject. It is not surprising, therefore, that deciding whether or not to tell someone he is dying is often seen as problematic. When asked, most people anticipate that they would want to be told if they were dying; doctors themselves, it seems, are unexceptional in this respect. Such hypothetical questions are clearly of limited value, however: how many relatively young and healthy people can accurately predict how they will feel as death approaches? Interestingly, American research suggests that doctors may be changing their attitudes toward telling patients they are dying. Novack et al. (1979), for example, report that whereas in 1961

90% of the doctors they questioned indicated a preference for not telling a cancer patient his diagnosis, in 1977 97% indicated a preference for passing on the diagnosis, 'a complete reversal of attitude'. The authors conjecture that this 'reversal' may be due to the availability of improved therapies for many forms of cancer, and hence to less pessimism among doctors, and to changes in public perception of cancer (that is, to a partial de-stigmatization of cancer).

Cartwright et al. (1973), who interviewed relatives of a national sample of people who had died in the preceding year in Britain, were told by the relatives that 37% of those dying knew as much, and a further 20% 'half-knew'. Nearly three-quarters of the relatives felt they had themselves known. It was also apparent from this study that the relatives received more information from all sources than did the people who were dying. If death occurred in a hospital less information was forthcoming than if it occurred at home; in *both* contexts, however, the general practitioner was the key informant.

Awareness of dying

Glaser and Strauss (1965) have noted that there are four particularly prevalent types of 'awareness context' in relation to the dying. They define 'awareness context' as follows: 'what *each* interacting person knows of the patient's defined status, along with his recognition of others' awareness of his own definition'. The four types are:

1. *Closed awareness.* The situation in which the patient does not recognize his impending death even though everyone else does.

2. *Suspected awareness.* The situation when the patient suspects what others know and attempts to confirm or invalidate his suspicions.

3. *Mutual pretence awareness.* The situation where each party defines the patient as dying but each 'pretends' that the other has not done so.

4. *Open awareness.* The situation where health care personnel and patient are both aware that he is dying, and where they act on this awareness fairly openly.

Some commentators have assumed that 'closed', 'suspected' and 'mutual pretence' awareness contexts are intrinsically undesirable and that health workers, especially doctors, are to blame for the fact that they not infrequently exist. As a study by McIntosh (1977) suggests, however, such assumptions can be naive and misleading. Interviewing doctors and selected patients with diagnosed but undisclosed cancers, McIntosh focussed on how both doctors and patients cope with the *uncertainties* that often attend talk about dying.

The doctors

The doctors told McIntosh that decisions to tell or not to tell rested on their assessments of individual cases; many added that these decisions were often complicated both by clinical uncertainties concerning diagnosis and prognosis and by uncertainties about whether or not patients 'really' wanted to know. These statements of policy, however, did not accord with actual medical practice. There were, in fact, *no* disclosures unless they were deemed absolutely necessary: that is, unless patients persistently demanded 'the truth' or even went so far as to refuse treatment. Doctors, in short, were biased against telling: 'the cornerstone of the doctors' philosophy on telling was the belief that the great majority of patients should not be told'.

The patients

Most patients spoken to suspected malignancy. The majority sought information from members of the hospital team but, according to McIntosh's estimate, two out of every three did not 'really' want their diagnostic suspicions confirmed, and fewer still 'really' wanted information about the prognosis. 'They sought exclusively information which would reinforce an optimistic conception of their condition': uncertainty afforded hope. Patients also felt that doctors would tell them everything *if asked*.

To some large extent both doctors and patients are victims of contemporary culture. One implication of a policy of not communicating diagnoses of cancer, for example, is that it helps perpetuate the lay belief that cancer is a 'dread and incurable' disease: if patients recover they will probably not have been told, but if they die their cases will always be known. Doctors often say, however, that they cannot pass on diagnoses of cancer because of lay beliefs about cancer, that educating the public is a prerequisite of change in hospital policies about telling. It is one vicious circle among many in this area.

If one thing is clear it is that there is no easy, general answer to the question 'To tell or not to tell?'. Hinton (1967) offers doctors the following counsel: 'although it is not an infallible guide to how much the dying patient should be told, his apparent wishes and questions do point the way. This means that the manner in which he puts his views should be closely attended to — the intonations and the exact wording may be very revealing. It also means that he must be given ample opportunity to express his ideas and ask his questions. If the questions are sincere, however, then why not give quiet straight answers to the patient's questions about his illness and the outcome? It makes for beneficial trust'. A recent study by Hinton himself (1980) highlights the importance of giving dying patients the opportunity to talk. Hinton interviewed 80 patients with terminal cancer at a mean of 10 weeks before death; 66% told him that they recognized they might or would soon die, 8% were non-committal and 26% spoke only of improvement. Some patients spoke of dying to either their spouse or the staff and not to the interviewer, but they tended to say less to their spouse than to the interviewer and less still to members of the staff. This tendency is illustrated in Fig. 3. Hinton concludes that people are often ready to share their awareness *if someone is prepared to listen.*

Stages of dying

The manner in which people come to terms with the prospect of imminent death depends on such factors as the nature of the illness, age, familial circumstances and support, 'quality of life', religious convictions, and so on. There is enormous individual variation and, hence, unpredictability in any given case. Kubler-Ross (1970) has claimed, however, that people who know they are dying *typically*, but by no means always, pass through five 'stages'.

First stage: denial and isolation

Many people, on being told they are dying, experience a temporary state of shock. When the 'numbness' disappears, a

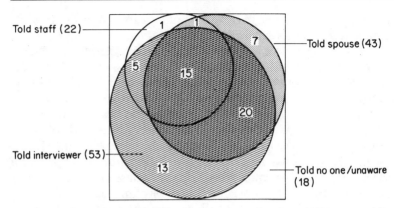

Fig. 3   Awareness of possibly dying as shown to different people by 80 patients with terminal cancer. The square represents the 80 patients and the three shaded circles their communicated awareness to staff, spouse and interviewer. (*From Hinton 1980*)

common response is: 'No, it can't be me'. One's own death is almost inconceivable. 'Denial' is usually a temporary defence, but some take it further, perhaps 'shopping around' for a more amenable medical opinion (only three of the 200 patients in Kubler-Ross' study attempted to deny the approach of death to the very end). A deep feeling of 'isolation' is normal at this stage.

Second stage: anger

When the first stage of denial can no longer be maintained, it is often replaced by feelings of anger, rage, envy and resentment. The question 'Why me?' is posed. The anger can be 'displaced in all directions and projected onto the environment at times almost at random' (although it can, of course, be justified as well as unjustified). The hospital team, especially the nursing staff, often bear the brunt of these outbursts.

Third stage: bargaining

The third stage of 'bargaining', Kubler-Ross argues, has only rarely been acknowledged. The point is that terminally ill patients will sometimes negotiate — openly with the hospital staff or secretly with God — to postpone death: postponement will be the reward for a promise of 'good behaviour'. For example, many patients in the study promised to donate parts or the whole of their bodies 'to science' if the doctors undertook to use their knowledge of science to extend their lives.

Fourth stage: depression

When terminally ill patients can no longer deny their illness, when they are compelled to endure more surgery, when they grow weaker, the numbness or stoicism or anger gives way to 'a sense of great loss'. This 'depression' may be *reactive*, for example a woman with cancer of the uterus may feel she is no longer a woman, or what Kubler-Ross terms *preparatory*, that is, based on impending losses associated with death itself.

Fifth stage: acceptance

The final stage of 'acceptance' is one in which dying patients commonly find a sort of peace, a peace which is largely a function of weakness and a diminishing interest in the world. 'It is as if the pain had gone, the struggle is over . . . '. Kubler-Ross adds that this is also the time during which the family usually needs more help, understanding and support than the patient himself.

A number of commentators have criticized Kubler-Ross' specification of discrete 'stages' of dying, usually on the grounds that they represent an over-generalization based on subjective data. As yet, however, there have been few attempts to evaluate Kubler-Ross' theory empirically, and none which have led to decisive results.

Place of death

Those, like Ariès, who argue that death has been increasingly 'hidden from view' in the twentieth century attach considerable importance to the fact that since the 1930s and 1940s death has been substantially removed from the community or 'hospitalized'. In the hospital, the argument runs, death is no longer an occasion of ritual ceremony over which the dying

Table 14.   *Total deaths and percentages of deaths occurring in non-psychiatric hospitals (N.H.S. and other) and at home, England and Wales, 1965 and 1970–74*

	All deaths			Cancer deaths		
Year	Total ('000)	Non-psych. hospitals	Home	Total ('000)	Non-psych. hospitals	Home
1965	549	50%	38%	107	60%	37%
1970	575	54%	33%	117	61.5%	33%
1971	567	55%	32%	118	63%	32%
1972	592	55.5%	32%	120	63%	31%
1973	587	55%	32%	121	63%	31%
1974	585	56%	31%	123	64%	31%

From Ford (1978).

person and his relatives and friends hold sway. The doctors and the hospital team are the new 'masters of death' — of its moment as well as its circumstances. This interpretation of changing events is once again open to criticism, but there is no doubt that the hospitalization of death has continued (Table 14). It does not follow, however, that the role of *home care* for dying patients has correspondingly diminished. Ward (1974) studied the last days of 279 people in Sheffield who died of cancer and found that, in spite of the fact that most of them died in hospital, out of a total of 7812 days in the last four weeks of their lives 5387 days were spent at home and only 2425 in hospital; the mean for the total of 279 people was 8.7 days in hospital.

There is a growing feeling that the hospital is too frequently an inappropriate place in which to die. Most are designed to provide for acute illness, for example, and terminally ill people in acute wards can both disturb other patients and members of ward staff and be disturbed by them; most hospitals do not set aside a whole or part of a ward for terminally ill patients, perhaps because they are anxious to avoid the stigma of a 'death ward'. Several alternative locations exist in Britain, including special units within conventional hospitals, but the most discussed are the home and the hospice.

The home

For many people, despite the statistical trend to hospitalization, the home remains the 'natural' and 'proper' place in which to die. Health workers too recognize its advantages. As Cartwright et al. (1973) discovered, however, dying people and their relatives are likely to require a good deal of help (see also Chapter 11). McNulty (1978), from the perspective of the health worker, has specified a number of 'basic essentials' for home care:

1. Adequate, trained staff who are familiar with the special needs of patients with terminal malignant disease.
2. Good communication between hospital and community and between all members of the team.
3. Sufficient time for patients and families to be able to voice their fears, anxieties and difficulties to the staff.
4. A full 24-hour coverage, both medical and nursing, on an internal rota system.
5. Foresight and planning so that adequate drugs are available for emergencies, and frequent assessments of the changing needs.
6. A bank of nursing aides available for loan at a moment's notice.
7. A day centre and an out-patient clinic for those who are well enough, with volunteer car drivers to ensure quick and easy transport.
8. Quick and easy access to beds should admission be needed suddenly, with the possibility of discharge always in mind and the certainty of continuity of attitude and care.
9. A follow-up service to the bereaved with help and support in starting life again.

The hospice

The 'hospice movement' was founded in the mid-nineteenth century in Dublin by Mary Aikenhead, founder of an order of nuns, the Irish Sisters of Charity. The movement is still most advanced in Britain, where its favoured pattern is to build small units in the grounds of general hospitals, using their facilities but remaining administratively independent. The range of care provided in a hospice is intermediate between that of a long-stay hospital and that of an acute hospital. The staffing ratios are similar to those of an acute hospital, but the call for diagnostic and other 'support' services is much less. The average length of stay is also closer to that of patients in an acute hospital than that of patients in a long-stay hospital. The costs are in keeping with this. One week's stay at St Christopher's Hospice in London, for example, cost £184 in 1976–7; at the time the cost of a week in a NHS long-stay hospital was £142, in an acute, non-teaching hospital it was £264 and in a London Teaching Hospital £375. Central to the philosophy of the hospice is the view that the whole caring team should work in unison to develop the skills the dying person needs.

One rider ought to be appended to this discussion. It is that there is a 'subjective' component to people's choice of place of death. In one study the care given in four radiotherapy wards of an acute hospital, in a Foundation Home visited by two general practitioners and in a hospice were compared (Hinton 1979). Little difference was found between the acute hospital and the Foundation Home, but there was some evidence that patients were less depressed and anxious in the hospice and preferred the more frank communication available there. It was also found, however, that patients gave most praise to the out-patient system of care, *despite experiencing more anxiety or irritability at home*. The author concluded: 'treatment cannot be judged solely by the mental quiet it brings; freedom or hope may be preferred even if they bring worry'. It has been found that home-centred patients tend to experience more pain than hospital-centred patients; it does not follow, however, that, even knowing this, people would *necessarily* choose to leave home.

Patterns of death in hospital

Sudnow (1967) has drawn a distinction between *biological* and *social* death. The problem of how to define biological death has recently been resolved by the medical profession in favour of the irreversible cessation of higher brain activity. Sudnow uses the term 'social death' in a general sense to refer to how organizations deal with different modes of dying and death. More specifically, social death is marked, within the hospital setting, by that point at which a patient is treated essentially as a corpse, although still perhaps biologically alive. He gives an example of social death preceding biological death. A nurse on duty with a woman she explained was 'dying' was observed to spend two or three minutes trying to close the woman's eyelids. After several unsuccessful attempts she managed to shut them and said, with a sigh of relief, 'Now they're right'. When questioned, she said that a patient's eyes must be closed after death, so that the body will resemble a sleeping person. It was more difficult to accomplish this, she explained, after the muscles and skin had begun to stiffen. She always tried to close them *before* death. This made for greater efficiency when the time came for ward personnel to wrap the body. It was a matter of consideration toward those workers who preferred to handle dead bodies as little as possible.

Glaser and Strauss (1968) list seven 'critical junctures' in what is sometimes called the 'career' of the dying patient:

1. The definition of the patient as dying.
2. Staff and family then make their preparations for the patient's death, as the patient may do if he or she knows that death is near.
3. At some point there seems to be 'nothing more to do' to prevent death.
4. The final descent, which may take weeks, days or merely hours.
5. The 'last hours'.
6. The death watch.
7. Finally death itself.

When these critical junctures occur as expected — as it were, on schedule — then all those involved, including sometimes the patient, are prepared for them. When, however, critical junctures occur unexpectedly, hospital staff and the patient's family are alike somewhat unprepared. If a patient is expected to die quite soon, for example, but vacillates sufficiently often, then both staff and family are likely to find the experience stressful.

Predictability, then, makes the work of hospital teams easier. Miscalculations in forecasting can play havoc with the organization of work. When crises do occur, the staff attempt to regain control as quickly as possible; but sometimes the disruption of work is accompanied by a shattering of what Glaser and Strauss (1965) have called a ward's characteristic 'sentimental mood' or order. They cite the following example:

'in an intensive care unit where cardiac patients die frequently, the mood is relatively unaffected by one more speedy expected death; but if a hopeless patient lingers on and on, or if his wife, perhaps, refuses to accept his dying and causes "scenes", then both mood and work itself are profoundly affected'.

Glaser and Strauss (1968) differentiate between a number of patterns of death, or *dying trajectories*, paying special attention to the distinction between 'quick' and 'slow' dying. Quick dying, they claim, may take three forms: 'the expected quick death'; 'unexpected quick dying, but expected to die'; and 'unexpected quick dying, not expected to die'. They report that, in general, unexpected and expected quick deaths have different impacts on the hospital staff and the family: the former are more disturbing. Even expected quick deaths, however, can give rise to distinctive difficulties. Glaser and Strauss focus on staff–family interaction and note, for example, that the likely presence of the family at the bedside when death occurs requires careful handling by the staff, since a 'scene' will disrupt ward-order and worry other patients. Slow dying, in the authors' words, 'is fraught with both hazard and opportunity'. On the one hand, the dying may take 'too long', be unexpectedly painful or unpleasant and so on; on the other hand, a slow decline may allow time, for example, for wills to be made or families to come together, and may provide the setting for quiet and dignified endings. All these consequences are less likely to occur with quick dying.

Many of the authors cited in this chapter close their own contributions to the literature on death and dying by asserting that students of the health professions — both in Britain and in the USA — receive inadequate preparation for terminal care. Glaser and Strauss argue that much non-technical conduct toward, and in the presence of, dying patients is profoundly influenced by common-sense assumptions, 'essentially untouched by professional considerations or by current knowledge from the behavioural sciences'. The argument for the provision of a good training in those aspects of terminal care — psychological, social and organizational — which are now relatively neglected is a strong one.

References

ARIÈS, P. (1974) *Western Attitudes Toward Death: From the Middle Ages to the Present.* Baltimore, Md: John Hopkins University Press.

CARTWRIGHT, A., HOCKEY, L. & ANDERSON, J. (1973) *Life Before Death.* London: Routledge & Kegan Paul

FORD, G. (1978) Terminal care in the National Health Service. In: *The Management of Terminal Disease,* ed. C. Saunders. London: Edward Arnold.

GLASER, B. & STRAUSS, A. (1965) *Awareness of Dying.* Chicago, Ill.: Aldine.

GLASER, B. & STRAUSS, A. (1968) *Time for Dying.* Chicago, Ill.: Aldine.

GORER, G. (1965) *Death, Grief and Mourning in Contemporary Britain.* London: Cresset Press.

HINTON, J. (1967) *Dying.* Harmondsworth: Penguin.

HINTON, J. (1979) Comparison of places and policies for terminal care. *Lancet,* **1**, 29–32.

HINTON, J. (1980) Whom do dying patients tell? *Br. med. J.*, **281**, 1328–30.

KUBLER-ROSS, E. (1970) *On Death and Dying.* London: Tavistock.

LOFLAND, L. (1978) *The Craft of Dying: The Modern Face of Death.* Beverly Hills, Ca.: Sage Publications.

McINTOSH, J. (1977) *Communication and Awareness in a Cancer Ward.* London: Croom Helm.

McNULTY, B. (1978) Out-patient and domiciliary management from a hospice. In: *The Management of Terminal Disease,* ed. C. Saunders. London: Edward Arnold.

NOVACK, D., PLUMER, R., SMITH, R., OCHITILL, H., MORROW, G. & BENNETT, J. (1979) Changes in physicians' attitudes toward telling the cancer patient. *J. Am. med. Ass.*, **241**, 897–900.

SUDNOW, D. (1967) *Passing On: The Social Organization of Dying.* New York: Prentice-Hall.

WARD, A. (1974) Terminal care in malignant disease. *Soc. Sci. Med.*, **8**, 233.

8

Communication in Medical Practice

David Locker

Communication is a key process in medicine, whether this be communication between doctors and patients, between the various professionals involved in providing health care or between those professionals and the general public (Jefferys 1976). Perhaps the most important of these is the communication that takes place between doctors and patients since this provides the foundation of diagnosis and treatment. Given the prevalence of chronic illness, effective communication between doctor and patient is of increasing significance. Many of these conditions have profound consequences for both patient and family such that the doctor's role is no longer one of treating disease but of assisting in the management of and adjustment to the problems that disease creates. Information, advice and support are essential in helping patients adapt to new and more limited life-styles. For many chronic illnesses communication is virtually the only form of treatment there is.

Although communication is a two-way process this chapter will concentrate on the transmission of information from doctors to patients.

Patients' views about communication

The most consistent finding of studies of patients' views of medical care is that more tend to be dissatisfied with the amount and nature of the information they receive than with any other aspect of their treatment. For example, McGhee (1961) interviewed patients in their homes 10–14 days after they were discharged from hospital and asked about various aspects of their stay. While less than 40% expressed dissatisfaction with the medical or nursing care they received, or with the food, noise and amenities, 65% were dissatisfied with communications. Only 14% were completely satisfied and the remaining 21% were satisfied with some reservations. On the basis of data like these other authors have concluded that the greatest single defect in hospital care is the poor exchange of information, stemming from a failure to recognize the social and psychological needs of patients in hospital (Cartwright 1964).

Failures in communication are not confined to the relatively complex environment of the hospital. Kincey et al. (1975) provide some data on general practice in their study of communication and compliance. Patients were asked if they had received enough information about diagnosis, aetiology, treatment and prognosis during a visit to a general practitioner: 70–79% said they had received enough information about diagnosis, treatment and prognosis. However, only 61% said they had received sufficient information about aetiology, with as many as 31% claiming they had received none at all. Using a more stringent criterion of satisfaction with information given based on response to questions about the four categories, only 56% felt they had been fully informed.

These studied indicate that patients wish to know more about their condition and its treatment. But what do they want to know and how much information would they like? Reader et al. (1957) report that two-thirds of their sample of out-patients wanted more information about the nature and cause of their condition, over half wanted to know how serious it was and two-fifths wanted the results and implications of any tests conducted. Cartwright (1964) found that 75% of her sample wanted to know as much as possible about their illness.

Some reasons for failures of communication between doctors and patients

Professional attitudes

While some doctors claim that health education takes up a large proportion of their time and consider this to be one of their most important activities, studies of professional attitudes show that not all view information transmission in this way. Comaroff (1976) interviewed general practitioners at length about the amount of information they were prepared to give patients and found wide variations in their attitudes and practice. Some gave the patient as little information as possible: patients who asked for information were given limited explanations and those who did not ask were given none. These doctors saw their job as one of allaying fear and anxiety and withheld information on the grounds that it only caused the patient to worry. Other doctors saw the communication of information as integral to their role, irrespective of whether or not it was requested by the patient. These doctors gave the patient as much information as possible in the time available, although they did vary the amount given according to their judgements about the patient's ability to understand.

These attitudes regarding patient education were related to more general attitudes concerning the nature of the doctor–patient relationship. The first group of doctors tended to stress their professional status, the competence gap between themselves and patients and the need to exercise tight control over the consultation. Their image of patients and their own role was quite different from that of the second group of doctors, who saw the relationship as egalitarian and reciprocal and recognized the part the patient has to play in medical practice.

The problem of uncertainty

Many writers have commented on the extent to which modern medical practice is characterized by uncertainty. As far as many chronic conditions are concerned, their aetiology is not well-understood and no explanation is therefore available to convey to patients. Similarly, prognoses cannot be specified with any certainty since the course of the illness and its outcome may be subject to wide variations. One reason why information may not be given to patients is that there is little information to give. However, others have pointed to the fact that this uncertainty is rarely communicated to the patient and even when doctors are certain about the course of a disease or the outcome of treatment information may be withheld. Davis (1963) studied the families of children with poliomyelitis and found that communication of the child's prognosis to the parents was delayed long after the doctor had a clear idea about the level of residual disability. Reviewing this and other evidence Waitzkin and Stoekle (1972) suggest that maintaining uncertainty is one way doctors can retain control over both the patient and the treatment. Failure to inform patients masks the doctor's own uncertainty, maintains patients' beliefs in the efficacy of medicine and limits their role in decision-making.

Patient diffidence

Poor communication has frequently been attributed to barriers created by differences in class and status between doctors and their patients. Such differences have an effect on what information patients convey to doctors and their ability to obtain information in return. In a study of patients in hospital only 45% obtained the information they desired by asking doctors or nurses (Cartwright 1964). The remainder either waited to be told or received no information at all. Cartwright reports that there were social class differences in the way patients acquired information. While 65% of patients in social class I asked for information, only 40% of those in social class V did so. Those in manual occupations more often waited until they were told, or failed to discover what they needed to know. Similar results emerged from Cartwright and O'Brien's (1976) later study of general practice consultations with elderly patients. On average, consultations with middle-class patients were longer than those with working-class patients, and middle-class patients asked more questions and discussed more problems with the doctor even though they mentioned fewer symptoms to an interviewer prior to the consultation (Table 15). The relative disadvantage of working-class patients can be attributed to the social distance between the doctor and themselves and the assumption on the part of doctors that if patients do not ask questions they do not want to know.

Doctors may also contribute directly to patient diffidence by the way they respond to patients who seek information. Cartwright and O'Brien (1976) found that the doctors involved in their study tended to be more satisfied with consultations where the conversation time was not more than five minutes and where the patient asked only one question. It is not unreasonable to suppose that patients become aware of their doctors' unwillingness to continue discussion and modify their behaviour accordingly.

Table 15.   General practice consultations with middle- and working-class patients aged 65 and over

	Middle class	Working class
Average length of consultation (min)	6.2	4.7
Average number of questions asked by patient	3.7	3.0
Average number of problems discussed with doctor	4.1	2.8
Average number of symptoms mentioned to interviewer prior to consultation	2.2	3.0

Adapted from Cartwright and O'Brien (1976).

Failures of communication and memory

While the factors already discussed are important in accounting for poor communication they do not tell the whole story. Even when doctors make special efforts to inform patients or improve communications many patients remain dissatisfied. Ley and Spelman (1967) consider that this is due to failures in comprehension or memory. Table 16 lists a number of studies showing that a large proportion of what patients are told is not recalled even a few minutes after the consultation.

A number of factors which may be a feature of doctor–patient consultations are known to influence comprehension and memory. Firstly, doctors may talk in a highly technical language which is unfamiliar to the lay person. Messages couched in these terms may not be understood. Even when ordinary language is used patients' limited knowledge of illness and other medical matters may result in misunderstanding and confusion. Because patients are diffident they are unlikely to ask for clarification of what they do not understand. Secondly, many patients find encounters with doctors anxiety-provoking and anxiety has a negative effect on what is remembered. Finally, even when patients are given information couched in every-day language they may be told too much too quickly.

Socio-psychological research on memory has indicated that the more information given at any one time the greater the

Table 16. Summary of studies of patients forgetting medical information

Investigators	Type of patient	Time between consultation and recall	% Forgotten
Ley and Spelman (1965)	47 out-patients	10–80 min	37.2
Ley and Spelman (1967)	(*a*) 22 out-patients	10–80 min	38.7
	(*b*) 22 out-patients	10–80 min	40.6
Joyce et al. (1969)	(*a*) 30 out-patients	Immediately after consultation	52.0
	(*b*) 24 out-patients	1–4 weeks	54.0
Ley et al. (1973)	20 general practice patients	Less than 5 min	50.0

Source: Ley, 1976.

proportion forgotten. Consequently, if people are given more information than they can absorb they select some and discard the rest. In addition, what is heard first tends to be recalled the best, more information is retained if its importance is stressed and people remember more of what *they* consider to be important. Advice and instructions about treatment tend to be forgotten more readily since they are given at the end of the consultation and are probably considered less important by patients than the diagnosis of the problem presented. Experiments using these findings as guidelines have been able to improve substantially the amount of information patients understand and recall (Ley 1976).

The effects of improved communication

The transmission of information from doctor to patient has a number of effects which are of direct clinical benefit and enhance patient care. There is evidence that effective communication with patients can improve their physiological and psychological responses to therapy, increase compliance with medical advice and contribute to overall satisfaction with the treatment and care received.

The management of postoperative pain

Pain is a complex phenomenon which is affected by a number of socio-psychological factors. For example, anxiety is related to the experience of pain in such a way that a reduction of anxiety can reduce pain. An important part of the effects of a narcotic analgesic like morphine lies in its ability to reduce anxiety. Research suggests a 'loop' effect whereby pain is influenced by anxiety which in turn is influenced by uncertainty arising from lack of information and control, with pain increasing both uncertainty and anxiety. The reduction of anxiety by the preoperative instruction and encouragement of patients has been shown to reduce the level of postoperative pain. In a study by Egbert et al. (1964) the beneficial effects of warning patients what to expect after surgery was demonstrated. Ninety-seven patients undergoing abdominal surgery were randomly assigned to an experimental and a control group. The patients in the control group were not told about postoperative pain, whereas those in the experimental group were visited by the anaesthetist who discussed how they would feel after their operations. They were informed where they would feel pain, how severe it would be and how long it would last and were reassured that pain was normal following surgery. Following the operation the narcotic requirements of both groups of patients were recorded. The experimental group received significantly less narcotics than the controls (Fig. 4). Furthermore, the experimental group were more comfortable and in better physical and emotional condition than the control group, and they left hospital on average nearly three days earlier.

Other physiological effects of anxiety reduction

Going into hospital, especially for surgery, can create anxiety and stress for both patient and family (see Chapter 6). Reducing the general anxieties created by hospital life can have beneficial effects both pre- and postoperatively. It is known that preoperative anxiety significantly influences a patient's physiological state, such that the highly anxious patient requires

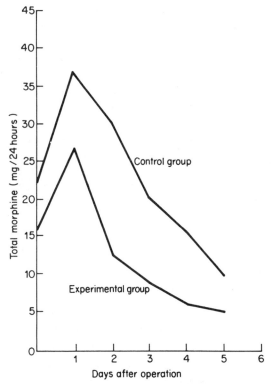

Fig. 4 Postoperative treatment with narcotics (means for each day ±standard error of the mean). (*From Egbert et al. 1964*)

more anaesthetic to induce anaesthesia. Consequently, the 'management' of preoperative anxiety is sometimes necessary to reduce the dosage of anaesthetic required and to maximize the patient's general physiological condition prior to surgery. Evidence from a number of small-scale studies has shown that care by a nurse specially trained in communication can result in reductions in the stress experienced by the patient and a decrease in somatic complications following surgery. These beneficial effects of communication can also be achieved through the patient's relatives. In a study by Skipper and Leonard (1968), 80 children having a tonsillectomy were randomly assigned to experimental and control groups. The experimental group was admitted by a special nurse whose job it was to provide the mother with information regarding the operation and its effects at time of admission and at several stages during the child's stay in hospital. The control group was subject to the hospital's usual procedure. The results indicated that the mothers of the experimental group of children experienced less stress during their child's stay in hospital. This led to less stress in the child and an improvement in postoperative physiological state. There were significant differences between the groups in blood pressure, heart rate, postoperative vomiting, voiding and fluid consumption, indicating a more satisfactory recovery from tonsillectomy for the experimental group. Each of these studies suggests a general process at work: the social environment influences psychological states which in turn influence physiological functioning.

Compliance with medical advice

Patients do not always take drugs as recommended by their doctor; some fail to take them at all. Stimson (1975) has summarized a number of studies showing that between 19 and 72% of patients do not take their drugs as prescribed. In most of these studies the proportion was over 30%. Similar observations have been made with regard to dietary, child-care and antenatal advice. A number of hypotheses have been advanced to explain this. The one most thoroughly investigated suggests that it is due to a failure in doctor–patient communication. A measure of support for this theory has come from Kincey et al. (1975) who found that patient satisfaction with the amount of information received during a general practice consultation was associated with reported compliance with the doctor's advice. Similarly, the extent to which mothers follow advice concerning their children seems to depend on the extent to which the doctor fulfils one of their goals in seeking care by providing an explanation of the child's illness. Korsch et al. (1969) found that non-compliance increased from 11 to 24% when an explanation of the nature and the cause of the illness was not given. On the basis of the research quoted earlier, Ley (1976) found that giving advice early in the interview, stressing its importance and providing information in the form of leaflets improved the amount of advice remembered and subsequent compliance.

Patient satisfaction with medical care

Since one of the goals of many patients in seeking medical care is to gain information about and develop an understanding of their illness and the problems it creates, improving communications can effect overall satisfaction with the care that is received. Many studies of satisfaction with general practitioner care have noted that patients tend to lay more stress on the personal qualities of the doctor than on his technical abilities. In this respect a willingness on the part of the doctor to give information and spend time explaining things to the patient is taken as an indicator of a general concern for patients and their welfare. Consequently, a willingness to listen, to explain and to take time are qualities in doctors most appreciated by patients (Cartwright 1967).

Methods of improving communications in medical care

On the basis of his experiments on comprehension and memory Ley (1976) has made a number of suggestions for improving practitioner–patient communication:

1. Give instructions and advice early in the interview.
2. Stress the importance of instructions and advice.
3. Use short words and short sentences.
4. Arrange the information given into clear sentences.
5. Repeat advice.
6. Give specific detailed information rather than general statements.

He also advocates giving patients instructions in written form so they can be referred to as and when necessary. Cartwright (1964), commenting on poor communications in hospital, suggests that there should be someone whose specific duty it is to keep the patient informed. Outside hospital the patient has a personal doctor in the form of the general practitioner. In hospital, where the onus is on team care, no single individual fulfils that role. Consequently, information may not be passed to the patient because staff assume that someone else has already told the patient what he or she wants or needs to know.

Allocating this task to a specific individual is one way of reducing the failure induced by the complexity of hospital care.

While suggestions such as this provide some guide as to how communications may- be improved, they presuppose recognition of the importance of giving patients information. It must be remembered that doctors and patients do not always share the same objectives or interpretation of events (see Chapter 5). The attitudes of staff, their views of patients and their ideas about their own roles are all important in determining whether realistic attempts are made to communicate (see Chapter 7). It is only after practitioners have become convinced of the value of effective communication that the other barriers to effective information exchange can be overcome.

References

CARTWRIGHT, A. (1964) *Human Relations and Hospital Care.* London: Routledge and Kegan Paul.

CARTWRIGHT, A. (1967) *Patients and Their Doctors,* London: Routledge and Kegan Paul.

CARTWRIGHT, A. & O'BRIEN, M. (1976) Social class variations in health care and in general practitioner consultations. In: *The Sociology of the NHS,* Sociological Review Monograph No. 22, ed. M. Stacey. Keele: University of Keele.

COMAROFF, J. (1976) Communicating information about non-fatal illness: The strategies of a group of general practitioners. *Sociol. Rev.,* **24,** 269–90.

DAVIS, F. (1963) *Passage Through Crisis: Polio Victims and Their Families.* Indianapolis: Bobbs-Merrill.

EGBERT, L., BATTIT, G., WELCH, C. & BARTLETT, M. (1964) Reduction of post-operative pain by encouragement and instruction of patients. *New Engl. J. Med.,* **270,** 825–7.

JEFFERYS, M. (1976) Sociology and communication in medicine. In: *Seminars in Community Medicine,* **1,** ed. R. Acheson & L. Aird. London: Oxford University Press.

KINCEY, J., BRADSHAW, P. & LEY, P. (1975) Patients' satisfaction and reported acceptance of advice in general practice. *J. R. Coll. gen. Practnrs.,* **25,** 558–62.

KORSCH, B., GOZZI, E. & FRANCIS, V. (1969) Gaps in doctor–patient communication: patients' response to medical advice. *New Engl. J. Med.,* **280,** 535–40.

LEY, P. (1976) Towards better doctor–patient communication. In: *Communication Between Doctors and Patients,* ed. A. Bennet. London: Nuffield Provincial Hospital Trust.

LEY, P. & SPELMAN, M. (1967) *Communicating With the Patient.* London: Staples Press.

McGHEE, A. (1961) *The Patient's Attitude to Nursing Care*. Edinburgh: E. and S. Livingstone.

READER, G., PRATT, L. & MUDD, M. (1957) What patients expect from their doctor. *Mod. Hosp.*, July, 19–21.

SKIPPER, J. & LEONARD, R. (1968) Children, stress and hospitalization: a field experiment. *J. Hlth soc. Behav.*, **9**, 275–87.

STIMSON, G. (1975) Obeying doctor's orders: a view from the other side, *Soc. Sci. Med.*, **11**, 149–56.

WAITZKIN, H. & STOEKLE, J. (1972) The communication of information about illness, *Adv. psychosom. Med.*, **8**, 180–215.

Part III
Social Structure and Health

9

Inequality and Social Class

David Blane

In Bethnal Green in the year 1839 the average age of deaths in the several classes was as follows: 'Gentlemen and persons engaged in professions, and their families...45 years; Tradesmen and their families...26 years; Mechanics, servants and labourers, and their families...16 years' (Chadwick 1842). Although the average age of deaths in the different classes varied somewhat from area to area, the differences between the classes existed in all areas of the country.

The population's general level of health has improved dramatically since then, but subsequent investigations have shown that a relationship between mortality rates and social class remains. This has been repeatedly confirmed and shown to apply to morbidity measures as well (DHSS 1980). It is important, therefore, to understand both what is meant by 'social class' and why it should be related to health indicators of many kinds. With this in mind the chapter starts with details of some modern inequalities and different ways of accounting for them, the most influential of which draw on concepts of social class; it then goes on to examine the relationship between social class and health.

Some dimensions of inequality in the United Kingdom

Wealth

The distribution of personal wealth, defined in terms of marketable assets, is shaped like an inverted cone. The richest 1% of the population own approximately a quarter of the total personal wealth, and the richest 10% approximately two-thirds. This leaves 90% of the population with one-third of the total personal wealth, once again disproportionately concentrated, with a large percentage of the population owning virtually nothing. The form of this wealth varies with its distribution. Among the richest 10% it consists mainly of land and company securities, while what wealth the rest possess consists predominantly of owner-occupied houses and life insurance policies (Royal Commission on the Distribution of Income and Wealth 1980).

Income

The distribution of income, as distinct from ownership, is also shaped like an inverted cone, but the differences are smaller than in the case of wealth. After income tax has been deducted, the top 10% of income-earners receive a quarter of total personal income, and the top 50% three-quarters. Thus the bottom 50% of income-earners receive approximately the same as the top 10%. Within this bottom 50% the inequality continues, the lowest 20% of income-earners receiving just 7% of total personal income (Royal Commission on the Distribution of Income and Wealth 1980).

Living conditions

As would be expected in a market economy, these differences in income and wealth result in differences in such things as housing, possessions and diet. Some 10% of unskilled workers' homes are officially overcrowded (more than 1.5 persons per room) and 11% have no shower or bath; these conditions are virtually unknown among the families of professional workers and managers (OPCS 1973). Unskilled workers' homes are more likely to be in areas where the air is polluted with industrial waste; lacking gardens, their children are more likely to have to play in an already overcrowded flat or in the street. The homes of managers and professionals are likely to possess central heating (80%), a telephone (88%), a car (91%) and a refrigerator (99%); in contrast, only 29% of unskilled workers' homes have central heating, 27% a telephone, 19% a car and 81% a refrigerator (OPCS 1976). Compared to that of the better paid, the diet of the low paid contains far less fruit, significantly less meat, dairy products and fresh vegetables and considerably more highly refined bread and sugar (Ministry of Agriculture 1977).

Working conditions

The differences in income and wealth are also associated with differences in the way money is earned. A small minority who receive adequate investment income do not have to work. For the rest, manual work is more physically demanding, noisier and more dangerous than the work of professionals and managers. Manual workers work on average seven hours per week longer than professionals or managers and, whereas just under 25% of all manual workers are on some form of shift system, less than 5% of professionals and managers join them in this. Furthermore, manual workers usually have three or four weeks paid holiday per year compared with professionals' and managers' four to six weeks (Department of Employment 1977). Manual work is often more boring than the work of professionals and managers, and manual workers are subject to closer supervision and tighter discipline. One study found that 98% of manual workers have to clock into work (managers 6%), 90% automatically lose money when late (managers 0%) and 84% are likely to be sacked if continually late for work (managers 40%) (Wedderburn 1972). In addition, manual workers' lives are less secure and less predictable because their income and jobs are much more vulnerable to changes in the business cycle.

Social stratification

Many other areas of inequality could have been discussed in addition to those listed above, including, for example, education, career prospects and leisure activities. Furthermore, these inequalities tend to go together: they affect the same people. Sociologists use the term 'social stratification' to refer to this kind of socially *structured inequality*.

Most societies to date have been structured in some way. Historical forms of stratification have included, for example, the Hindu caste system and the various estates of feudal society. Some social theorists, drawing on the work of the early German sociologist Max Weber, consider that the stratification of modern industrial societies like that of Britain involves three main dimensions: social class, social status or honour and the political power of organized groups. Although class, status and power are usually related, so that, for example, unskilled labourers generally have low social status and little political influence, they are analytically distinct and can vary independently of one another. While it is generally agreed that social class is the most fundamental dimension of stratification, sociologists often differ in their precise definition and treatment of class and there are thus many competing theories of social class.

The one most commonly propounded involves the division of the population into two stereotyped groups of roughly equal size. 'Middle-class' people tend to earn monthly salaries in non-manual jobs, borrow money to buy their own houses and encourage their children to get as much formal education as possible; 'working-class' people are likely to earn weekly wages in manual jobs, rent their homes from the council and try to get their children started in a good job as soon as they are allowed to leave school. While this division is based on general life-style, a second, deriving from the work of Marx, is based on a group's relationship to the processes which produce society's wealth. This results in a division of the population into two social classes of markedly different size: a small 'capitalist class' which can live off the profits it makes from its ownership and control of the land, factories and financial institutions, and a 'working class' consisting of the overwhelming majority of the population, which has to sell its labour power to live.

Social scientists engaged in research generally need a more precise definition of social class and in this context the Registrar General's classification (Table 17) is normally used. This classification divides the population into five social classes (one of which is further subdivided into two), according to the general social standing of different groups of occupations. Men are allocated to a particular social class on the basis of their occupation, married women on the basis of their husband's occupation, children on that of their fathers' and the retired and unemployed on that of their last significant period of employment. Single women are classified on the basis of their own occupation. On the whole, the classification is less satisfactory for women than for men, all of whom are classified by their own occupation. The classification does have the

Table 17.   *The Registrar General's social class classification*

Social class	Description	Examples	% of population
I	Professions Business	Lawyers Large employers	5
II	Lesser professions Trade	Teachers Shopkeepers	20
IIIN	Skilled non-manual	Clerical workers	15
IIIM	Skilled manual	Electricians Lorry drivers	33
IV	Semi-skilled manual	Farm workers Machine operators	19
V	Unskilled manual	Building labourers	8

Adapted from Morris (1975).

advantage, however, that it allows virtually the whole population to be assigned to one of five social classes. An additional advantage is that it is very widely used by researchers and therefore facilitates the comparison of findings.

Social class and health

The vagueness of the concept 'health' ensures that there is no perfect way of measuring it (see Chapter 18). Use of doctors' records falls down because of variability in doctors' diagnoses and the fact that not all illnesses reach a doctor (see Chapter 4). Use of self-reporting surveys is open to the objection that people vary in the interpretation of their symptoms. The use of mortality rates, while having the advantage that death is an unambiguous event and is the one time that a person has to be seen by a doctor, has the obvious disadvantage that it ignores all minor illnesses and those major illnesses such as depression and arthritis which rarely cause death.

As mortality statistics are readily available they are most often used to examine the relationship between social class and health. That this can by and large be justified is indicated by a comparison of Tables 18 and 19, which show that there are

Table 18.   *Social class and death from all causes (1970–72)*

Social class	Stillbirth rate*	Infant mortality rate†	Standardized mortality ratio‡	
			1–14 years	15–64 years
Males				
I	9	14	74	77
II	10	15	79	81
IIIN	11	17	95	99
IIIM	12	19	98	106
IV	13	22	112	114
V	17	35	162	137
Females				
I	9	10	89	82
II	10	12	84	87
IIIN	12	12	93	92
IIIM	13	15	93	115
IV	13	17	120	119
V	18	27	156	135

*   No. of deaths per 1000 live and dead births.
†   No. of deaths in the first year of life per 1000 live births.
‡   The ratio of the observed mortality rate in a subpopulation to the mortality rate expected from the total population, multiplied by 100.
   Adapted from OPCS (1978).

comparable social class differences in self-reported acute and chronic sickness rates and in various mortality measures. Tables 18 and 19 also show that health, whether measured by mortality or by self-reported morbidity, consistently deteriorates from social class I to social class V; that the deterioration occurs at all ages and among both males and females; and that this gradient between social class I and social class V becomes somewhat less extreme as one moves from infancy to adult life.

Table 20 examines the relationship between social class and the main causes of death for men of working age. The seven specific causes of death examined together account for over half

Table 19.   Social class and sickness from all causes (1976)

Social group	Acute sickness rate*		Chronic sickness rate†	
	Male	Female	Male	Female
Professionals	11	16	80	86
Employers and managers	13	12	121	131
Intermediate and junior non-manual	15	18	149	163
Skilled manual and own account non-professional	17	16	160	143
Semi-skilled manual and personal service	14	20	178	213
Unskilled manual	22	21	234	299

*   Average number of restricted activity days per person per year (all ages).
†   Rate per 1000 reporting limiting long standing illness (all ages).
   Adapted from OPCS (1978).

Table 20.   Social class and main causes of death (1970–72) (standardized mortality ratios for males aged 15–64)

Cause of death	Social class					
	I	II	IIIN	IIIM	IV	V
Ischaemic heart disease	88	91	114	107	108	111
Lung cancer	65	65	81	102	132	193
Cerebrovascular disease	80	86	98	106	111	136
Bronchitis	36	51	82	113	128	188
Motor vehicle accidents	77	83	89	105	121	174
Pneumonia	41	53	78	92	115	195
Suicide	110	89	113	77	117	184

Adapted from OPCS (1978).

the deaths in this group. The relationship between social class and death rates is found to hold for all these separate causes of death, although it is weakest in the cases of ischaemic heart disease and suicide.

Interpretations of the relationship between social class and health

The association between social class and health shows that death and disease are not randomly distributed throughout the population and that inequalities in health go along with those inequalities in standard of living detailed earlier. However, such an association says nothing about the direction of causation. 'Social class determines health' and 'health determines social class' are both interpretations consistent with the data.

Health determines social class?

Examining this alternative first: one possibility is that when individuals become seriously ill they are unable to hold down their jobs and have no option but to move to occupations in a less advantaged social class. Although such downward 'social drift' undoubtedly takes place, especially in the case of some forms of mental illness (Farris & Dunham 1939), there is little evidence to suggest that it occurs on the scale which would be necessary to account for the strength of the relationship between social class and health. In addition, there are theoretical reasons for doubting the power of this explanation: downward social drift would be confined to the years of working life, whereas the health differences between social classes exist at all ages and if anything are greater in the pre-work age groups; secondly, incapacitating illness is as likely to lead to unemployment, early retirement or a move to a similar but less demanding job as it is to lead to a move to a worse and therefore often physically more demanding job.

A second possibility is that health determines social class because illness has caused downward social drift over several generations. If this were true, it would follow that disease predisposing genes would be concentrated in social class V and become progressively less frequent as one moved up the social class scale. There is no direct evidence to support this theory; indeed, given that successive waves of immigration to a country have usually involved migrants starting at the bottom of the occupational ladder, one would expect the opposite, namely, that the gene pool would become less varied and therefore less healthy, if anything, as one moves from social class V to I.

Social class determines health?

Turning to the alternative explanation: as social class embraces many interrelated inequalities, it is necessary to specify which particular aspect of social class is responsible for the differences in health. One possibility is that the inequalities in health result from differences in the social classes' access to medical care. Examples of evidence that such differences exist are presented in Table 21 for (a) the use of health services by children and (b) the ratios of the prevalence of chronic handicapping illnesses among adults to general practitioner and hospital out-patient consultation rates (the General Practitioner Index and the Hospital Out-patient Index). However, medicine's lack of success in preventing and curing those diseases which are the main causes of death (see Table 20) suggests that differences in access to medical care cannot be primarily responsible for social class differences in health.

An alternative possibility is that social class differences in health result from differences in exposure to those factors which may cause disease and/or differences in access to those factors which enable the body's immune system to prevent disease developing. Although the specific aetiological factors will vary from disease to disease, and although the evidence is still patchy, diet, stress, cigarette smoking, housing, atmospheric pollution and social isolation have all been implicated in one way or another and all these have been shown to vary with social class. It has also been found that middle-class patients are more knowledgeable than working-class people about the nature of disease and more likely to take preventive action.

A further debate concerns the relative contribution of work and way of life to these differences. Although the distinction is to some extent artificial, the similarity of male and female rates and the results of social class standardization to these rates suggest that differences in the general way of life, rather than factors associated with specific occupations, are primarily

Table 21. Social class and use of health services (1970–72)

Social class	Visited a dentist	Percentage of those under 7 years who have never		
		Been immunized against		
		Smallpox	Polio	Diphtheria
I	16	6	1	1
II	20	14	3	3
IIIN	19	16	3	3
IIIM	24	25	4	6
IV	27	29	6	8
V	31	33	10	11

Social class	General practitioner index*		Hospital OPD index[†]	
	Male	Female	Male	Female
I	1.2	2.0	1.3	1.6
II	1.0	1.3	1.0	1.1
IIIN	0.9	1.3	1.0	1.1
IIIM	0.8	1.2	0.9	0.8
IV	0.8	0.8	0.7	0.6
V	0.6	0.7	0.6	0.5

* Ratio of prevalence of chronic handicapping illnesses among adults to general practitioners' consultation rates.
† Ratio of prevalence of chronic handicapping illnesses among adults to hospital out-patient consultation rates.
Adapted from OPCS (1978) and Blaxter (1976).

responsible for social class differences in health (Fox & Adelstein 1978).

The overall picture

The relationship between social class and health is unlikely to be the result of a single process. The Victorians were familiar with the vicious circle of 'poverty causes disease which causes poverty'. Although this may be re-formulated to read 'limited opportunity to lead a healthy life combined with inadequate medical care is likely to result in illness and disability which may lead to further deprivation', the logic of the vicious circle remains. However, for the reasons already given, the most important part of this circle, and therefore the main explanation of the relationship between social class and health, is almost certainly the social-class-related differences in exposure to factors implicated in the aetiology of disease.

The differences in health status between the various social classes are worrying. Brotherston (1976) has voiced the concern felt by many of those working in the health professions: 'For the most part, the evidence suggests that the gaps remain as wide apart as a generation ago, and in some instances the gaps may be widening'. These inequalities are a source of perplexity and disappointment to those who support the NHS as a means of improving health or increasing opportunities for health within our society. There is no easy answer to changing inequalities in health, which have complex, multi-causal explanations, rooted in the general nature, conditions and styles of living of the different social classes. Reduction in health inequalities depends on major social changes both in work and outside work, as well as clearly organized and concerted efforts by central government and individual citizens to attack directly the sources of inequality described in this chapter.

References

BLAXTER, M. (1976) Social class and health inequalities. In: *Equalities and Inequalities in Health*, ed. C. Carter & J. Peel. London: Academic Press.

BROTHERSTON, J. (1976) Inequality: is it inevitable? In: *Equalities and Inequalities in Health*, ed. C. Carter & J. Peel. London: Academic Press.

CHADWICK, E. (1842) *Report on the Sanitary Condition of the Labouring Population of Great Britain*. Reprinted by Edinburgh University Press, 1965.

DEPARTMENT OF EMPLOYMENT (1977) *New Earnings Survey*. London: HMSO.

DEPARTMENT OF HEALTH AND SOCIAL SECURITY (1980) *Inequalities in Health*. London: HMSO.

FARRIS, R. & DUNHAM, H. (1939) *Mental Disorders in Urban Areas*. Chicago: University of Chicago Press.

FOX, J. & ADELSTEIN, A. (1978) Occupational mortality: work or way of life? *J. Epidem. commun. Hlth*, **32**, 73–8.

MINISTRY OF AGRICULTURE (1977) *Household Food Consumption and Expenditure.* London: HMSO.

MORRIS, J. (1975) *Uses of Epidemiology.* Edinburgh: Churchill Livingstone.

OFFICE OF POPULATION CENSUSES AND SURVEYS (1973) *General Household Survey.* London: HMSO.

OFFICE OF POPULATION CENSUSES AND SURVEYS (1976) *General Household Survey.* London: HMSO.

OFFICE OF POPULATION CENSUSES AND SURVEYS (1978) *Occupational Mortality, Decennial Supplement, 1970–72, England and Wales.* London: HMSO.

WEDDERBURN, D. (1972) Inequality at work. In: *Labour and Inequality*, ed. P. Townsend & N. Bosanquet. London: Fabian Society.

10

Ethnicity, Health and Health Care

Ellie Scrivens and Sheila M. Hillier

Despite the steady accumulation of evidence suggesting that ethnicity can play a crucial role in the experience of illness, the special health problems of the many ethnic minorities in Britain have generally been neglected, not least in medical education. If health workers are to meet the varying needs of people from different ethnic groups, it is important that this is rectified. A good deal is already known about the diseases to which different ethnic *minorities* are particularly susceptible, the effects of cultural background and conditions in the 'host' community on their health, and their perception and use of services available in the British health care system.

Asian and West Indian communities in Britain

This chapter concentrates on minorities in Britain from the New Commonwealth and Pakistan (N.C.W.P.), and especially on Asians and West Indians, largely because much of the relevant British research concerns these groups. Fig. 5 gives a breakdown of the population of N.C.W.P. ethnic origin in the UK in mid-1971 and mid-1976. It shows clearly that the largest group is of West Indian origin. It also shows that, because migrants from the Caribbean began to arrive before migrants from the Indian subcontinent, a relatively large proportion of people of West Indian origin were born in the UK. It has been estimated that in 1976 approximately 40% of the population of N.C.W.P. ethnic origin was born in the UK. By contrast, the number of those of Indian or Pakistan origin born in the UK is small.

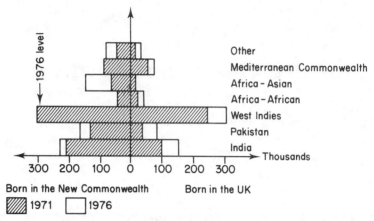

Fig. 5   Population of N.C.W.P. ethnic origin according to ethnic origin and birthplace in Britain, mid-1971 and mid-1976. (*OPCS Immigrant Statistics Unit 1975*)

The bulk of migration from the N.C.W.P. to Britain occurred within the legal framework of the British Nationality Act of 1948. It was not the legal possibility of entry, however, which caused the migration. Unemployment or underemployment and poverty in the colonies and ex-colonies, the anti-immigration policies of other countries and, most significantly of all, the demand for labour in Britain were the principal reasons for migration. Peach (1968) has argued convincingly that the great wave of West Indian migration to Britain in the late 1950s and early 1960s can be explained largely in terms of the active recruitment policies of British employers. London Transport, for example, set up a recruiting office in Barbados to attract new employees because of the difficulty of recruiting British people to their semi-skilled and unskilled jobs.

It is necessary also to distinguish between two kinds of migrants, namely 'settlers' and 'sojourners'. Settlers intend to remain permanently in the host country; sojourners plan to earn sufficient money to permit a return to their home society. Migrants to Britain from the West Indies and Asia include both types.

Bagley (1975) has identified two 'ideal' types of relationship between migrants and hosts: *assimilation*, in which the migrant group is dispersed and absorbed into the host community; and *plural accommodation*, in which the migrant group retains its own culture and separate identity whilst at the same time being accepted by the host community. He claims that West Indian migrants to Britain have typically tried to assimilate into British society, while Asian migrants have typically tried to establish a situation of plural accommodation. He further claims that both minority groups have largely failed to achieve their goals because of racial prejudice and discrimination in the host society.

There is indeed strong evidence in the labour market of racial discrimination against West Indians and Asians. Such discrimination, whether tacit or overt, can result in workers either not being employed at all or being recruited at a lower level than their abilities may warrant. Smith (1976) found that 40% of white men work in professional, managerial and white collar jobs, compared with 8% of West Indian and Bangladeshi men, 20% of Indian and 30% of African Asians. By contrast, 18% of white men were in semi-skilled or unskilled jobs, compared with 32% of West Indians, 36% of Indians, 58% of Pakistanis and Bangladeshis and 26% of African Asians. These differences in job grades were not explicable solely in terms of differences in qualifications: for example, 79% of white men with degree level qualifications were in professional/managerial jobs compared with 31% of Asian/Afro–Caribbean men with that level of qualification.

Special health problems of ethnic minorities

Physical illness

Available information suggests that Asian babies in Britain have low birth weights and high levels of perinatal and infant mortality compared with the indigenous population. In its evidence to the Royal Commission on the National Health Service, the Community Relations Commission (1977) expressed concern that there had been no adequate investigation into the reasons for weight differentials and for the low utilization of antenatal and postnatal care services by Asians. The Commission also drew attention to certain dietary deficiences amongst Asians. Anaemia caused by iron deficiency or vitamin B12 deficiency has been shown to be more common among Asians, particularly amongst vegetarian Hindus whose diet is devoid of easily assimilated iron from animal sources. In addition, two specific anaemic conditions are known to affect certain ethnic groups: sickle cell anaemia, an inherited difficulty in the manufacture of haemoglobin, affects West Indians and Africans, and thalassaemia, another inherited anaemia, affects Cypriot babies. These conditions are much rarer among the indigenous white population.

Rickets and its adult equivalent, osteomalacia, are thought to be caused by vitamin D deficiency and are also particularly prevalent among the Asian minority. The vitamin D content of an Asian diet, which is largely based on rice, chapatis made from refined flour and ghee, is low; some groups may have negligible vitamin D intake if their diet is vegan (vegetarian, but also forbidding fish and eggs). The traditional styles of dress adopted by Asian girls and women mean that this deficiency cannot be compensated for by exposure to sunlight, although recent research has suggested that Asian women who have adopted western styles of dress *also* suffer from osteomalacia: one implication of this research, then, is that the aetiology of osteomalacia may be more complex than is currently thought (Compston 1973). As yet prophylactic measures have been poorly organized and no account of an effective preventive campaign has been published. Since 1979, however, Asian children in Glasgow have been receiving vitamin D supplementation on the initiative of the Greater Glasgow Health Board, and the results are expected to be encouraging (Dunnigan et al. 1981).

It seems clear from the discussion so far that certain ethnic groups are genetically susceptible to specific conditions and *culturally* vulnerable, through their dietary customs, to others; they may also, however, be *socially* vulnerable to illness: in other words, they may be liable to illness which is causally related to general social disadvantage (e.g. employment, poor housing, lack of education and so on). In this context it is useful to distinguish analytically between the negative effects of ethnicity *per se* and the negative effects of, for example, social class. In practice, however, such lines are often very difficult to draw.

Mental illness

Recent research on ethnicity and mental illness, much of it

based on notes of admission to psychiatric hospitals, has highlighted some of the difficulties involved in identifying the role of cultural and social factors in the aetiology of disease. For example, some authors have maintained that migrating from a poor agricultural village in Jamaica or India to an industrial city in Britain is a stressful experience in itself and that this may be compounded by the experience of racial discrimination and of a culture which threatens key values of the migrant. The predictable consequence will be higher rates of psychiatric breakdown amongst certain migrant communities. While some studies, often of West Indian migrants, have been cited in support of this hypothesis, others, often of Asian migrants, appear to refute it. Rack (1979) has argued strongly that such hypotheses cannot be tested adequately until more is known about the access of particular ethnic groups to treatment facilities and about differences in the perception and reporting of symptoms of illness by people from cultures which are very different from that of most doctors.

Rack, a psychiatrist, goes on to argue that diagnosing mental illness is largely dependent on how patients report their symptoms. He claims that Asians tend to concentrate on physical symptoms and to identify illness in terms of the extent to which they remain capable of discharging normal social responsibilities rather than in terms of internal distress. He also contends that diagnosis of paranoid states can be difficult when patients come from cultures where beliefs in supernatural forces are widespread. Ballard (1979) makes the point particularly well: 'in a situation where magico-religious beliefs are persuasive, the "rational" and the "magical", the physical and the mental, are not always easy to separate. Very often allegations about supernatural forces may be a means of making statements about real social relationships. However, in the absence of an understanding of the code, such communications may seem bizarre and deluded, evidence perhaps of schizophrenia'.

Before some of these issues are elaborated further, in the context of the perception and use of health care services, it ought to be noted that the cultures or subcultures of ethnic minorities can serve to *decrease* as well as to increase the risk of illness. Particularly pertinent to the preceding discussion is Ananth's (1978) claim that certain Indian cultural systems may afford protection against mental illness.

In this connection, a study of coronary heart disease (CHD) in Japanese–Americans is worth citing in more detail (Marmot & Syme 1976). Japan has the lowest mortality from CHD of any industrialized country, and the USA, by contrast, has one of the highest CHD rates. Marmot and Syme set out to test the hypothesis that social and cultural differences may account for the CHD differences between Japan and the USA. They classified 3809 Japanese–Americans in California according to the degree to which they retained a 'traditional' Japanese culture. They found that the most traditional group had a CHD prevalence as low as that observed in Japan and that the group that was most acculturated to Western culture had a three- to five-fold excess in CHD prevalence. The difference in CHD rate between these two groups could not be accounted for by differences in the major coronary risk factors known to be associated with CHD.

Perception and use of health care facilities

There is enormous diversity among ethnic minorities in Britain. It is a mistake, for example, to see the Asian population as in any way homogenous. Table 22 shows the location of the many Asian communities and gives some indication of the extent of the variations that exist in religion and language and, consequently, in beliefs and practices. While it is important to avoid wide generalizations about Asian culture in Britain, certain patterns of belief and behaviour concerning illness are discernible in most Asian communities (Henley 1979). For example, sick people in Asian cultures are normally expected to express their feelings of pain, worry and grief openly and to retire passively to bed until the illness has taken its course. The whole of the extended family — embracing the male head of the family and his wife, their sons and their wives, and their sons' children — is expected to want to gather round the sick person; they feed and tend the patient, share in any suffering and perform his or her duties and chores until health is restored. In many British hospitals the staff remain insensitive to such cultural differences: Asian patients who lie passively in their beds, perhaps crying and groaning, are often made to feel unwelcome and uncomfortable, as are their families who wish to

Table 22. *Main Asian Communities in Britain*

People from	Called	Their religion	Their first language	They may speak some	They first settled in
India					
Punjab	Punjabis	Sikhism	Punjabi	Hindi	Chatham, Gravesend, Smethick, Leeds, West London, West Midlands
Gujarat (central and south)	Gujaratis	Mainly Hinduism, some Islam	Gujarati	Hindi	Preston, Birmingham, north London
North	Kutchis or Gudjaratis	Mainly Hinduism, some Islam	Kutchi or Gujarati	Hindi	Gudjarati Moslems in Bolton, Leicester, Preston
Pakistan					
Punjab	Punjabis	Islam	Punjabi	Urdu	Bedford, Glasgow, High Wycombe
Mirpur	Pirpuris	Islam	Mirpuri (Punjabi dialect)	Punjabi, Urdu,	Sheffield, Slough, West Midlands, West Yorkshire
North-west Frontier Province	Pathans	Islam	Pashto	Urdu, Punjabi	
Bangladesh (mainly from Sylhet)	Bengalis	Islam	Bengali		Bolton, Bradford, east and north-east London, Luton, Oldham, Scunthorpe
East Africa Kenya, Malawi, Tanzania, Uganda, Zambia		Hinduism, Islam or Sikhism	Gujarati or Punjabi	Hindi, English, Swahili	Birmingham, Croydon, Leicester, north and south London, south-east England

Adapted from Henley (1979).

be with them and support them at all hours, which is what would happen in the Indian subcontinent.

The fundamental importance of the extended family to Asians can be further illustrated with reference to stigma. A number of physical conditions, such as tuberculosis, Hansen's disease, asthma and eczema, carry a strong stigma in Asian culture, especially among more conservative or less educated people. In all families, however, the diagnosis of a stigmatizing condition may have very serious consequences, not only for the patient but for the whole family. When a marriage is being arranged, each family investigates thoroughly the character, reputation and health of the intended bride or bridegroom *and* of his or her whole family. The marriage chances of *all* the siblings may be ruined if one member of the family has a stigmatizing condition.

The extent to which Asian migrants use the available health care services in Britain is dependent not just on their cultural conceptions of health and illness, but also on their previous experiences of health care. Poor migrants from a rural area of India, for example, will have had very different experiences from wealthy migrants from urban communities in East Africa. The former may never have been in a hospital in their lives and hence be apprehensive or frightened of British hospitals; by contrast, the latter may be fully acquainted with western-style medical facilities, supported by a bureaucratic administration, and may miss a highly personalized service which in Britain is often available only in private hospitals. More specifically, some Asian women, particularly in their early years in Britain, may fear both hospitals and doctors because of the possibility of having to be examined by a man. Some women decline to go to surgeries or clinics, even if they think there is something wrong with them, because they fear they will be seen by a male doctor. Henley (1979) writes: 'the anguish and embarrassment of many women during a vaginal examination cannot be over-emphasized'.

Alternative medicine

In many parts of the N.C.W.P. two different systems of medicine coexist, namely, the western system and one or more 'folk' systems. In Jamaica, for example, one folk system, derived from West Africa, explains ill health in terms of witchcraft and a neighbour's malice. The sick person consults the 'obeah man' (or woman) in pursuit of a diagnosis. The obeah healer generally uses the laying on of hands in the form of massage with balm oil: it is believed that evil influences inside the body 'come out of your skin' and can be drawn forth by massage (Kitzinger 1980). Such practices have often survived after migration to Britain and may either complement or substitute for conventional treatment by western-trained doctors.

On the Indian subcontinent there are few western-trained doctors outside the towns, only one for every 50 000 people; there is one 'hakim' or folk healer, however, for every 5000 inhabitants. Moreover, it has been estimated that there are at least four or five hakims in full or part-time practice in every large town in Britain (Davis & Aslam 1979). It is quite common for Asian migrants to consult one or more hakims instead of a general practitioner, or to seek the help of hakims and NHS doctors simultaneously. While this continued reliance on the 'dubious' arts of folk healing may, from the vantage point of the medical profession, be a cause for concern, there is little doubt that hakims fulfil a need in Asian communities. For example, the hakim respects, and makes provision for seeing and involving, a patient's whole family. Hakims also have insight into the special problems of Asian migrants. For instance, some aches and pains may be misdiagnosed by general practitioners and analgesics routinely prescribed. Such symptoms may, however, be signs of neurosis. An Asian patient may complain of 'wind filling his stomach and going to his head'. The hakim interprets this as a family problem and the family is brought together to solve it. Davis and Aslam (1979) suggest that hakims and other folk healers be encouraged to form professional associations in Britain and to register those who conform to the high standards of practice which obtain in India and Pakistan.

Employment and the National Health Service

It is sometimes not appreciated that the NHS is one of the principal employers of members of ethnic groups. The Community Relations Commission (1977) has reviewed the data available and shows that in the mid-1970s, up to one-fifth of hospital ancillary workers were either of N.C.W.P. ethnic origin or from foreign countries; nearly one-quarter of the student and pupil nurses and pupil midwives in training in NHS hospitals were born overseas, mostly in the N.C.W.P.; and over one-third of all NHS hospitals doctors and nearly one-fifth of general practitioners were born overseas. Some commentators have argued that the NHS is unusual in that the migrants are not clustered in the lowest-paid jobs; it is claimed that this is because the British immigration laws have been used selectively to allow particular types of skilled labour into the country, and nurses and doctors have been among the few categories of workers able to obtain immigration vouchers in recent years (Sivanandan 1976).

Nurses born overseas, however, are over-represented in hospitals dealing with mental illness, mental subnormality, mental handicap and geriatrics, and relatively few are to be found in the 'prestige' teaching hospitals. It seems that they are used to compensate for the shortage of native recruits into less well paid and sometimes more taxing work. The picture is similar for doctors born overseas. In 1975 they comprised 35% of all hospital doctors in the NHS: 14% of consultants, 28% of senior registrars, 57% of registrars and 60% of senior house officers. They were heavily under-represented in the more popular specialties, especially at consultant level; overseas doctors formed, for example, only 9% of consultants in general surgery compared with 34% in geriatrics (Community Relations Commission 1977). The Community Relations Commission reflects on the possibility that these 'imbalances' can be attributed, at least in part, to varied discrimination and recommends that steps be taken to ensure that the skills of nurses and doctors born overseas are adequately rewarded.

The research on ethnicity, health and health care in Britain is as yet fragmentary. There is little doubt, however, that members of ethnic minorities are often unusually vulnerable, both to particular diseases and, largely because of disadvantages in the labour and housing markets, to general poor health. Often there are also cultural barriers to help-seeking. Some of these difficulties may be overcome by time and health education programmes, others by increased awareness among health workers and by changes in medical procedure and organization. Some difficulties, however, have deep roots in the socioeconomic structure of British society and are unlikely to be solved by small-scale social engineering.

References

ANANTH, J. (1978) Psychopathology in Indian females. *Soc. Sci. Med.*, **12B**(3), 177–8.

BAGLEY, C. (1975) Sequels of alienation: a social psychological view of the adaptation of west Indian migrants in Britain. In: *Case Studies in Human Rights and Fundamental Problems*, Vol. 2, ed. K. Glasser. Amsterdam: Martin Nijhoff.

BALLARD, R. (1979) Ethnic minorities and the social services. In: *Minority Families in Britain*, ed. V. Khan. London: Macmillan.

COMPSTON, J. (1979) Rickets in asian immigrants. *Br. med. J.*, **2**, 612.

COMMUNITY RELATIONS COMMISSION (1977) *Evidence to the Royal Commission on the National Health Service.* London: Community Relations Commission.

DAVIS, S. & ASLAM, M. (1979) *The Hakim and His Role in the Immigrant Community.* London: DHSS.

DUNNIGAN, M., McINTOSH, W., SUTHERLAND, G., GARDEE, R., GLEKIN, B., FORD, J. & ROBERTSON, I. (1981) Policy for prevention of Asian rickets in Britain: a preliminary assessment of the Glasgow rickets campaign. *Br. med. J.*, **282**, 357–360.

HENLEY, A. (1979) *Asian Patients in Hospital and at Home.* London: King Edwards's Hospital Fund for London.

KITZINGER, S. (1980) Caribbean conceptions. *Gen. Practnr*, May.

MARMOT, M. & SYME, S. (1976) Acculturation and coronary heart disease in Japanese–Americans. *Am. J. Epidem.*, **104**, 225–47.

OFFICE OF POPULATION CENSUSES AND SURVEYS IMMIGRANTS STATISTICS UNIT (1975) Country of birth and colour 1971–74. *Pop. Trends*, **2**.

PEACH, C. (1968) *West Indian Migration to Britain.* London: Oxford University Press.

RACK, P. (1979) Diagnosing mental illness: Asians and the psychiatric services. In: *Minority Families in Britain*, ed. V. Khan. London: Macmillan.

SIVANANDAN, A. (1976) *Race, Class and the State: The Black Experience in Britain*, Race and Class Pamphlet No. 1. Nottingham: Russell Press.

SMITH, D. (1976) *The Facts of Racial Disadvantage.* London: Political and Economic Planning.

The Family and Illness

David Locker

In all societies it is possible to identify a social unit that may be called a family. This unit, consisting of a set of social relationships established by marriage and parenthood, performs functions essential to the stability and survival of society. Although the family is found in all cultures and historical periods its structure, the functions it performs and the extent to which those functions are shared with other social institutions vary.

One approach to the study of the family is the analysis of its functions and the way these have been modified as a result of industrialization and urbanization. Such an analysis has given rise to a lively debate. On the one hand, it is argued that the family is outmoded: since some of its functions have been taken over by other institutions such as the welfare state, it has lost its role in society and will gradually be replaced by alternative social groupings. Some have argued that it is oppressive, the source of the subordination of women and the emotional and behavioural problems labelled mental illness (Laing & Esterson 1964). On the other hand, it has been argued that the family is essential to the health of the individual and society. This view is supported by the claim that the family is now a highly specialized unit responsible for procreation, the primary socialization of children, the fulfilment of the psychological, emotional and sexual needs of its members and the care and nurturing of the sick and dependent. While both these viewpoints have provided insights useful in understanding the nature and conduct of family life, it is the latter position which informs much of our current social welfare provision.

Another way of looking at the family is in terms of the socially stereotyped roles occupied by the individuals who constitute it. These roles are defined in terms of the sex of the occupant: the male role tends to be instrumental and the female role expressive. That is, the tasks performed by the family such as household management, the care and control of children and economic provision are divided according to sex. The woman's role in the family is that of wife and mother. Her occupation and interests are domestic, concerned with the home and the daily needs of the family for care and nurturing. The reward for such work is almost entirely emotional. On the other hand, men are active producers. They occupy a place in the labour market where their main interest is securing material rewards to provide for the economic needs of the family. Women thus occupy an economically subordinate position in the family. These roles, which are learned by children during their socialization within the family, are often assumed to be natural, necessary and inevitable. They are also generalized to the wider society. When women do enter the labour force they tend to have jobs in the poorly paid service and caring occupations (see Chapter 17). The woman's role in the family and the way her role is changing in modern society have important implications. To the extent that the functions of the family are realized through the tasks performed by women there is a sense in which women are the family. Consequently the growing independence and equality of opportunity for women may require corresponding changes in the nature and conduct of family life.

The role of the family in health care

Whatever the merits of the argument that the family is losing its traditional functions it continues to assume the major burden of caring for the sick. The contribution of the family is particularly important in chronic illness where care is continuous and long-term.

Some impression of the extent of family support for the sick can be gained from surveys of the numbers cared for in the community as opposed to institutions. In 1969 a national study by Harris (1971) estimated that approximately 116 000 very severely handicapped, elderly persons were living in private

Table 23.   Distribution of the disabled population between private
households and residential care including hospitals

	No. in private households	No. in institut-ional care	Total no. of disabled	No. in private households % Total no.
Under age 65	1453 000	75 400	1528 400	95.1
Over age 65	1782 000	267 000	2049 000	87.0
All ages	3235 000	342 400	3577 400	90.4

From Topliss (1979).

households. These were people who were senile, bedfast, unable
to feed or wash themselves, needed help to use the toilet, were
doubly incontinent or could not be left alone. There were a
further 380 000 appreciably handicapped individuals living at
home who could do some things for themselves but still needed
assistance. Table 23 shows that only one-tenth of the physically
disabled in UK are in residential care or live in hospital.
Similarly, in 1971 only 5% of the population which had reached
statutory retirement age were cared for in institutional settings.
Moreover, it is not necessarily the less severely handicapped
who are cared for at home. In a national study of the care of the
terminally ill, Cartwright et al. (1972) found that 84% of those
dying at home had very disturbing symptoms such as
incontinence or senility compared to 64% of those dying in
hospital.

Table 24 shows the percentage of elderly bedfast people who
received help from different sources. The local authority
services were the main source of help for only a minority of those
studied. In her study Harris (1971) found that 37% of the *very*
severely handicapped elderly were not receiving help from any
of the community services available. Cartwright et al. (1972)
reported similar findings and also found that it was female
rather than male relatives who provided most of the help
received by the dependant. Consequently, the availability of
female relatives often determined the place of care: 60% of those
with unmarried daughters were nursed at home before they died
compared with 34% of those who only had unmarried sons.

Table 24. *Percentage of elderly people needing assistance receiving help from different sources*

	Housework	Heavy housework	Bathing
Spouse	31	18	15
Child in household	22	25	28
Child outside household	13	11	5
Other relatives			
in household	9	7	6
outside household	13	11	5
Privately paid help	—	11	1
Social services	4	9	7
None	7	13	37

Adapted from Shanas (1968).

The effect on the family of providing care for the chronically ill

A common finding of studies of the utilization of community services such as home helps, meals-on-wheels and home nursing is that the elderly or chronic sick living alone are much more likely to receive help than those living with relatives. If the person is living with others, services are often withheld on the assumption that the family will provide the care that is needed. While few families are unwilling to provide support many have to bear an enormous burden in so doing. Chronic illness handicaps not only the individual concerned but also the family as a whole. Sainsbury and Grad de Alarcon (1974) have documented the consequences of treating the mentally ill at home (Table 25). Similar effects have been noted in the families of mentally handicapped children (Holt 1958).

Such problems may become so severe that support within the family cannot be maintained. For example, one of the major reasons for the admission of an elderly person to institutional care is to relieve the burden imposed on the family (see Chapter 13). The provision of community services can ease or alleviate many of these difficulties. Even so, Sainsbury and Grad de

Table 25.   Family problems as a result of home care of the mentally ill

Effect on	% reporting effect
Health of relatives	
Mental	60
Physical	28
Social and leisure activities	35
Children	34
Domestic routine	29
Income of family	23
Employment of family members	23

Adapted from Sainsbury and Grad de Alarcon (1974).

Alarcon found that 20% of the families they studied remained disrupted two years after being in contact with services.

The extension of community care

Since the early 1960s policy concerning the care of the elderly, the mentally ill and handicapped and the physically handicapped has sought to extend the family's role still further by having more of these clients cared for in the community rather than in institutions. There is also an increasing tendency to shorten periods of hospitalization following childbirth, surgery or acute episodes of mental illness, so that the patient returns to home care sooner. While this trend has been justified on economic and social grounds, an extension of the family's role needs to be seen in the context of changes that are taking place in the family. These may affect either the ability or the willingness of the family to provide care or cope with the hardship that results. Whether care at home is feasible will depend upon *structural* and *attitudinal factors*.

It has been generally believed that industrialization brought about a structural change in the family, transforming the extended family, large and complicated with several generations living together, into the relatively isolated nuclear family, consisting solely of parents and their offspring. Historical research has shown this belief to be false. Though birth rates were high, so were death rates and large family groups did not materialize. While the households of the rich were large, owing to the number of servants they employed, the households of the poor were small. It would appear that the nuclear family of today, existing within a network of related families, has been the dominant pattern for six centuries or more. Consequently, the image of the extended family as the sole source of welfare for the sick and dependent is also false. These individuals were often cared for within the family but financial and other forms of support have always been provided by the wider community (Laslett 1980).

Improvements in mortality rates over the last century have not produced an increase in family size since there has been a corresponding fall in birth rates. The decrease in family size from an average of seven children in 1860 to an average of two in 1960 has meant that the availability of support within the nuclear family remains limited. In addition, the increase in the divorce rate and prevalence of one-parent families and the continuing disparity in mortality rates between men and women mean that increasing numbers of individuals have no spouse on whom they can rely. In a study of the physically handciapped in Lambeth over half were found to be single, widowed or divorced, 24% lived alone and a further 36% lived with just one other person (Patrick et al. 1981).

Another characteristic of the modern family is its high degree of geographical mobility. This has been brought about by the needs of the economic system for a workforce that can change its place of residence often and easily and the post-war housing policy in Britain which created new towns some distance from traditional urban centres. More than a third of the adult population moves every five years and almost 10% move yearly. Consequently, while family members may exist, they may be too remote to provide the necessary degree of care.

A third, and perhaps more significant, change is that concerning the growth in opportunities for women. This is reflected in the increase in the proportion of married women working. In 1921 less than one in ten married women worked outside the home. By 1980 changes in the labour market had meant that over half of married women had a job in addition to that of housewife. Many women work to achieve a sense of self-fulfilment and to develop social contacts not provided by the domestic role. Other women are the main providers for their families or need to work to supplement the family income and maintain a desirable standard of living. This means that many women may be unavailable or unwilling to provide care for the dependant or, more likely, that they will find it necessary to perform this role as well as those of housewife and worker.

This situation is further complicated by changes in the age structure of the population. As mentioned in Chapter 13, the proportion of elderly people in the population is increasing relative to younger age groups. Consequently, the pool of potential careers is decreasing. Assuming that most of the care of the elderly is likely to be provided by women aged 45–60, in 1901 there were 83 such women for every 100 retired persons in the general population. By 1971 demographic changes had reduced this ratio to 49 per 100. These changes are particularly sharp if the numbers of single women between 45 and 60 are considered. A decrease in the proportion of women remaining unmarried has meant that there are now only five single women aged 45 to 60 per 100 elderly compared to 13 per 100 in 1901. The proportion of women who might make their prime commitment the care of elderly parents or relatives has thus declined substantially.

Marriage, the family and illness

While the chronically sick patient can have an effect on the conduct and quality of family life, it is also the case that the family can have an effect on the patient. There is an accumulating body of evidence showing that the family may influence both the *onset* of illness and its *course or outcome*. The mechanisms which link family characteristics and illness are not yet understood, but some research suggests that the structure of the family and the nature of relationships within it are important. These factors may play a direct or a mediating role and they may operate at different points in the course of illness. For example, the family situation may:

1. Constitute a pathological agent in itself.
2. Affect the chances of an individual coming into contact with agents which produce disease.

Table 26. *Mortality, all causes: ratio of mortality rate of the unmarried by the mortality rate of the married, whites aged 25–64, USA, 1960*

Marital status		Ratio
Single	Male	1.96
	Female	1.68
Widowed	Male	2.64
	Female	1.77
Divorced	Male	3.39
	Female	1.95

Adapted from Gove (1979).

3. Affect the chance of onset of disorder following such contact.
4. Affect the severity of the disorder.
5. Affect the likelihood of treatment being received.
6. Influence the response to treatment.

A specific factor may be linked to a number of diseases but by different mechanisms. For example, loss of a parent in childhood by death, divorce or separation is associated with the onset of tuberculosis, suicide and serious accidents in later life (Chen & Cobb 1960). Since these are different types of event it is likely that parental deprivation operates differently in each case. This can be illustrated further by an examination of the association between marital status and mortality. The single, widowed and divorced have consistently higher mortality rates than the married, the difference being much larger for men than for women. Widowhood and divorce appear to have a particularly significant effect on mortality for men (Table 26).

One possible explanation for these differences is that marital status has an influence on psychological states and life-styles (Gove 1979). Studies have shown that the married tend to be happier and more satisfied than the unmarried, they are less likely to live a socially isolated existence and they have more interpersonal ties. In a society in which marriage and the family are valued, being married gives meaning and importance to existence, promotes a sense of well being and is a source of social and emotional support. This explanation tends to be supported

Table 27.   Mortality, specific causes: ratio of mortality rate of the unmarried by the mortality rate of the married, whites aged 25–64, USA, 1960

Marital status	Suicide	Lung cancer	Cirrhosis	Tuberculosis	Diabetes
Single					
Male	2.00	1.45	3.29	5.37	2.69
Female	1.51	1.11	1.19	3.31	2.03
Widowed					
Male	5.01	2.24	4.61	7.70	2.46
Female	2.21	1.20	3.45	3.31	1.71
Divorced					
Male	4.75	3.07	8.84	9.27	4.32
Female	3.43	1.11	4.43	3.10	1.67

Adapted from Gove (1979).

by the observed relationships between marital status and specific causes of death. Variations in mortality rates are large where psychological states or aspects of life-style play a direct role in death, as in suicide and accidental death, or are associated with acts such as smoking and alcohol consumption, as in deaths from lung cancer and cirrhosis of the liver. Large differences are also observed in diseases such as tuberculosis and diabetes where family factors may influence entry into care, willingness to undergo treatment or the availability of long-term social support (Table 27). In this way, factors associated with marital status appear to act differently with regard to specific diseases.

The influence of marriage and the family on the onset of illness

The association between mortality and marital status suggests that the unmarried are at greater risk from a number of physical illnesses. The data on mental illness show a more complex picture. While mental illness is more frequent among the single, widowed and divorced than among the married, single women are less likely to become mentally ill than single men but married women become mentally ill more frequently than married men. Again, this would suggest that men find marriage more advantageous than women. In explaining these findings Gove (1972) has claimed that their role within the family predisposes women to mental illness. This is attributed to the frustrations and restrictions of being a housewife, the inferior occupational position, the strain of performing the conflicting roles of wife, mother and worker and the contradictory expectations which confront women. In support of this theory there is evidence to show that women more often find marriage constraining and are more likely to be socially isolated and dissatisfied than men. In a more specific study based on original data Brown and Harris (1978) have identified a number of factors associated with marriage and family life which predispose some women to depression following a severe life event (see Chapter 1). Of particular importance was the absence of an intimate and confiding relationship with a husband or other person and lack of a job outside the home.

The emotional relationships and patterns of communication within the family are central to Laing's controversial view of the family as inherently psychopathological. He has claimed that schizophrenia is not an illness but a rational response to family life. That is, the apparently bizarre behaviour and thought patterns of the individual diagnosed as schizophrenic do not appear bizarre when interpreted in terms of their family context (Laing & Esterson 1964). Integral to this is a confusion of identity brought about by the shifting and contradictory images conveyed to the person concerned during interaction with members of the family.

A more limited and more conventional view is adopted by those who seek to establish a link between what is defined as an inadequate family life in early childhood and a variety of pathologies in later life. A number of illnesses and behavioural disorders have been attributed to maternal deprivation. Studies reporting such an association have been based on the traditional assumption that the mother is the key individual in a child's life. The more enlightened view is that, while failure to provide for a child's emotional needs may have negative consequences, such needs can be met outside the confines of the nuclear family (Rutter 1972). In addition, the exclusive relationship between a mother and child engendered by modern family life may give rise to a level of dependence that can itself be pathological.

While the family may sometimes contribute to the onset of illness, the social support it provides can play a protective role in reducing the impact of stress. Gore (1978) studied a group of men for two years following enforced redundancy and assessed their health in terms of the number of symptoms they experienced and their serum cholesterol levels. The men were divided into supported and unsupported groups depending upon their relationships and social activities with wives (if present), relatives and friends. The unsupported group suffered more economic and psychological deprivation than the supported group, they reported more symptoms over the two years following unemployment and had higher serum cholesterol levels. Like much of the work in this field, the mechanisms which link social support and illness are not fully understood. These findings do, however, give some indication of the way in which social and psychological variables affect physiological processes and point to the fact that disease is always multicausal.

The influence of the family on the course and outcome of illness

In the 1950s Parsons and Fox (1958) argued that the nuclear family was an inappropriate place to care for the ill. They claimed that because the family was concerned with providing for the emotional needs of its members, emotional involvement with the patient would encourage dependency and inhibit recovery. In fact, research seems to suggest that while emotional relationships within the family do affect the course of an illness they may operate to inhibit or encourage recovery. The important factor seems to be the nature of those relationships.

Brown et al. (1972), in attempting to explain why some schizophrenic patients suffered a relapse after discharge from hospital to the home environment, investigated the effect of the emotional involvement of the family with the patient. Patients and their families were studied over a period of one year and as a result of a series of interviews a measure of *expressed emotion* was obtained. This was based on the amount of criticism of the patient by the family, hostility in the family and expressions of warmth and concern. Brown et al. reports that where expressed emotion was high the chance of relapse was greater: where there was a high degree of expressed emotion 58% of patients were returned to the hospital, compared with 16% of those from families where expressed emotion was low.

Other studies have shown that the family can have a positive influence on the patient's progress. Litman (1966) studied 100 orthopaedic patients undergoing rehabilitation. Response to rehabilitation and level of residual disability were related to the type of family from which the patient came and the family's attitudes. Those who were married with children or single but living at home with family had a more favourable outcome than those who were married with no children or single and living alone. The extent to which the family held positive attitudes and encouraged the patient also influenced how well he did, pessimistic attitudes have a retarding effect on the patient's progress.

While care by the family is often assumed to be the ideal and informs much health and social policy it is not necessarily the case that it is best for the patient or other members of the family. Some families have an adverse effect on the course or outcome of a person's illness and the burden of providing care imposes severe strain on some families. Consequently, the kinds of issues addressed by the studies described above need to be taken into account in decision-making about the most appropriate setting in which to provide care.

In this respect knowledge about the structure of the patient's family, the nature of the relationships within it, the attitudes of the family towards the patient and the resources available to the family in providing care is essential. Such information assists in identifying those patients who may need additional support and encouragement from professionals to compensate for a lack of family support and also those families who need services to help cope with the problems of caring for the sick.

References

BROWN, G. W., BIRLEY, J. & WING, J. W. (1972) Influence of family life on course of schizophrenic disorders: a replication. *Br. J. Psychiat.*, **121**, 241–58.

BROWN, G. W. & HARRIS, T. O. (1978) *The Social Origins of Depression*. London: Tavistock.

CARTWRIGHT, A., HOCKEY, L. & ANDERSON, J. (1972) *Life before Death*. London: Routledge and Kegan Paul.

CHEN, E. & COBB, S. (1960) Family structure in relation to health and disease. *J. chron. Dis.*, **12**, 544–67.

GORE, S. (1978) The effects of social support on moderating the health consequences of unemployment. *J. Hlth soc. Behav.*, **19**, 157–65.

GOVE, W. (1972) The relationship between sex roles, marital status and mental illness. *Soc. Forces,* **51,** 34–44.

GOVE, W. (1979) Sex, marital status and mortality. *Am. J. Sociol.,* **79,** 45–67.

HARRIS, A. (1971) *Handicapped and Impaired in Great Britain,* OPCS Social Survey Division, London: HMSO.

HOLT, K. (1958) The home care of the severely retarded child. *Pediatrics, Springfield,* **22**(4), 744–55.

LAING, R. & ESTERSON, A. (1964) *Sanity, Madness and the Family.* Harmondsworth: Penguin.

LASLETT, P. (1980) Characteristics of the Western Europe family. *Lond. Rev. Books,* **2**(20), 7–8.

LITMAN, T. (1966) The family and response to rehabilitation. *J. chron. Dis.,* **19,** 234–40.

PARSONS, T. & FOX, R. (1958) Illness, therapy and the modern urban American family. *J. soc. Issues,* **8,** 31–4.

PATRICK, D., WIGGINS, R., LOCKER, D., GREEN, S., DARBY, S. & HORTON, G. (1981) Screening for disability in the inner city. *J. Epidem. commun. Hlth,* **35,** 65–70.

RUTTER, M. (1972) *Maternal Deprivation Reassessed.* Harmondsworth: Penguin.

SAINSBURY, P. & GRAD DE ALARCON, J. (1974) The cost of community care and the burden on the family of treating the mentally ill at home. In: *Impairment, Disability and Handicap,* ed. D. Lees & S. Shaw. London: Heinemann Educational.

SHANAS, E. (1968) *Old People in Three Industrial Societies.* London: Routledge & Kegan Paul.

12

Women as Patients and Providers

Sheila M. Hillier

The special issues surrounding women's health are important for several reasons. First, epidemiological evidence shows that there are differences in the disease patterns of women and men. Second, female symptomatology and what is defined as illness in women are particularly good examples of the introduction of *social* definitions into what are often thought of as the purely scientific exercises of diagnosis and treatment. Third, looking at the way women are treated as patients is informative not only about how medical practices incorporate many of the socially derived stereotypes of sex and gender, but also about how this helps to confine women to certain limited and limiting roles in society. Fourth, women form the major part of the health care labour force, although they are under-represented in the higher echelons of the medical and administrative hierarchies.

The health of women

Mortality

In modern industrialized societies like Britain or the USA, women live longer than men and at every age there is an excess of male over female mortality. Life expectancy for both males and females has steadily increased over the last hundred years, but the average life expectancy of women is longer: in 1976 in the UK it was 75 years for females and 69 years for males (Office of Health Economics 1979a).

These differences appear to be related to social factors. For example, in less developed countries female life expectancy is lower than that for males; moreover, there is little difference in

Table 28. *Major causes of higher mortality in men*

Ratio of male/female death rates	Cause of death	Death rate (per 100 000 population)	
		Male	Female
5.9	Malignant non-secondary neoplasms of respiratory system	50.1	8.5
4.9	Other bronchopulmonic disease (71% emphysema)	24.4	5.0
2.8	Motor vehicle accidents	39.4	14.2
2.7	Suicide	15.7	5.8
2.4	Other accidents	41.1	17.4
2.0	Cirrhosis of liver	18.5	9.1
2.0	Arteriosclerotic heart disease	357.0	175.6
1.6	All causes	1081.7	657.0

From Waldron (1976).

female and male rates of death from the epidemics which afflict developing societies or which have occurred in the past in developed ones. The major change affecting the mortality of women over the last 100 years in Britain has been the change in patterns of child-bearing and the consequent decline in maternal mortality and in deaths from diseases affecting the female reproductive system. The average woman married in 1880 would expect to bear about five live children, whereas a woman married in 1980 will probably have only two. The other side of the coin — the excess of male mortality — seems to be related at least partly to the different living patterns of men and women. Typically, men are more likely to engage in activities which are injurious to health, both at work and during leisure activity: they drink more, smoke more, drive faster and work in more physically hazardous occupations (Waldron 1976) than do women. This is reflected in Table 28, which summarizes the main causes of higher mortality in men.

The excess of male mortality over female might be even greater were it not that a considerable number of women die of cancers of the breast, cervic and uterus: 39% of deaths in women aged 25–44 are from cancer, a third of these being malignant cancers of the breast. Even after the age of 44, when diseases of the circulatory system take over as the major cause of death in women as in men, breast cancer accounts for one in ten female deaths (Office of Health Economics 1979a) (Table 29).

Changes in mortality rates from particular diseases have affected the male/female ratio of deaths. Among these are the decline in maternal mortality referred to above and the rising number of deaths among women from cancer of the breast, cervix and lung and from cirrhosis of the liver. Lung cancer and cirrhosis seem to be related to the increasing consumption of cigarettes and alcohol among women (Camberwell Council on Alcoholism 1980). Cancer of the cervix appears to be related both to the number of sexual partners and to early sexual intercourse (Martin 1967). It might be, then, that changes in patterns of sexual behaviour among women underlie those changing rates. The reason for the rise in breast cancer remains something of a mystery, but the association between the disease and a first pregnancy after the age of 30, which is more likely to occur in women who have a well-established professional career, might link with changing career patterns among women. Overall, women enjoy a more favourable mortality experience than men and social changes have, on the whole, been beneficial to them. Men, on the other hand, largely for cultural and social reasons, are less fortunate. It has been suggested that the mortality patterns of women might eventually come to resemble those of men, as differences in life-styles diminish, but this could just as well come about as a result of a decline in male mortality resulting from changes in male behaviour as by an increase in that of females.

Morbidity

Much illness and suffering is occasioned by diseases which do not in themselves kill, but are often chronic and disabling. About a quarter of the population suffers from chronic ill health, and more women than men are affected. Women are more likely, for example, to suffer disability from strokes, rheumatoid arthritis, diabetes and varicose veins. In fact, two-thirds of the

Table 29.   Top 20 causes of death in 1976, death rates per million population, England and Wales

Females	Rate	Males	Rate
1. Cerebrovascular disease	1861	1. Acute myocardial infarction	2678
2. Acute myocardial infarction	1886	2. Cerebrovascular disease	1200
3. Pneumonia	1263	3. Cancer of trachea, bronchus and lung	1110
4. Myocardial degeneration	992	4. Myocardial degeneration	1051
5. Cancer of breast	466	5. Pneumonia	994
6. Cancer of trachea, bronchus and lung	275	6. Bronchitis	717
7. Arteriosclerosis	262	7. Cancer of stomach	289
8. Cancer of large intestine except rectum	251	8. Cancer of prostate	192
9. Bronchitis	239	9. Cancer of large intestine except rectum	186
10. Cancer of stomach	196	10. Motor vehicle traffic accidents	171
11. Hypertensive disease	168	11. Aortic aneurysm (non-syphilitic)	152
12. Influenza	165	12. Hypertensive disease	142
13. Chronic rheumatic heart disease	148	13. Cancer of rectum	139
14. Cancer of ovary, fallopian tube and broad ligament	147	14. Arteriosclerosis	138
15. Cancer of uterus	146	15. Cancer of bladder	123
16. Accidental falls	130	16. Cancer of pancreas	119
17. Diabetes mellitus	120	17. Influenza	106
18. Cancer of rectum	116	18. Suicide	97
19. Cancer of pancreas	110	19. Chronic rheumatic heart disease	87
20. Aortic aneurysm (non-syphilitic)	83	20. Diabetes mellitus	86
All causes	11 829	All causes	12 527

From OPCS mortality statistics DH2.

disabled and handicapped population of four million in the UK are women (Office of Health Economics 1979*b*).

Because women live longer than men, they are more likely to experience the greater morbidity associated with age. At almost every age, however, women appear to exhibit greater morbidity than men and this fact, compared with their relatively favourable mortality experience, requires some explanation. Figures on morbidity are collected from general practitioners, from hospitals, from the DHSS and occasionally from community studies or surveys like the General Household Survey. All these sources of information suggest higher morbidity among women, but difficulties in interpretation exist. For example, statistics from general practice indicate that women are more likely than men to consult their doctors: on average, women visit their general practitioners 3.7 times per year, men 2.9 times (OPCS 1976). These visits cannot be regarded as a true measure of illness, however, since not every symptom leads to a consultation (see Chapter 4). There may even be under-reporting of female morbidity because of women's domestic responsibilities; or it may be culturally more acceptable for women than for men to admit 'weakness' and seek help, which would suggest an under-reporting of *male* morbidity. It remains likely, however, that the various statistics on morbidity, while not affording a complete picture, give a fairly accurate approximation of actual morbidity (for example Table 30).

The greater morbidity of women and their greater use of the health care system can be partly explained by the likelihood of their experiencing disabling conditions or pregnancy which necessitate the use of general practitioner or hospital services. It has also been suggested that they might report more illness than men and that their relatively high consultation rate is a function of 'illness behaviour' rather than of true morbidity. The evidence on this is conflicting, however, as it is in relation to the suggestion that 'being sick' is more compatible with a woman's other role responsibilities than it is with those of a man. It is known that, in general, consultation rates are affected not only by susceptibility to disease but also by age, sex, marital status and a variety of personal and cultural factors (see Chapter 4). Few studies have concentrated on women, although one of women in London showed that brevity of stay in the neighbourhood, lack of basic household amenities and difficulty

Table 30.　Morbidity in the UK population: proportion of the population by sex who, in the 14 days before interview reported

	Males (%)	Females (%)
No health problems	23	15
Done something about a health problem	42	53
Taken medicine	43	57
Seen general practitioner	8	11
Advice from other source (e.g. chemist)	12	14
Had chronic health problems	56	70
Take special care (all the time)	67	71
Taking medicine 'all the time'*	18	28

* Of the group who reported 'chronic health problems'.
  From *Social Trends* (1979).

in running the household were related to a high patient-initiated consultation rate (Beresford et al. 1977).

Some popular stereotypes exist to the effect that women are either intrinsically weaker or less stoical than men or more fussy about their physical condition. It is equally plausible, however, to suggest that women are more sensitive to and commonsensical about matters of health and sickness and that there are social pressures on men which lead them to take more risks with their health and to fail to protect themselves.

The special problems of women

Sex and gender

In all known societies, assumptions are made about what is appropriate behaviour for men and for women. These assumptions cover not only behaviour but also personal attributes. Social scientists refer to them as sexual stereotypes. Such stereotypes are extremely powerful, deriving much of their strength from the belief that behaviour is biologically based and that the most fundamental aspect of any person's identity is their sex. From this it is but a short step to deduce that the behaviours that men and women are expected to exhibit, for example competitiveness and aggression in men, passivity and nurturing in women, somehow reflect basic differences between the sexes. Evidence from other cultures, however, shows that the personality traits and behaviour stereotypes attributed to men and women in societies like Britain are not always similarly attributed elsewhere. Thus it seems that whatever the ultimate biological bases for the behaviour of males and females may be, the stereotypes result mainly from cultural values.

It may be useful at this stage to distinguish between the biological and the cultural by using the word *sex* to refer to those elements of the male and female which are indisputably biological and the term *gender* to refer to the socially assigned meanings given to sexual differences. For example, differences in sex determine who has menstrual periods and who nocturnal emissions; but it is gender assignment to regard tender loving care as a female characteristic and skill with a surgeon's knife as a male one.

Bearing these distinctions in mind, it is appropriate to turn to a discussion of women as patients and to consider how far the medical management of their illnesses incorporates socially derived sexual stereotypes.

Sexual stereotypes in medical practice

One of the commonest stereotypes of women is that they are 'by nature' more delicate and more susceptible to illness because of their reproductive function. This view was often expressed in the nineteenth century by male doctors, who argued that women's physiology made them more prone to hysteria (a term itself derived from the Greek for womb). Some writers have even suggested that doctors contributed to the debate on women's political and legal rights by suggesting that they were biologically unfit to participate in national affairs because of their propensity to 'nervous excitation'. Further, it was argued that women should not be admitted to medical school because they would faint in anatomy lectures and their reproductive organs would be damaged by study, rendering them 'repulsive and useless hybrids' (Gardner 1870).

Although such ideas would be thought silly today, others, possibly as pernicious but less obvious, are still around. For example, teaching in medical schools today rarely covers psychosexual development and recent evidence concerning the nature of female sexuality appears to have received little consideration; lectures tend to be limited to female hormonal reactions and the mechanisms of pregnancy and childbirth.

The sexual stereotypes of the woman as potentially sick — 'the product and prisoner of her reproductive system' — and emotionally unstable have militated against a rational approach to women's illnesses. Cystitis, premenstrual tension, dysmenorrhoea and menopausal symptoms have sometimes been written off as 'not real' illnesses or as 'psychogenic' in origin. The word 'psychogenic' is sometimes a polite way of saying 'imaginary'. Unfortunately, there has been too little application of accepted scientific methods to the study of disorders of allegedly psychogenic origin. Infertility, habitual abortion and premature delivery, as well as complications of pregnancy like nausea, vomiting and toxaemia, have been variously explained as 'failure to identify with the feminine role', failure to achieve maturity, the perpetuation of unacknowledged hostility towards the mother and psychosomatic defence. Many of the studies which purport to confirm such 'explanations' were carried out on small groups of patients and lacked controls. They were usually retrospective or, if prospective, did not assess personality variables before pregnancy (Oakley 1979).

It is useful to remember that many findings are reported in such a way as to create a picture of women that is congruent with social stereotypes of weakness and instability. The consequence of this can be two-fold: either symptoms will not be taken seriously or they will be dealt with in a way which reinforces and reflects women's lack of control over their own health. Some examples might be appropriate here; they relate exclusively to those aspects of women's health which are associated with being female, since it is these aspects, many researchers feel, which demonstrate most clearly the essentially oppressive use of sexual stereotypes.

Pregnancy and childbirth

Several recent studies have emphasized the lack of control over an essentially natural and healthy process which many women experience in obstetric hospitals today. The ceding of control begins with the diagnosis of pregnancy. Women are now persuaded that it is the doctor who must make the initial pronouncement (Oakley 1979). Not until this has happened will the woman trust her own judgement and feel free to communicate with her friends. She is also dependent on her doctor's validation before she can begin to make arrangements for her antenatal care and confinement. The definition of pregnancy and childbirth as something which is likely to entail pathology for mother or child is introduced during antenatal care (Comaroff 1976). It has even been suggested that procedures at this time are such that women's own views and knowledge are ignored. In one absurd but possibly revealing consultation (Oakley 1979) the following exchange took place:

Doctor (reading case notes): 'Ah, I see you've got a boy and a girl'.
Patient: 'No, two girls'.
Doctor: 'Are you sure? I thought it said ... [checks in notes] Oh no, you're quite right, two girls.'

The 'are you sure?' can only have been uttered by a doctor who had learned to treat women's own experience as irrelevant and hence not worth listening to.

Today there is widespread use of technological devices in childbirth: 98% of British births take place in hospital and, although the induction rate is now declining, it reached a peak of over 40% in the mid-1970s. While intervention techniques can be of positive benefit, the style in which they are managed is often open to criticism. Writers have commented, for example, on the expectations of medical and nursing staff that maternity patients should be passive and cooperative and have little control over the process of giving birth (Kitzinger & Davies 1978). Many women feel cheated when control rests completely with those who administer drugs to induce birth, relieve pain or facilitate delivery and their own central part in the process is devalued.

Abortion

Views about the social role of women as wives and mothers or about their sexuality may be incorporated in judgements about abortion. There are inequalities in the provision of abortion in different parts of the UK which cannot be explained solely in terms of the facilities available. In a study of a clinic which gave antenatal care and also referred patients for abortion, different responses to the pregnancies of single and married women were noted (Macintyre 1977). For the former, pregnancy was assumed to be a disaster, for the latter a 'happy event'. No attempt was made to verify these assumptions. For single women, abortion was assumed to be the most likely outcome of pregnancy, for married women, childbirth. Single women seeking abortions tended to be labelled 'bad girls', 'good girls who've made a mistake' or 'almost married'. In the case of single pregnant women, the question of marriage was seen as crucial and doctors often felt it legitimate to obtain some understanding of the patient's 'character'. They posed such questions as 'who is the father of your baby?' and 'are you still sleeping with him?', questions which they never asked of married women (Macintyre 1976).

These examples suggest that stereotypes of women's roles and allied beliefs about the causes of women's diseases may serve to divert attention from the serious consideration, as well as the research, still needed for a proper understanding of women's health problems. A change in emphasis which treats the health problems of women as worthy of the same kind of scientific attention as is afforded to the pathological problems which are not confined to women is clearly desirable.

Women as health workers

In the National Health Service, approximately 70% of the work force are women. There are doctors, nurses, orderlies, physiotherapists, occupational therapists, technicians and midwives; but the great majority of women work in the more subordinate positions and are relatively poorly paid. Women have struggled to be allowed to train as doctors and to have nursing recognized as an important and integral aspect of health care. These struggles still continue.

Women doctors

In medieval times both women and men attended medical schools, but from the late Middle Ages onwards attempts to

Table 31.   Hospital medical staff analysis by grade and sex (England)

	Males	*Females*	Female % of all posts in each grade (*1963*)	*Males*	*Females*	Female % of all posts in each grade (*1974*)
Consultant	34.2	15.5	5.8	31.0	18.4	8.4
Senior registrar	5.2	4.6	11.3	6.3	7.0	16.1
Registrar	16.5	18.7	14.4	13.4	16.0	17.3
SHO	13.0	16.2	16.0	20.0	28.0	19.9
HP Pre-reg.	7.8	13.9	22.9	6.2	11.0	26.4
SHMOs and medical assistants	7.6	10.9	18.0	3.5	8.0	32.7
Para. 94 appts.*	15.7	20.2	16.5	18.2	30.0	24.1

* Mainly those carrying out part-time hospital appointments.
Computed from DHSS (1976) *Health and Personal Social Services Statistics, 1975.*

professionalize medicine by basing it in the universities led to the exclusion of women. Women were still expected to be skilled in the treatment of minor ailments and female bonesetters and surgeons continued to practice until their work was outlawed by the professional associations of apothecaries and barber surgeons in the time of Henry VIII. The first woman to be trained at a 'modern' medical school was Elizabeth Blackwell, an American who went to the medical faculty at the University of Geneva and graduated in 1849. During the remainder of that century a tiny number of women were admitted to medical school, but it was not until 1944 that it was recommended that women should be admitted to the previously single-sex London medical schools and not until 1978 that restrictions on the admission of women students were outlawed by the Sex Discrimination Act.

Women doctors do not occupy senior posts in the same proportions as men. A comparison of the figures between 1963 and 1974, however, does show slight improvement (Table 31).

Much has been made of the problems of 'wastage' of women doctors. A survey conducted in the 1960s showed that only a fifth of women with young children and a third of women with older children were working full-time (Elliot & Jeffreys 1966). Importantly, however, employment of female doctors varied depending upon the part of the country they lived in. The majority wanted to work full-time but no career opportunities were available. Later data suggest that the situation has changed slightly. Between 1965 and 1976 the proportion of women doctors active in medicine rose from 66% to 83%, which suggests that, when opportunities exist, these will be taken (Editorial 1980). The wastage of male doctors receives much less attention, although the loss of men through migration, disability, disqualification and death is a reminder that wastage is not a problem confined to women.

The number of 'part-time' women has almost doubled since 1963 (Table 31). This solution of part-time work, which combines with family responsibilities, has traditionally been open to women doctors. Women in part-time posts, however, cannot pursue their careers as effectively as men. Moreover 'part-time' positions, when occupied by married women with children, carry some *stigma*: it is felt that such women must lack commitment. Interestingly, the same stigma does not attach to the part-time NHS consultant grade, which provides opportunities for private practice. Part-time opportunities are in fact still limited below consultant level.

At present women who seek consultant posts are most likely to find them in the low status 'shortage' specialties like geriatrics or mental subnormality. It has been argued that this fact serves to reinforce the ideas, on the one hand, that the patients dealt with by such specialties are 'second-class' and, on the other hand, that women, who are seen as 'second-class' doctors, are the ones most suitable to deal with them. The notion that women, unlike men, have a special or even an innate capacity to 'care' for patients remains a popular rationalization for the existing sexual division of labour within medicine. It has also been suggested that there is a structural requirement in medicine to maintain a pool of doctors whose skills can be used to do the work that other doctors do not wish to undertake, for example in community medicine (Elston 1977).

Women form the majority of the patients and providers of health care. As patients, they suffer rather than benefit from views which presume their physical and/or psychological weakness. Such views not only affect what will happen to them as patients, but also serve to reinforce existing social attitudes towards women. As workers, they suffer from inequality of opportunity, low status positions and poor pay, for within the health service, the distribution of power and the social relationships which exist often mirror the general relationships of inferiority and superiority between women and men in society. The position is slowly changing, however, and it remains to be seen whether increasing numbers of women doctors, coupled with increasing self-confidence on the part of women patients, will fundamentally alter the picture described in this chapter.

References

BERESFORD, S. *et al.* (1977) Why do women consult doctors. Social factors and the use of the general practitioner. *Br. J. soc. prev. Med.*, **31**, 220–6.

CAMBERWELL COUNCIL ON ALCOHOLISM (1980) *Women and Alcohol*, pp. 181–3. London: CCa.

CENTRAL STATISTICAL OFFICE (1979) *Social Trends*. London: HMSO.

COMAROFF, J. (1977) Conflicting paradigms of pregnancy: managing ambiguity in antenatal encounters. In: *Medical Encounters: the experience of Illness and Treatment*, ed. A. Davis & G. Horobin. London: Croom Helm.

BRITISH MEDICAL JOURNAL EDITORIAL (1980) Women in hospital medicine. *Br. med. J.*, **281**, 693–4.

EHRENREICH, B. & ENGLISH, D. (1974) *Complaints and Disorders: the Sexual Politics of Sickness*, Glass Mountain Pamphlet No. 2. London: Compendium.

ELLIOT, P. & JEFFREYS, M. (1966) *Women in Medicine*. London: Office of Health Economics.

ELSTON, M. (1977) Women in the medical profession: Whose problem? In: *Health and the Division of Labour*, ed. M. Stacey, M. Reid, C. Heath & R. Dingwall. London: Croon Helm.

GARDNER, A. (1870) *Conjugal Sins*. New York: J. S. Redfield.

KITZINGER, S. & DAVIES, J. (ed.) (1978) *The Place of Birth*. London: Oxford University Press.

MACINTYRE, S. (1976) 'Who wants babies?' The social construction of 'instincts'. In: *Sexual Divisions in Society. Process and Change*, ed. D. Barber & S. Allen. London: Tavistock.

MACINTYRE, S. (1977) *Single and Pregnant*. London: Croom Helm.

OPCS (1976) *General Household Survey*. London: HMSO.

OAKLEY, A. (1979) *Women Confined: Towards a Sociology of Childbirth*. Oxford: Martin Robertson.

OFFICE OF HEALTH ECONOMICS (1979a) *Mortality*. London: HMSO.

OFFICE OF HEALTH ECONOMICS (1979b) *Morbidity*. London: HMSO.

MARTIN, C. (1967) Epidemiology of cancer of the cervix II: marital and coital factors in cervical cancer. *Am. J. publ. Hlth*, **57**, 815–29.

WALDRON, I. (1976) Why do women live longer than men? *Soc. Sci. Med.*, **10**, 340–62.

13

Elderly People and Health

David Blane

Elderly people are major users of health services. Throughout the 1970s half the patients in non-psychiatric NHS hospitals were more than 65 years old and the greater use of general practitioner services by elderly people is financially recognized in the form of a higher capitation fee for those over retirement age. As a group they are therefore of major concern to all who work in the health services. This chapter examines the proportion of elderly people in the population, their social situation and the help they need.

Profile of elderly people

Changes in the age structure of the population have resulted in elderly people forming an increasingly large proportion of the total population. As Table 32 shows, during this century those over retirement age have increased from 6% to 17% of the total population. For 1978 this represented 3.1 million men aged over 65 years and 6.4 million women over 60 years. Table 32 also shows that the proportion of the population over 75 years has increased rather faster than the elderly as a whole, so that by the late 1970s some three million people, or about one in 20 of the population, were aged 75 years or more. It is expected that the proportion of very elderly people in the population will continue to rise, at least until the early twenty-first century.

Elderly people form a growing proportion of the population partly because fewer people are being born but to a greater extent because of the improvement in life expectancy at younger ages. In 1870 the birth rate was 35 per 1000 population; it then

Table 32. *The elderly as a proportion of the total population*

	1901	1931	1978	2001
Over retirement age	6.3	9.8	17.0	16.0
Over 75 years	1.3	2.2	5.2	6.1

Adapted from CSO (1980).

fell steadily until it had approximately halved by 1930; since then it has fluctuated, but the range of these fluctuations has been small compared with the earlier fall. Improved contraception and its wider availability provided the technology for this fall in birth rate, while women's desire to control their fertility and the reduction in infant mortality probably provided the motivation.

While life expectancy at birth has increased dramatically since the end of the nineteenth century, the increase in life expectancy after middle age has been more modest. Life expectancy at birth in 1901 was 50 years; in 1976 it was 73 years. However, because this improvement was due mainly to a reduction in infant and childhood deaths, further life expectancy at age 45 years has only increased from 24 years in 1901 to 30 years in 1976.

Figures such as these make some people wonder if the working population will be able to support the increasing proportion of elderly people in our society (see Chapter 11). However, not only has industrial productivity increased far faster than the population has aged, but, as has been seen, much of the proportionate increase in the elderly is a result of the reduction in the number of infants and children who used to die before they could join the workforce. Thus, there is no absolute material reason why old age should not be a time of plenty.

So far the figures used have referred to men and women combined. More women than men survive into old age, however, and this sex differential widens with increasing age. In 1976, women's life expectancy at birth was 76 years compared with men's 70 years, and whereas women made up 69% of the over-75s they constituted 80% of the over-85s. Thus the very elderly as a group are predominantly elderly women and widowhood is now the most common way for a woman to spend the last years of her life.

Table 33.   Changing life expectancy by sex

Life expectancy		Male	Female	Male–female difference	Percentage growth in difference 1901–76
At birth:	1901	48	52	4	50%
	1976	70	76	6	
At age 45:	1901	23	25	2	150%
	1976	28	33	5	

Adapted from CSO (1980).

Women's greater life expectancy is often explained in terms of their physiological differences from men, for example the menstrual cycle's hormonal fluctuations. However, the data contained in Table 33 suggest that social factors are also important. The growth in the difference between the life expectancies of men and women from 1901 to 1976 cannot be due to physiological differences between the sexes. It is more likely to reflect the effect of fewer pregnancies and smaller families on women's health, there having been no such dramatic changes in men's lives over the same period.

Social situation

Whereas the biological process of ageing involves progressive physical deterioration, 'old age' is a label which tends to be applied abruptly to individuals at a certain age, irrespective of their physical abilities or personal wishes. The age at which this usually happens is that of retirement from work and an important part of the image of 'old age' involves the consequent loss of work income. Various negative connotations may be associated with this; for example, the elderly are sometimes seen as 'a burden on society' or objects of charity. The negative stereotype attached to old age in our society is in marked contrast to the honour and high status which has been accorded the elderly in some other types of society.

All human societies need special arrangements for the physical reproduction of the next generation and for the distribution of the necessities of life. In societies such as ours the former is achieved mainly by means of the nuclear family, while the latter takes place primarily through work income. In old age, however, an individual becomes marginal to both of these social institutions which, as a result, fail to meet the needs of a large minority of the elderly.

Nuclear families can be isolating. The process starts at marriage when the partners begin to see less of their old friends; it is consolidated during the years of child-rearing when the parents' energies are directed inwards towards their children; and it becomes acute when the children leave home, especially where the children's search for work, housing, freedom or education takes them a long way from their parents. Elderly couples are often extremely dependent on one another and when one of them dies the survivor may be left living not only alone but also isolated, feeling lonely and empty.

Many elderly people live alone and the proportion doing so increases with age. In 1978 a quarter of those aged 65–9 years were living alone, as were 40% of those over 70 years. Social isolation is not the same as living alone and is rather more difficult to measure. One survey considered anyone to be socially isolated who had taken part in less than 20 ten-minute conversations during the previous week. Defined in this way, it was found that two-thirds of elderly people who lived alone were socially isolated (Tunstall 1966). Isolated elderly people tend to be over 70 years old, single or widowed, not to have children or other relatives living near by and infirm or chronically sick (Shanas et al. 1968).

While the emphasis on securing separate living accommodation for the nuclear family seems to entail a substantial number of elderly people being lonely and isolated, the distribution of resources through work income seems to ensure that many also have to live in poverty or on its borderline. This remains the case in spite of financial provisions such as retirement pension, occupational pensions, and supplementary benefits. Everyone over retirement age is automatically entitled to a statutory retirement pension. However, this often falls below the official poverty line, as defined by the income below which a person is entitled to a supplementary pension. For

Table 34.   Poverty among the elderly

	Percentage of those over 65 who are	
	In poverty	*On margin of poverty*
Men	13.8	36.8
Women	16.8	42.9

Adapted from Townsend (1979).

example, in 1980 the weekly retirement pension for a single person was £23, while the basic supplementary benefit for a single person without other sources of income was £23.70 *plus* the rent. Thus to avoid poverty the retirement pension needs to be increased by an occupational pension or by supplementary benefits.

Occupational pensions, being related to income during working life, vary enormously in value; even the smallest, however, helps to raise their recipients above the poverty line. While most managers and white-collar workers get an occupational pension, many manual workers do not. It is therefore mostly manual workers who on retirement will need supplementary benefits to save them from poverty. Unfortunately, the intricacies of the supplementary benefit system meant that over a quarter of a million old age pensioners received benefits which failed to bring them up to the official poverty line in 1965, while a further 850 000 who were eligible failed to apply, mainly through ignorance of their rights, dislike of the means-test or fear of being thought scroungers (Atkinson 1975).

A recent study found that some 50% of men over 65 years and 60% of women over 65 either live below the official poverty line or can be forced below it for varying periods of time by extra expenses such as large heating bills (Table 34). As most of their income is spent on rent, food and heating, and as rent cannot be reduced, any additional expenditure such as that for new clothes may well mean less food and/or heat. Combined with apathy, which may be an effect of social isolation, these can result in hypothermia and nutritional deficiencies. Some of the effects of poverty on elderly people are reflected by the lack of amenities in their homes (Table 35).

Table 35. *Housing conditions of the elderly*

Percentage with	Over 65 years	Over 80 years
No bath or shower	16	20
No inside toilet	20	23
No central heating	76	82

Adapted from Wroe (1973).

Elderly people do have some financial advantages, however. At the official level they are exempt from health service prescription charges and in many areas of the country they benefit from reduced transport fares; equally important, at the unofficial level many shopkeepers make special 'bargain offers' to their elderly customers. Many pensioners have mixed feelings about such concessions and point out that they would not need to be the objects of charity if the retirement pension were adequate. They argue that compulsory retirement, inadequate pensions, separate housing estates for the elderly and the need for supplementary benefits amount to systematic discrimination against the elderly, a form of discrimination for which the term 'ageism' has been coined.

State of health

The elderly population obviously has the highest morbidity and mortality rates. Morbidity rises steeply with age and multiple disabilities often combine to limit severely the physical activities of elderly people. One study in 1976 found that more than half those aged over 65 years recognized that they suffered from some disability. For 4% of the over-65s the disabilities were sufficiently severe to confine them to their beds or their homes, while a further 10% could leave their homes only when aided (Hunt 1978). To this one million over-65s can be added the many more who experienced great difficulty with tasks such as taking a bath, getting into bed or putting on shoes. Obviously these difficulties, in combination with the poor housing experienced by many of them, make accidents and falls likely.

Many of the disabilities of elderly people are caused by

illnesses such as chronic bronchitis and heart disease, which occur in younger age groups as well, but they are much more common in old age, as are foot disabilities, visual defects, hearing defects, dental problems and joint disease. Some conditions such as osteoporosis, partial paralysis following strokes, and senile dementia are almost always confined to elderly people. Chapter 4 has shown that not all disease reaches the health services or, if it does, is medically treated. Studies such as that by Williamson et al. (1964) have illustrated that this is certainly the case among elderly people. This is particularly tragic because comparatively simple treatments can do much to improve many of the handicaps suffered by the elderly. For example, chiropody can help those with foot disabilities; spectacles or medical/surgical treatment are helpful for many visual defects; hearing aids may transform the lives of the partially deaf; properly fitting dentures can assist those with few or no teeth; and physiotherapy can restore mobility and independence after strokes. Untreated, these conditions can produce a vicious circle: for example, poor vision combined with foot disabilities make a fall more likely; fear of a fall in traffic may make the person housebound; being housebound can result in social isolation and an inadequate diet; this in turn may lead to depression and nutritional deficiencies; and if a fall does occur, the osteoporosis makes a fracture and prolonged hospitalization likely. This chain can be broken by early detection and treatment of physical disabilities, allowing the elderly to continue leading an independent life.

Social support

Many of the elderly become progressively less able to lead an independent life in the community and rely increasingly on others for help. This help comes primarily from the elderly person's family, with varying degrees of assistance from the health and welfare services. A study in East London in the 1950s found that 70% of the elderly received regular help from their families, and that it was only the families' support which allowed 15% of elderly people to stay out of hospital; only 10% of elderly people received no help from their families (Willmott & Young 1957). Families usually give as much help as they are able, but as the elderly person's need for care increases the effort

Table 36. *The elderly's use of health and welfare services*

Percentage using (*per month*)	65–74 years	Over 75 years
Home helps	2.4	9.8
District nurse	1.7	5.8
Chiropodist	0.8	4.2
Meals on wheels	1.0	2.7
Social worker	0.8	1.7
Health visitor	0.7	1.6

Adapted from Wroe (1973).

can be an enormous burden which may involve loss of paid work, financial difficulties, family discord, loss of social life and holidays and an adverse effect on the health of other family members (see Chapter 11).

As the elderly person's need for help increases there comes a point beyond which the family can no longer cope on its own, although reaching this point can be delayed by the provision of official assistance from the health and welfare services such as the various discretionary allowances, domestic help and nursing care. Table 36 gives details of some of these services and the extent to which they are used. About 6% of the 65–74s and 19% of the over-75s used one or more of these services per month. Home helps and district nurses were the most frequent helpers but they, like the other services, were extremely short-staffed. There were only a quarter of the estimated number of home helps necessary to meet assessed needs, a tenth of the chiropodists, and a sixteenth of the meals-on-wheels (Brown 1974). Additional problems faced by those caring for elderly relatives include lack of knowledge of the types of official help available and great difficulty in obtaining accommodation suitable for those with disabilities. In short, many elderly people at present do not get the social and nursing support services they need. Unfortunately those who do get them may be put off by the 'rushed' service such overworked staff are forced to provide.

Attempts are usually made to admit into an institution those who can no longer manage in the community. Apart from the usually expensive private nursing home, the five main types are the local authority housing department's sheltered housing, its social service department's Part III accommodation, the NHSs geriatric hospitals and general hospitals and residential homes operated by voluntary associations which often cater to those of a particular religious denomination. Sheltered housing, Part III accommodation, voluntary organization homes and hospital geriatric beds in many areas are inadequate in number and often have long waiting lists for admission.

As a result of this general practitioners and relatives often attempt to have old people who can no longer manage at home admitted into acute hospital beds or geriatric units. Although the elderly may be happy with this arrangement, hospital staff often regard geriatric admissions for social reasons as 'blocking acute beds' (see Chapter 6). Such attitudes reflect the priorities of both the acute health services and hospital doctors in the acute specialties. The fact that elderly patients may have to spend weeks or months in an acute ward, waiting for a bed to become available in a geriatric ward or for a place in a local authority home, is a result of the shortage of facilities in these sectors. Geriatric medicine is one of the health service's worst-funded specialties; for example, in 1972, the last year for which this information is available, the cost per in-patient per week in an acute hospital was £76.56 while in the mainly geriatric chronic hospitals the comparable figure was £30.50 (DHSS 1980). Making optimum use of the already inadequate facilities for the elderly is hampered by the fact that control of these facilities is split between the health service and the local authority's housing and social service departments, although it is hoped that the recently established joint committees will minimize this problem (DHSS 1978). The priorities of the medical profession do not lead it to challenge seriously the inadequacy of the facilities for the elderly, because its emphasis on curative medicine as the most rewarding aspect of medical practice inevitably makes the primarily caring services the elderly need seem less attractive. In general, one can see the type of services available to the elderly both as a reflection of, and as reinforcing, the low esteem in which elderly people are held in our society.

References

ATKINSON, A. (1975) *The Economics of Inequality*. London: Oxford University Press.
BROWN, (1974) *On the National Health*. BBC broadcast.

CENTRAL STATISTICAL OFFICE (1980) *Social Trends.* London: HMSO.

DEPARTMENT OF HEALTH AND SOCIAL SECURITY (1978) *A Happier Old Age.* London: HMSO.

DEPARTMENT OF HEALTH AND SOCIAL SECURITY (1980) *Health and Personal Social Services Statistics for England.* London: HMSO.

HUNT, A. (1978) The elderly at home. *Social Trends,* Central Statistical Office. London: HMSO.

SHANAS, E., TOWNSEND, E., WEDDERBURN, D., FRIIS, H., MILHOJ, P. & STEHOUWER, J. (1968) *Old People in Three Industrial Societies.* New York: Atherton Press.

TOWNSEND, P. (1979) *Poverty in the United Kingdom.* Harmondsworth: Penguin.

TUNSTALL, J. (1966) *Old and Alone: a Sociological Study of Old People.* London: Routledge and Kegan Paul.

WILLIAMSON, J., STOKOE, I., GRAY, S., FISHER, M., SMITH, A. McGHEE, A. & STEPHENSON, E. (1964) Old people at home: their unreported needs. *Lancet,* **1,** 1117–20.

WILLMOTT, P. & YOUNG, M. (1957) *Family and Kinship in East London.* Harmondsworth: Penguin.

WROE, D. (1973) The elderly. *Social Trends.* London: HMSO.

Part IV
Deviance and Social Control

14

Medicine and Social Control

Sheila M. Hillier

In recent years medicine has been subject to increasing criticism from the press, social analysts, the public and doctors themselves. These criticisms share a common theme: despite medicine's acknowledged contribution to public welfare it *can* be dangerous to life, liberty and happiness. Different critics have addressed the medicalization of human affairs, professional dominance in medical organization, the deleterious consequences of medical intervention and technology and the influence of political and economic structure on medicine. Such criticism needs to be analysed carefully, since perceptions of the role of medicine in society have changed greatly over the last hundred years. The number of hospitals, of doctors and of specialists has increased and in the light of this apparent growth it is important to consider how the institution of medicine has changed as a social force, and what the effects of the change are on doctors, patients and the organization of medical care.

The institution of medicine has been described as having a function of *social control* (Zola 1975). This means that it has the power to instill order in society, to inhibit disorder or fundamental change. This power depends on the agreed values and behaviour patterns of members of society and every social group or force, such as law, religion, medicine or education, can be viewed from the standpoint of the social control which it exercises. Thus, the power that *medicine* might exercise over people's behaviour exists to some degree because of the importance society attaches both to good health and to the role of medicine in maintaining and improving it.

Medicine and the exercise of control

Legitimation of illness

All societies experience disease and have evolved ways of dealing with it. This is because disease threatens life and the capacity for living and can affect all classes, ages and sexes. At the extreme, it can also threaten the order and stability of society. Parsons (1951) suggested that modern western society generates great need for dependence, nurturing, stability and security in the individual, while at the same time emphasizing independence, competition and materialism. If the status quo is to be maintained, illness must be controlled and managed to meet these needs. It is also argued that these needs provide the foundation for the authority of medicine and doctors. People cannot simply declare themselves sick and opt out of their social responsibilities (see Chapter 5). Before people are considered legitimately ill by other members of society, they generally require some declaration, either verbal or written, from licensed medical practitioners.

Professional control

In western society the practise of medicine is under professional control (see Chapter 17). People simply cannot set themselves up as medical doctors. They must follow a recognized and rigorous period of training and their professional status, based upon their specialized knowledge and the recognition that certain procedures may be carried out *only* by them, has a very important consequence for medicine as a social force: it gives doctors considerable power over patients.

Power resides firstly in the 'competence gap' which exists between doctors and their patients. On the whole patients do not share the knowledge and skills of doctors and when they come to doctors for treatment they are in a sense surrendering themselves. The question is to what degree the 'competence gap' is a *necessary* feature of relationships between doctors and patients? To what extent does the gap serve to increase professional dominance by preventing doctors from interacting as equals with well-informed patients?

The second area of power concerns the doctors' ability to define what is or is not illness, and what is or is not a good way of dealing with it. As Hughes (1958) succinctly puts it: 'Collectively they tell society what is good and right for the individual and society at large in some aspects of life ... indeed they set the very terms in which people may think about it'. According to this argument doctors do not simply provide a service, they also control the way the service is organized and evaluated.

The influence of professional control on the organization and delivery of services may have several consequences:

1. *Inequality of access.* In countries with fee-for-service payments, or where the cost of medical care is covered by various insurance schemes, there may be a temptation to put material interests over the interests of patients. This can be seen most dramatically where patients with low incomes cannot afford medical care.

2. *Inequality of care.* Since doctors have the authority to define what illness is, they are more likely to concentrate on those areas of medicine which are more rewarding professionally, materially or intellectually. An example of the tendency to 'shed' those diseases or disabilities which are not deemed rewarding can be seen in the relatively low status of certain specialties, like geriatrics, psychiatry, community medicine and care for the mentally handicapped or disabled. Work in these specialties does not accord with the still-predominant professional view of medicine as 'curative'. The hope of many doctors who work in these specialties is that they will eventually be allotted proportionately equal shares of resources. At a time when resources are scarce, however, it may be that medical involvement in these areas will lessen, more work being done by relatives and self-help groups, or by other lower-status health professions like nursing (Davis 1979).

3. *Narrowness of practice.* Professional control also ensures the dominance of certain styles of practice. Newer health occupations are subordinated to medicine, since doctors have the final control over health work. The potential for change which such occupations might bring to health care is therefore blocked. Such built-in conservatism extends into research and development, since it is likely that only those advances which fit the current medical model, or can be used by clinicians without radically altering their styles of work, will be incorporated into medicine. Thus, in the way medical practice is organized at the

moment, there may be a tendency to favour high-technology solutions which require professional expertise rather than low-technology ones which do not require specialized knowledge. There may also be an inclination on the part of the profession to emphasize or prefer those specialties which allow a style of practise where the superordinate position of doctor over patient is assured.

4. *Individualizing health care problems.* The very nature of the doctor–patient relationship is that it is a meeting of two individuals, but concentration on the problems of individual patients may make the work of health professionals less effective, particularly since the major causes of illness today are closely related to social and environmental factors. Drinking and smoking too much, poor working conditions, lack of exercise, faulty diet and, though less well demonstrated, social stress all seem to be of major causal importance. Strategies for tackling health problems, although acceptable to many patients, often result in exhortations to individuals to change their personal behaviour while ignoring the social pressures which may have driven them to behave in ways which are detrimental to their health. Such efforts also ignore the social processes by which *particular* individuals are identified as having a problem or are selected for certain types of treatment.

The individualistic perspective of medicine may, however, be of benefit to the patient. It is precisely the individual bond which exists between doctor and patient which can itself be of therapeutic benefit (Balint 1957). In addition 'social engineering' approaches to health problems may not be effective or may have social consequences which individuals might not enjoy or which, some would argue, constitute an attack on individual freedom (Szasz 1970). For example *Toxocara canis*, which is parasitic in dogs, constitutes a serious health hazard to children. Should failure to exercise adequate control over dogs result in banning an individual from dog ownership?

Medicalization

The question of medicalization is closely allied to the question of professional power and dominance, but the two are not synonymous. 'Medicalization' describes a process of expansion by which more and more areas of life become subject to medical definition and jurisdiction. Problems are defined in medical terms and medical treatments are seen as appropriate solutions. Although some writers have seen this as a wholly negative process (Illich 1975; Zola 1975), others have described the substitution of medical treatments for legal punishments as a social advance (Halmos 1966). They argue that it is better to attempt therapy with alcoholics, sex offenders, drug addicts and overdose patients than impose sentences of imprisonment. As an American dean, talking about an outbreak of witchcraft practices on campus, was reported as saying: 'a couple of hundred years ago we would have burned them; twenty-five years ago I would have expelled them. Now we simply send them all to psychiatrists' (Kosa 1970).

Debate has raged over the past 20 years as to whether or not 'mental illness' exists in the way that physical illness does or whether its treatment represents a clear example of a 'take-over' of behavioural problems and 'problems of living' by psychiatrists (Szasz 1961). One argument suggests that the label of mental illness is a convenient means to deal with socially disruptive problems. Most psychiatrists, on the other hand, contend that mental illness has a clear organic aetiology or is due to specific psychological disturbances and that it is not only legitimate but right and proper for psychiatrists to use every means at their disposal, such as drugs and electroconvulsive therapy, to alleviate the suffering involved.

Medicalization may be viewed in two ways. The first is from the viewpoint of 'supply'. Particularly in health care systems where financial incentives exist for doctors, it is postulated that medicine may extend into more and more areas of life. Doctors may actively promote their own involvement in current problems or seek to find ones for which only they can provide solutions. Evidence for such medical imperialism is hard to come by. The actual expansion that can be observed seems to suggest that the profession is offering 'more of the same' (at increasing cost) rather than diversifying into an ever-increasing number of fields. It also seems that the professions involvement with the control of deviant behaviour is not universally welcomed by its members (McKinley 1979).

The second approach to medicalization is to see the extension as a function of 'demand'. There may always be a willing market of consumers for whatever the medical profession has to offer in the way of surgical procedures and new drugs. Evidence of a large scale 'addiction to medical care', however, is hard to obtain and assess. Without better historical data the hypothesis that the concern of people with their health today is greater than it was in the past cannot be tested. All societies employ means of combatting disease and the historical evidence suggests that an interest in maintaining health and coping with illness is to be found in all cultures and ages. The change in perception may lie in the degree to which organized medical care and the activities of doctors are seen as the appropriate solutions to problems of disease or to the achievement of a better life.

Iatrogenesis

The term 'iatrogenesis' was used by Illich (1975) to describe social and physical pathology that originates in medicine and in the activities of doctors. He describes three kinds of iatrogenesis: clinical, social and structural.

1. *Clinical*. The pain, sickness and death that result from medical intervention he calls 'medical iatrogenesis'. Scepticism about the value of medical intervention is not new, but evidence of Illich's claim that medicine can be used in a way that is, at worst, clinically damaging and, at best, clinically irrelevant continues to accumulate. For example it was estimated that in 1974 the American public spent about four billion dollars on 2.1 million operations judged to be 'unnecessary', causing 12 000 unnecessary deaths and 503 000 non-fatal hospitalizations (McKinlay 1979).

2. *Social iatrogenesis*. Illich argues that this occurs 'when health policies enforce an industrial organisation which itself generates dependency and ill-health'. It is the result of manipulation by the medical care bureaucracy, which aims at creating a dependency upon itself and an artificial need for what it produces. An alternative explanation supports the view of an 'addiction to medical care', but sees this as a symptom of a more fundamental process rather than as manipulation.

3. *Structural iatrogenesis*. According to Illich, this occurs 'when medically sponsored behaviour or delusions restrict the vital autonomy of people by undermining their competence in growing up, caring for each other and ageing'. When he is discussing this level of functioning Illich slightly alters his analysis in that he no longer sees the damage as due solely to the

organization of medical care as such. Rather, he suggests that the nature of industrial society produces large-scale organizations like medicine and inhibits the growth of small-scale, low-technology, self-reliant groups.

The strategies which Illich sees as necessary to combat these forms of iatrogenesis involve the deprofessionalization of medicine by removing its license to exclusive practice, by demystifying its knowledge base, by maximizing individual responsibility for health and by halting economic growth and opting for middle-range technology.

The control of medicine

One counter-argument to those which contend that medicine exercises control over the lives of individuals is that medicine itself is controlled by societal forces. In this view, medicine is seen to be acting at the behest of society as a whole (Parsons 1951), or powerful segments within it (Navarro 1976; McKinlay 1979), rather than in its own interests.

Control of medicine may occur in two ways: firstly by its association with the forces of economic *production*, and secondly by its involvement in the promotion of the dominant ideas and values of society. According to these viewpoints medicine and the medical profession are, willingly or unwillingly, the agents of the capitalist class (Navarro 1976) or state bureaucracies (Illich 1976). This control of medicine can, it is argued, operate at two levels: at the *macro* level of society as a whole and at the *micro* level of the doctor–patient relationship.

Illich's argument is that *industrialization* has caused medicine to take the form of an all-enveloping bureaucracy, whose objective at the macro level is further growth and consumption of its products and at the micro level the mystification of knowledge and the elevation of the expert in the individual encounters.

Navarro (1976) suggests, however, that *financial capital* has invaded, transformed and dominated the medical/health care arena. At the level of production, this means that health care becomes a commodity to be bought and sold and the societal effects are such that decisions about health care will be made on the basis of their profitability. Activities where the result is unprofitable, or where it cannot be measured in terms of profitability, will never be given priority. For example, adequate legislation to protect the health of workers will not be passed or enforced if it affects an organization's level of profit. The effect at the individual level is to change the doctor–patient relationship from one of service and assistance to one where financial concerns are paramount. Further, Marxist writers maintain that capitalism influences the way in which medical definitions of disease are formulated. Tuberculosis, for example, was regarded as a 'constitutional weakness' rather than something which resulted from poverty and poor living conditions. Today, diseases like heart disease and lung cancer are seen as problems of *individual* life-style. In a micro setting, it is suggested that the values of dominance and hierarchy typical of capitalism are reflected in the relative levels of power which exist between doctor and patient. The articulation of these values in a setting which is characterized by intimacy and vulnerability renders them even more potent.

Navarro (1976) has drawn attention to the role of the modern state in the control of medicine. While some have seen the role of the state as merely to extend or support the interests of capital at the command of capitalists (Marx & Engels 1848) Navarro suggests that the state in capitalist countries acts on behalf of capitalism, but is not dominated by it. It has also been argued that there are features of state organization which occur in non-capitalist societies and capitalist societies alike, and the consequences for the control of medicine might have some similarities (Hillier & Jewell 1981).

Both capitalist and socialist governments have adopted a variety of strategies in relation to medicine. Often these strategies represent an attempt to resolve conflicts which exist between various objectives. For example, all sorts of governments might wish to have a healthy work force. On the other hand, they might not wish to endanger profitability or production levels or to bear the costs of setting up a comprehensive health care system. Governments might regard preventive health measures as an important objective, but not wish to surrender the revenue obtained from tobacco and alcohol or contribute to unemployment by reducing the consumption of motor cars. Governments may wish to 'buy off' political discontent by setting up a system of health care financing which makes health care more readily available, such as Medicare in the USA, the welfare state in the UK or the cooperative medical service in China. On the other hand, they might discover that attempts to cut back on such systems at a time of financial crisis generate social disruption. Governments might be eager to use the service of medicine in the control of deviants (USA, UK), political dissidents (USSR) or population growth (China), but might also wish to devote medical resources to other priorities (Hillier & Jewell 1981).

The role of the state in relation to medicine is a complex one. It does appear, however, that the state itself, over and above classes or dominant-interest groups within it, potentially possesses great power over the form and direction of medical care and should not be ignored in the analysis of the structural control of medicine.

For the present, criticisms apart, both doctors and patients seem able to accommodate themselves to the sort of social control exerted by doctors and on doctors. This is because the role of healer is an important and valued one. Yet the form of medical practise has consequences beyond the immediate healing role and it is for this reason that the claims made by medicine need to be examined and evaluated, and its activities reviewed. 'Medicine is too important to be left to the doctors'.

References

BALINT, M. (1957) *The Doctor, his Patient and his Illness*. London: Tavistock.

DAVIS, A. (1979) An unequivocal change of policy: prevention, health and medical sociology. *Soc. Sci. Med.*, **13A**, 129–37.

HALMOS, P. (1966) *The Faith of the Counsellors*. London: Constable.

HILLIER, S. & JEWELL, J. (1981) *Health Care in China*. London: Routledge and Kegan Paul.

ILLICH, I. (1975) *Medical Nemesis*. London: Calder and Boyars.

KOSA, J. (1970) Entrepreneurship and charisma in the medical profession. *Soc. Sci. Med.*, **4**, 25–40.

McKINLAY, J. (1979) Epidemiological and political determinants of social policies regarding the public health. *Soc. Sci. Med.*, **13A**, 541–58.

MARX, K. & ENGELS, F. (1848) *The Communist Manifesto* in Mendel, A. P. (1961) *Essential Works of Marxism*. New York: Bantam.

NAVARRO, V. (1976) Social class, political power and the State and their implications in medicine. *Soc. Sci. Med.*, **10**, 437–57.

PARSONS, T. (1951) *The Social System*. London: Routledge and Kegan Paul.

SZASZ, T. (1961) *The Myth of Mental Illness*. New York: Hocber/Harper.

ZOLA, I. (1975) In the name of health and illness. *Soc. Sci. Med.*, **9**, 83–7.

15

Deviance, Labelling and Stigma

Graham Scambler

Illness and deviance

'Deviance' refers to forms of behaviour which are considered *unacceptable* in a particular culture. Deviant *behaviour* is behaviour which, once it has become public knowledge, is routinely subject to correction, treatment or punishment by the appropriate agencies of social control (see Chapter 14). There are three main ways in which illness has been linked with deviance.

Illness 'as' deviance

Some have contended that illness itself is a type of deviance because 'being ill' is an unwelcome state. As Freidson (1970) points out: 'human, and therefore social, evaluation of what is normal, proper, or desirable is as inherent in the notion of illness as it is in notions of morality'. Illness, the argument runs, represents a deviation from culturally established norms or standards of 'good health'; thus, anyone acknowledged to be ill properly desires and is the recipient of 'treatment' to correct his state of body or mind.

Illness as affording special opportunities for deviant behaviour

Another line of argument is that illness makes possible new and distinctive kinds of deviant behaviour. Parsons (1951) maintains, for example, that, although a person who becomes (acutely) ill in developed countries like the USA is accorded certain 'rights', he or she at the same time acquires certain 'obligations', namely to be motivated to get well and to seek help from, and cooperate with, medical experts (see Chapter 5). These rights and obligations are culturally entrenched. If, on becoming ill, a person neglects his new obligations, he is likely to be chastised as a 'malingerer' or at least regarded as irresponsible or misinformed. His behaviour deviates from what is both expected and *required* of him.

Deviant or stigmatizing illnesses

A third argument is that a number of specific illnesses are regarded as deviant by lay populations: these are usually referred to as *stigmatizing conditions*. Thus victims of blindness, venereal disease, epilepsy, mental subnormality and numerous other diseases and symptoms of disease have been ridiculed, shunned or isolated by non-sufferers.

Sociologists have paid most attention to this last way of relating illness to deviance. It is here also that research promises to have the most immediate impact on medical practice by alerting doctors to the effects of such conditions, and of their own diagnostic labels, on patients' lives. This chapter therefore concentrates on stigma and its implications both for patients with stigmatizing conditions and for those who treat them.

The social meaning of stigma

The Greeks used the word 'stigma' to refer to bodily signs, usually inflicted cuts or burns, designed to expose the unfortunate bearer as a slave or criminal, as a social outcast (Goffman 1963). A person scarred in these ways was ritualistically excluded from normal social relations. Usage has changed: today stigma is applied more generally to any condition, attribute or trait which marks an individual as culturally unacceptable or 'inferior'.

Definitions of unacceptability vary: both lay constructions of stigma and professional or medical beliefs and assumptions concerning conditions that are stigmatizing have differed from epoch to epoch and across cultures.

Lay constructions of stigma

It is well established that conditions that are formally the same can have different meanings to laymen in different cultures. Anthropological studies have found, for example, that in societies such as those of Tibet, Burma and Turkey, the crippled and maimed are rejected as 'inferior' human beings, while in other societies, like Korea and Afghanistan, people with the same conditions are believed to possess special, valued abilities on the basis of which they are granted 'superior' social status. Similarly, while epilepsy is stigmatizing in most modern industrialized societies (see below), in some segments of the Brazilian population and in some African tribes people with epileptic seizures qualify for the most prestigious of all social roles, that of the witchdoctor or medium.

Medical interpretations of stigmatizing conditions

While the existence of considerable variation in lay constructions of stigma may be expected, it is perhaps less obvious that such variation extends to professional interpretations. Professional theory and practice do not develop in a cultural vacuum, however; they reflect lay conceptions of stigma, professional training, professional work organization and the demands of clienteles. Scott (1969) found that professional interpretations of blindness were not consensual, even in developed countries like the USA, Britain and Sweden, but subject to subtle variations which affected the treatment of blind people. In the USA a basic goal of medical care for blind patients was 'adjustment' to blindness; a blind person was seen as adjusted only when he had, with counselling help, accepted and learned to live with his disability. In Britain much more emphasis was placed by doctors on 'buoying up the spirits' of the blind: thus, centres for the treatment of the recently blinded were built around good-naturedness and 'cheerfulness in the face of adversity'. One blind man described his experience in such a centre in the following words: 'every member of the staff is making a tremendous effort to show us what a jolly place this is. Their actions, if not their words, say clearly, "Are we downhearted? No! Let's show the world how cheerful we are." We are being humoured and encouraged to put on a brave face' (Minton 1974). In Sweden, blindness was viewed rather as a 'technical' handicap to be compensated for by the mastery of new techniques and aids.

The force of a label

In most developed countries licensed medical practitioners have been granted the authority, in the last resort, to determine whether someone is really ill or not (and even, arguably, what illness really is) (see Chapter 14). They also have responsibility, of course, for applying the relevant diagnostic labels. The application of certain diagnostic labels, however, can have dire consequences for the patient. When a person is labelled 'blind' or 'epileptic', for example, he thereby acquires a new, deviant social status or identity; whereas previously, perhaps, he had possessed weak or bad eyesight or been subject to the odd dizzy spell or attack, he is now 'officially' blind or epileptic. It is in acknowledgement of the significance of the application of labels that some sociologists have chosen to re-define 'deviance' as follows: 'deviance is not a property inherent in certain forms of behaviour; it is a property conferred upon these forms by the audiences which directly or indirectly witness them' (Erikson 1964). Or, as Becker (1963) puts it: 'the deviant is one to whom the label has been successfully applied; deviant behaviour is behaviour that people so label'.

One possible unhappy consequence of being labelled in this way is that an individual's stigma can come to dominate the perceptions that others have of him and how they treat him. In the language of sociology, his deviant status becomes a *master-status*: whatever else he might be (e.g. father, car mechanic and so on), he is regarded primarily as a deviant. Even his past may be unsafe. A homosexual who is 'discovered', for example, may find that aspects of his past life are subject to retrospective interpretation by others: 'what he is now, "after all", he was all along'. Especially pertinent to this line of reasoning, also, are the concepts of 'cultural stereotyping' and 'secondary deviation'.

Cultural stereotyping

Those afflicted with a stigmatizing condition may be expected to conform to a popular stereotype. A study in the USA, for example, found that blind people are often attributed distinctive personality characteristics that differentiate them from sighted people: 'helplessness', 'dependency', 'melancholy', 'docility', 'gravity of inner thought' and 'aestheticism' (Scott 1969). However far-fetched or misleading such stereotyping may be, the blind person cannot ignore how others expect him to behave; to do so might well be to ignore key factors in his interaction with them. The authors goes on to claim that blind people adapt to cultural stereotyping in five major ways: by simply concurring; by 'cutting themselves off' to protect their self-conceptions; by deliberately adopting a facade of compliance for expediency's sake; by making people pay something for a 'performance' (i.e. begging); or by actively resisting. They may also have to adapt to stereotypes of blindness held by health professionals.

Secondary deviation

One distinction which has gained currency among those exploring links between *crime* and deviance is that between 'primary' and 'secondary' deviation (Lemert 1967). Study of the former focusses on how deviant behaviour (e.g. stealing) originates and study of the latter on how people are symbolically assigned to deviant statuses (e.g. 'thief' or 'criminal') and the effective consequences of such assignment for subsequent deviation on their part. The importance of studying secondary deviation has been increasingly acknowledged: it is now accepted, for example, that disapproving cultural and professional *reactions* to deviant behaviour can often foster rather than inhibit a continuing commitment to deviance. Similarly, some have claimed that a negative, stereotypical reaction to a stigmatizing illness or handicap can confirm individuals in their deviant status, can constrain them to see themselves as others see them and to behave accordingly. For example, a blind person who is expected to be and is treated as 'dependent' and 'helpless' may actually become so; he may find it less exacting to concur with and ultimately adopt his prescribed role than to resist it. Those in institutional or custodial care for long periods are particularly vulnerable in this respect (see Chapter 6).

Perhaps the area in which 'labelling theory' has had the most controversial impact in relation to medicine has been that of mental illness. In the mid-1960s an American sociologist,

Scheff (1966), claimed that labelling is the single most important cause of mental illness. He argued that there exists a residue of odd, eccentric and unusual behaviour for which the culture provides no explicit labels: such forms of behaviour constitute 'residual rule-breaking' or 'residual deviance'. Most psychiatric symptoms can be categorized as instances of residual deviance. There also exists a cultural stereotype of mental illness. When, for some reason or other, residual deviance becomes a 'public issue', the cultural stereotype of insanity becomes the guiding imagery for action. In time, a psychiatric diagnosis is made and procedures for hospitalization are put into effect. Problems of secondary deviation follow with a degree of inevitability.

Scheff's theory was attacked by Gove, another sociologist, on a number of counts (Gove 1970). Gove agreed that there is a cultural stereotype of mental illness, but not that people are treated as mentally ill because they inadvertently behave in a way that 'activates' this stereotype. If anything, he argued, 'the gross exaggeration of the degree and type of disorder in the stereotype fosters the denial of mental illness, since the disturbed person's behaviour does not usually correspond to the stereotype'. Scheff is also wrong, according to Gove, in suggesting that, once publicly noticed, the person will be routinely processed as mentally ill and put into an institution; public officials, he argued, 'screen out' a large proportion of those who come before them. Finally, Gove claimed that Scheff overstated the degree to which secondary deviance is associated with hospitalization for mental illness. Although the dispute between Scheff and others continues, it seems reasonable to conclude that he fell foul of the temptation to explain too much in terms of a single, if important, insight.

Living with a stigmatizing condition

Stigmatizing conditions vary in terms of their visibility and obtrusiveness and of the extent to which they are recognized. Not surprisingly, there is an equivalent degree of variation in their effects on individuals' lives. People who, for example, are 'discredited', to use Goffman's terminology, will often find they have to cope with situations made awkward or tense by their stigma: their problem will be one of managing impressions, the impressions others have of them (Goffman 1963). The physically handicapped, Davis asserts, typically pass through three 'stages' when meeting strangers: the first is one of 'fictional acceptance' — they find they are ascribed some sort of stereotypical identity and accepted on that basis; the second stage is one of 'breaking through' this fictional acceptance — they induce others to regard them as normal; and the third stage is one of 'consolidation' — they have to sustain the definition of themselves as normal (Davis 1964).

On the other hand, people who are 'discreditable', rather than discredited, will usually find they have to take care to manage information about themselves: to 'pass as normal' they will have to censor what others know about them. Thus, one homosexual writes: 'the strain of deceiving my family and friends often became intolerable. It was necessary for me to watch every word I spoke and every gesture that I made in case I gave myself away. When jokes were made about queers I had to laugh with the rest, and when the talk was about women I had to invent conquests of my own. I hated myself at such moments but there seemed nothing else I could do. My whole life became a lie' (Wildeblood 1955).

The case of epilepsy

Scambler and Hopkins (1975) found that people's responses when diagnosed as epileptic tended to follow a pattern. Firstly, the diagnostic label was unwelcome: patients were even less pleased with the diagnosis than they had been with the uncertainty that preceded it. Their concern derived mainly, if not completely, from their perception of epilepsy as a stigmatizing condition. Secondly, even whilst acknowledging the doctor's expertise in such matters, people often, 'irrationally' from the medical viewpoint, tried to negotiate a change of diagnosis. In this context, some would use the uncertainty that frequently attends a diagnosis of epilepsy. If the epilepsy was idiopathic, for example, a common reaction was: 'If he doesn't even know what causes my attacks, how can he possibly know they're epileptic?' Medical uncertainty, then, proved an incentive to disavow the label.

Once applied, such labels are difficult to shake off. Nevertheless, the stigma of people with epilepsy is dormant between seizures; for much of their time, therefore, they are discreditable rather than discredited, their chief problem in these circumstances being the management of information about themselves. Scambler and Hopkins found that, fearing discrimination, people tended to conceal their epilepsy whenever possible. Witnessed seizures were often 'explained away' (e.g. as 'faints') and 'stories' constructed to account for the fact that people could not drive, because of the law, or drink, because of their anticonvulsant therapy. Over half those suffering from epileptic seizures at the time of marriage hid the fact from their partners. Of those in full-time employment at the time of interview, just over a quarter had disclosed their epilepsy to their employers, and only one in 20 had done so before starting work (Scambler & Hopkins 1980). Interestingly, Tony Greig succeeded in hiding his epilepsy from players and public for the whole of his career in test cricket.

The authors made a distinction between 'felt' and 'enacted' stigma. The former refers to the fear of being discriminated against solely on the grounds of an imputed cultural unacceptability or inferiority, and the latter to actual discrimination of this kind. Paradoxically, the data suggested that felt stigma was more disruptive of the lives of those interviewed than enacted stigma. Thus, for example, although more than four out of every five in the sample made an unprovoked reference to epilepsy as a stigmatizing condition in the course of the interviews, only a third could cite even one incident when they suspected that they had been victims of enacted stigma or even of casual ridicule. Such is the fear of enacted stigma that people with epilepsy do their utmost to maintain secrecy about their symptoms and the diagnostic label: they disclose only when it strikes them as prudent or necessary. Non-disclosure, in turn, reduces the likelihood of enacted stigma. In sum, felt stigma leads to a policy of non-disclosure which has the effect of reducing the incidence of enacted stigma. Felt stigma itself, however, can be, and was among many of those studied, a potent source of stress and unease.

Doctors are unexceptional in that they resort to stereotypes to help them make sense of social reality. Inevitably, they develop, and are to some extent guided in their actions by, images of 'typical' patients. Medical expertise does not, however, confer *moral* expertise, and the images doctors have of patients will tend to reflect widely-held cultural values. One implication of this is that doctors may unwittingly perpetuate and give respectability to such values. For example, even after the myth of the 'epileptic personality' was finally debunked in the early 1960s some doctors proved reluctant to relinquish the concept: the confidential medical report British neurologists complete in order to assist the Disablement Resettlement Officers of the Department of Employment (Form DPIE) still specifically requests information about 'any personality problems' in epileptic clients. It is clearly important that doctors and other health workers both monitor their own values and remain sensitive to the likely consequences of 'labelling' patients with stigmatizing conditions.

References

BECKER, H. (1963) *Outsiders: Studies in the Sociology of Deviance.* Illinois: Free Press of Glencoe.

DAVIS, F. (1964) Deviance disavowal: the management of strained interaction by the visibly handicapped. *The Other Side*, ed. H. Becker. Illinois: Free Press of Glencoe.

ERIKSON, K. (1964) Notes on the sociology of deviance. *The Other Side*, ed. H. Becker. Illinois: Free Press of Glencoe.

FREIDSON, E. (1970) *Profession of Medicine.* New York: Dodd, Mead & Co.

GOFFMAN, E. (1963) *Stigma: Notes on the Management of Spoiled Identity.* New York: Prentice-Hall.

GOVE, W. (1970) Societal reaction as an explanation of mental illness: an evaluation. *Am. soc. Rev.*, **35**, 873–84.

LEMERT, E. (1967) *Human Deviance, Social Problems and Social Control.* New York: Prentice-Hall.

MINTON, H. (1974) *Blind Man's Buff.* London: Paul Elek.

PARSONS, T. (1951) *The Social System.* London: Routledge and Kegan Paul.

SCAMBLER, C. & HOPKINS, A. (1975) Some notes on how patients perceive their epilepsy. Paper given at British Sociological Association, Medical Sociology Group Conference.

SCAMBLER, G. & HOPKINS, A. (1980) Social class, epileptic activity, and disadvantage at work. *Epidem. commun. Hlth*, **34**, 129–33.

SCHEFF, T. (1966) *Being Mentally Ill.* Chicago, Ill.: Aldine.

SCOTT, R. (1969) *The Making of Blind Men.* New York: Russell Sage Foundation.

WILDEBLOOD, P. (1955) *Against the Law.* London: Weidenfeld and Nicolson.

Part V
Organization of Health Services

16

The National Health Service: Origins and Issues

Ellie Scrivens

All countries provide some kind of health and social care for their citizens, although there are marked differences in the way health services are financed and organized. Health care organization ranges from predominantly private-financed to predominantly public-financed systems of care, with all kinds of combinations and pluralistic alternatives in between. For example, in the USA private health insurance and 'fee-for-service' medicine is the principal means of finance, although a system of care exists which is government-financed through general taxation. In Britain, state provision of services financed through general taxation and 'free' at the time of delivery is the predominant mode, although a small but growing private insurance system exists in an emerging private sector. Canada, on the other hand, relies on a system of compulsory public insurance while most European countries have some combination of tax-supported and insurance-based health care organization.

The type of health care organization and financing found in a particular country depends on both the history and the prevailing political philosophy in that country. In view of these historical and philosophical foundations, all health care systems have their particular advantages and disadvantages when problems such as access, supply, resource allocation and priorities of services are considered. The British National Health Service (NHS) is a world-renowned model of 'socialized medicine' with the avowed goal of accessible cost-effective and reasonably equitable provision. It rests on a system of universal access to general practice and of referral through the general practitioner to specialist and hospital care. As a model system, it is important to examine both its origins and the major issues or stresses facing the NHS today and in the decades ahead.

Nineteenth and early twentieth century origins

During the nineteenth and early twentieth centuries, five major and overlapping systems of health care developed which paved the way for the welfare state and the NHS. The particular system or systems used by the population depended largely on the wealth and social standing of the prospective patients.

Fee-for-consultation practice

In the nineteenth century, for those who could afford it, a fee-for-consultation system of professionals with recognized qualifications replaced the care given earlier by apothecaries, physicians and surgeons. By the mid-nineteenth century, these doctors had become known as general practitioners.

Although many of these early general practitioners operated exclusively on revenue obtained from fees, organized bodies such as friendly societies and trades unions contracted with some of them to treat skilled workers enrolled in mutual benefit insurance schemes. An increasing proportion of general practitioners participated in these insurance schemes as the century wore on, since they were unable to secure enough private fees to maintain their practices.

The wealthy and those who were protected by the friendly societies and trades unions received care in the general practitioner's office or at home depending on the nature and seriousness of the medical condition. Hospitals were not used by the more fortunate until the very end of the nineteenth century, when developments in antiseptic surgery and anaesthesia made institutional care more safe, effective and appealing. Until that time, hospitals mainly served the indigent poor.

As more and more general practitioners were forced into contracts with the friendly societies and trades unions, they became increasingly resentful of what they saw as intrusions into their clinical autonomy from the insurance managers. Not unnaturally, the funding bodies sought to reduce the costs of their medical care by questioning prescribed habits and seeking to cut per capita fees.

The Poor Law

For many, sickness insurance, let alone private care, was undoubtedly a luxury they could not afford. In 1834 a New Poor Law was enacted to relieve the country of pauperism by providing a formal system for dealing with the indigent and unemployed based on unequivocable social values concerning the fallibility of human nature and the means for its improvement. In the legislation the common people were seen to be inherently hedonistic and lazy; public authority had the duty to inculcate the virtues of independence and work. Those people who through no fault of their own could not work were entitled to some care and compassion, but those who were fit and capable of work were encouraged to be financially independent through earning their own living. This goal could be achieved by using such deterrents to idleness as depriving individuals of their freedom by making them enter punitive institutions known as workhouses as a condition for obtaining any relief. Though pauperism due to unemployment was often explained in terms of idleness (the 'undeserving poor'), that of childhood, old age, mental illness and sickness (the 'deserving poor') was felt not to be due to individual failure by the New Poor Law and so treated with greater compassion. 'When an able bodied man who is unable to work on account of sickness applies for outdoor relief and it is ascertained that he cannot get along without assistance and that he endeavoured to make provision for himself it is recommended that outdoor relief should be granted if the man can be properly treated and attended to at home. If he cannot be properly nursed at home it would be better for all concerned to take the man into the hospital and to relieve his wife and family outside in kind' (Craighill 1898).

Shortly after the New Poor Law was passed, however, Chadwick (1842) published impressive reports which recognized, at least implicitly, the relationship between poverty, unsanitary conditions and ill health. It was then gradually accepted that the ill were generally blameless for their condition, but little was done by the poor law until the 1860s, except to allow outdoor relief in the case of illness, even to the able-bodied. A series of epidemics, particularly the widespread cholera outbreak of 1866 which took nearly 20 000 lives, stimulated public agitation about the conditions of the workhouse sick. During a remarkable period of reform in the late 1860s, a new policy was adopted whereby the sick poor were treated in workhouse infirmaries, established to provide care for their sick inmates. Unions were also encouraged to form 'sick asylum districts' large enough to support hospitals to which the sick could be removed from workhouses. A national hospital service was born.

Sick persons without income or savings were forced to resort to the poor law as their only source of help for both daily necessities and treatment. Not all cases required treatment within the workhouse infirmaries or new hospitals, so general practitioners were paid by the poor law to diagnose and prescribe treatment. Doctors prescribed medicines such as cod-liver oil and quinine and also stimulants such as alcohol. Like the friendly societies, poor law officials found prescriptions of food and alcohol hard to justify within their rigid framework of relief, and they tried to control the actions of doctors by preventing them from giving out 'inappropriate' help; this was again bitterly resented by the doctors concerned. Much of the antagonism which the profession has toward any outside control has its origin in these early confrontations with friendly society and poor law administrators. 'The medical officer alone is the judge of what medicines his patients should have. He is responsible for the treatment and any outside interference with that treatment from non-professional quarters is as unjustifiable as it is mischievous' (*Br. med. J.* 1883).

General hospitals

As mentioned previously, hospitals in the nineteenth century and earlier were considered primarily for the sick and poor. Voluntary hospitals were financed by subscription and the patients paid no fees for their treatment. Chartered institutions founded in the middle ages, such as St Thomas's and St Bartholomew's in London, were supported by endowments and fees paid by the patients. They were the main centres of training for doctors and admission to their facilities was generally made available by the grace and favour of members of the governing bodies of these institutions (Abel-Smith 1964).

Hospital consultants and practitioners with private paying patients tended to regard poor law and sickness society doctors as 'second class'. They were largely successful in excluding such doctors from hospital practice and in resisting the efforts to ease tension and maintain the unity of the profession which had been achieved formally in 1858 with the establishment of the General Medical Council (see Chapter 17). Hospital consultants agreed to accept referrals only from general practitioners; but it is clear that many found ways around this and by the first decade of the twentieth century the referral system had nearly broken down. The British Medical Association (BMA) whose provincial predecessor began in 1832, was established largely to represent general practitioners as opposed to the profession's elite which came to be included in the Royal Colleges. The BMA had no desire to modify practice conditions and was hostile to ideas of national health insurance for workers, a scheme for providing free medical care. Doctors who had been forced to accept poor law or friendly society work, on the other hand, welcomed the proposals, which they saw as a way of guaranteeing their incomes in a competitive world and of reducing the threat to their independence.

Public Health Services

Outbreaks of infectious diseases such as smallpox were considered a matter for public health officials. The Public Health Act of 1848 established a Public Health Service with local boards of health who could appoint medical officers of health with duties (including house-to-house searches) for infectious disease, vaccination, school and factory inspection, sanitary improvements and the ascertainment of the causes of unexpected death. The local boards of health had the powers to organize drainage, street cleaning, water and street paving. Later in the century, public health isolation hospitals were also established to treat the victims of infectious disease.

Many of the provisions of the 1848 Public Health Act were not compulsory and it was not until 1872 that the appointment of medical officers of health became obligatory and preventive medicine became a recognized state service. Compulsory notification of infectious disease, and medical certification of causes of death, also began in the 1870s, practices which continue to this day.

By the turn of the century, the mortality rate for adults had fallen dramatically, but the rate of infant deaths was much the same as in 1800. Public health improvements did not appear to lower mortality in the early months of life. Health visitors, who had been established in the 1860s, began to be appointed generally at the turn of the century to advise on infant care and, in particular, to combat gastroenteritis. Once again, the provision of health visiting was voluntary and it was not until 1918 that it became a statutory service. This and other developments in maternal and child welfare, such as free and cheap meals for poor mothers, infant welfare centres and maternity benefits, led to a rapid decline in the infant death-rate during the early twentieth century.

State-administered health insurance

By the turn of the century other events were contributing to a growing crisis in the provision of health care. The Boer War (1894) had great public support, but large numbers of volunteers for the army had to be turned down because of their poor physical condition. Hitherto the extent of physical debility in the general population had not been fully recognized and there was concern that in the event of another war there would not be sufficient people fit enough to fight. Furthermore there was considerable fear of internal social unrest. There had been uprisings in Germany and the 1905 revolution in Russia. The trades union movement in Britain was growing very rapidly and the Labour party, the new political party of the unions, was gaining a foothold in parliament. Socialist ideas spreading from the continent were causing many of the basic nineteenth century values to be questioned and the Liberals, especially, were actively seeking ways of halting the spread of socialist ideas. Balfour, a prominent MP, made his famous statement in 1895: 'Social Legislation is not merely to be distinguished from Socialist Legislation, but is its most direct opposite and its most effective antidote' (Navarro 1978). Germany had been following the same ideas and, under Bismark, had introduced a state-run social insurance scheme. Lloyd George visited Germany in 1909 and returned home convinced that this was also the best policy for Britain, specifically to defuse increasing social unrest (Bruce 1972).

In 1911 a system of state-administered health insurance was introduced. This legislation was designed solely to assist lower-paid manual workers and excluded manual workers earning more than a certain sum, all dependants, agricultural workers and nearly all non-manual white-collar workers. Insured persons were entitled to both cash and treatment, which included general practitioner care and drugs. It excluded, however, the cost of hospital and specialist treatment. The scheme was administered through insurance committees which were specially set up for this purpose. This had the unfortunate effect of splitting the administration of the state-provided health services. In 1919 a Ministry of Health was created to absorb all the existing health services. Even so, many organizational and administrative problems lingered on (Bruce 1972).

For the general practitioners this new system had many advantages. They received better remuneration; they could treat as many patients as they chose privately or through the insurance schemes; and although the friendly societies continued to deal with the day-to-day administration of the insurance, their control over the doctors' professional work was effectively removed. Access to hospital care and the division between primary and hospital care, however, were still unsatisfactory. General practitioners claimed that they were overworked and it was well known that hospital facilities were unequally distributed throughout the country and that voluntary hospitals were finding it difficult to raise sufficient funds. Hospital nurses shaking collection boxes on street corners were a common sight in the 1930s. By the end of the 1930s a comprehensive health service, free at the point of delivery, existed only for manual workers who could satisfy the means test requirements of the voluntary hospitals and those who could afford to pay for care.

Advent of the welfare state

During the 1920s and 1930s the right of every individual to have optimal health care began to emerge as a political goal (Ministry of Health 1920). The Local Government Act of 1929 merged the poor law and local authority services and provided the basis for planning, utilization and development of the hospital service as a whole. Pressure groups inside and outside government were calling for a health service funded from general taxation.

World War II, and the effective ending of the great depression of the 1930s, brought with it not only a need for changes in social policies but the opportunity for their wholesale implementation. At the beginning of World War II it was assumed that there would be a need for medical services for armed forces personnel and an Emergency Medical Service (EMS) was set up at the outbreak of war in 1939. With heavy bombing in Britain, especially in London, civilian casualties were more numerous than expected and the EMS was extended to include injured civilians. It became the first free service and took over two-thirds of all the local authority and voluntary hospitals.

The creation of the EMS had significant effects on both doctors and health care facilities. Many specialists were brought out of their well-endowed hospitals in London to man provincial hospitals. They discovered how many of these hospitals had little in the way of facilities and modern equipment. The extra demands of caring for the war-injured created more beds and operating theatre facilities and increased the availability of specialist treatment. More importantly, the possibility of a state-run service was realized and the obvious benefits of centralizing planning to provide health care became clear to some influential doctors. Furthermore the population shared a common experience of the deprivations of war, regardless of social class, and this also led to increased public acceptance of a universal service.

The philosophy of a universal health service was generally accepted as policy when Beveridge included it as part of this blueprint for post-war reconstruction in 1942 (Beveridge 1942). He proposed a 'welfare state' to combat the five 'giants' on the road to post-war reconstruction: want, disease, ignorance, squalor and idleness. To combat disease and disability from accidents Beveridge proposed a free system of health care to be available to anyone on British soil in need of medical treatment. It was not clear, however, how the system would be organized and paid for.

After a number of proposals from parliamentary leaders and the BMA, the system which was finally adopted was introduced into parliament by the Labour Party's forceful Minister of

Health, Aneuran Bevan, and reached the statute books in 1946 without the formal agreement of the BMA; many of the details were left to be worked out in the 18 months that remained before the appointed day in 1948 when the service would begin. Bevan, in order to achieve the tacit support he needed from doctors, made special concessions to hospital consultants, allowing them to work part-time in NHS hospitals for high salaries while keeping their private practices and, more importantly, allowing consultants to have pay-beds in NHS hospitals with no limit on the fees they could charge. Bevan is claimed to have said that he 'choked their [the consultants] mouths with gold' (Tudor Hart 1973).

The NHS: 1948–74

The organizational structure of the NHS in 1948 was popularly described as tripartite, because responsibility for it was carried by three statutory authorities: the regional hospital boards, the local authorities and the local executive councils. The earlier ideal of a fully integrated service run at local level by a single body was not realized and this failure was held over the following two decades to be the cause of many of the problems that the NHS faced. To some extent this was true: the divided administrative structure created problems for patient care and resource allocation. The roots of discontent with the NHS, however, were more fundamental than this.

Beveridge (1942) had envisaged 'a comprehensive health and rehabilitation service for the prevention and cure of disease and restoration of capacity to work, available to all members of the community at the time of need'. He believed that an improvement in health services would lead directly and immediately to an improvement in the health of the population and that, once an optimum level had been attained, it would be maintained except in the unavoidable case of accidents. His optimism was expressed in the estimated costs of the NHS, which he put at £170 million in 1945 and the same in 1965, 'it being assumed that there will actually be some development of the service and as a consequence of this development, a reduction in the number of cases requiring it'. In short, his view of health and health care was limited and, with hindsight, naive.

By 1953 the cost of the NHS had reached such a level that the

Minister of Health set up a committee chaired by Mr Guilleband to inquire into this wholly unexpected drain on resources (Ministry of Health 1956). The medical profession had been vehement in its criticisms of what they felt was the abuse of the service by the general public to which they attributed the unexpected costs. In the event, the committee reported that many of the problems stemmed from post-war inflation rather than from either administrative deficiencies or public abuse. By 1960 it was clear that the demand for health services was not a simple matter and that it would not automatically diminish with improvements in such measures of health as mortality rates.

During the 1960s the belief that it was primarily the administrative structure of the NHS which was at fault took a firm hold. Many reports were published and discussed on the administrative and management structure of hospitals and their nature and size. Some recommendations of the reports were implemented and the management structure of the health service changed slowly. The most dramatic change was that resulting in a new senior nursing staff structure (Ministry of Health and Scottish Home and Health Department 1966).

At the same time changes in attitudes were occurring concerning the basic nature of the health care system. As more people with chronic diasbilities survived, it was realized that parts of the health service must be concerned with caring rather than curing. Hospitals, the major consumer of resources allocated to the health service, were seen as contributing little in this respect, especially in the field of mental health. In 1946 the NHS Act had a clause about 'after care' to describe care outside institutions, but it was not until 1961 that a shift of emphasis to community care occurred. Enoch Powell, then Minister of Health, announced a policy of 'running down' mental hospitals to halve the number of mental patients in institutional care. Sociological work on the harmful effects of institutional care, most notably Erving Goffman's *Asylums* (see Chapter 6), gave humanitarian backing to the desire to reduce public expenditure, it being assumed that care outside hospitals would require less resources. Sociological investigations in other areas of institutional care, such as that for elderly people and children, led to the same conclusions.

These new ideas, concern about the increasing costs of the NHS and the realization that even when hospitals could contribute to health they were out-of-date, poorly equipped and unequally distributed throughout the country, led to some major rethinking about the NHS. In 1962 two documents were published which led to radical change in health and welfare policy. *A Hospital Plan for England and Wales* called for new hospitals in the light of projected population growth and recommended district general hospitals based on populations of about 125 000 (Ministry of Health 1962). *Health and Welfare* (1963) officially recognized for the first time the unsuitability of hospitals for providing long-term or non-acute care. The report concentrated on the elderly, the mentally and physically handicapped, the mentally ill and women in childbirth. The general conclusion was reached that hospital and community services needed to be coordinated under one administrative structure.

NHS reorganization: 1974–82

In 1968 the Labour Minister for Health, Kenneth Robinson, made proposals for reorganizing the NHS. He suggested 40–50 area authorities which would take over the functions of the existing administrative bodies and merge hospital and community services under each area authority. The BMA and other bodies raised many objections and when Richard Crossman succeeded Robinson as Secretary of State a second proposal was made taking into account many of these criticisms. This time the suggestion was that there should be 90 health authorities and a number of regional health councils for some supra-authority purposes. In 1970 the Conservative Party came to power and it was their policies for the health service which were enacted in 1973 although they were implemented in 1974 when the Labour Party was once more in office. Fig. 6 shows the resulting administrative structure.

The tripartite structure was substantially modified with the reorganization. Local authorities were no longer responsible for domiciliary health support services. These and the hospitals became the responsibility of area health authorities (AHAs) which were accountable to regional health authorities (RHAs). The day-to-day management of the health services was to be carried out by district management teams. An area could have from one to five districts depending on the size and density of

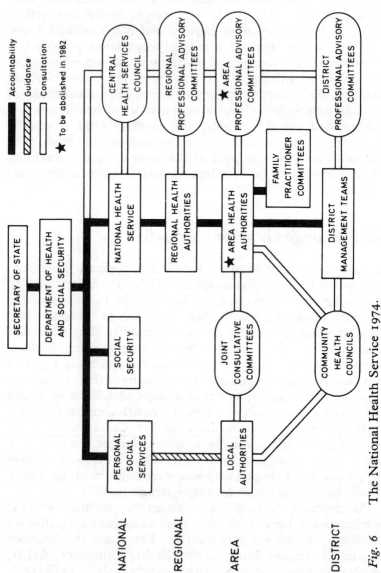

Accountability

Guidance

Consultation

★ To be abolished in 1982

SECRETARY OF STATE

DEPARTMENT OF HEALTH AND SOCIAL SECURITY

SOCIAL SECURITY

PERSONAL SOCIAL SERVICES

NATIONAL HEALTH SERVICE

CENTRAL HEALTH SERVICES COUNCIL

REGIONAL HEALTH AUTHORITIES

REGIONAL PROFESSIONAL ADVISORY COMMITTEES

★ AREA HEALTH AUTHORITIES

★ AREA PROFESSIONAL ADVISORY COMMITTEES

FAMILY PRACTITIONER COMMITTEES

JOINT CONSULTATIVE COMMITTEES

LOCAL AUTHORITIES

COMMUNITY HEALTH COUNCILS

DISTRICT MANAGEMENT TEAMS

DISTRICT PROFESSIONAL ADVISORY COMMITTEES

NATIONAL

REGIONAL

AREA

DISTRICT

Fig. 6   The National Health Service 1974.

the population. General practitioners, supported by the BMA, objected to the Labour Party proposals to unify their administrative bodies with the rest of the health service, and the Conservatives conceded to their demands for a separate body, the family practitioner committee, with direct access to the minister.

Another feature of the 1974 NHS reorganization was the complaints procedure. In each district there is a community health council (CHC) which has the right to monitor the running of the district, to receive information from district management, to send one member to AHA meetings and to be consulted on development and planning. Its members are not paid, but it has a paid secretary and occasionally a research officer. The CHCs have no managerial responsibility or power and have been alleged to be ineffective authorities. The other important function which the CHC performs is to act as a 'shop window' for NHS developments for the general public. The CHC can also advise and help a member of the public to make an official complaint (for further information see Levitt 1977).

The belief that the NHS would be fine if its administration were improved is still strongly held. In December 1979 the Conservative Secretary of State, Patrick Jenkin, put forward proposals for yet another reorganization to be completed by 1983. As shown in Fig. 6, the area health authorities and professional advisory committees are to be abolished. The area authorities will be replaced by district health authorities (DHAs) which will strongly resemble the AHAs but will be smaller geographical units, coterminous with local government areas which are larger than the present districts. Instead of 90 AHAs there will be approximately 160 DHAs.

Major issues facing the NHS

Issues concerning the economy have provoked considerable debate on where the NHS is going in the decades ahead. Indeed, the same issues are being debated in other countries without a government-run health service, since decisions on rationing of health services have become necessary in most economies. Six major issues are listed in Table 37 along with the direction of current policy on the NHS in England (Stevens 1981).

Table 37. Six issues for debate on the NHS

Issue	Current Policy on the NHS
Central versus local control	Efforts to encourage local decision-making within a national structure and with national priority-setting
Consumer representation	Limited inclusion of organized interests, particularly consumer, in decisions about NHS
Private versus public services	Restoration or transfer of health services to the private sector
Equality in resource allocation	Distributions of health resources across geographical areas according to need
Rationalization	Planning services with constricted budgets and with stated priorities
Administration	Development of management skills necessary to administer the NHS more efficiently

Adapted from Stevens (1980).

Central versus local control

The main idea behind the current NHS reorganization is to make the health service more responsive to local needs by bringing decision-making nearer to patients and communities. In functional terms, the issue is at what level and with whom should control over decisions reside? The unit for day-to-day management of the health services in the 1974 reorganization was the district and the 1982 reorganization will strengthen the district even further.

Consumer representation

The effectiveness of consumer participation in the NHS remains an open question, although the informal relationships between NHS managers and the public, including CHCs, has been important, for example in agreeing on the closure of a hospital. The functions of management and the functions of public representation remain separate, however, and the issue is still who is the 'public' and what kind of involvement is desirable?

Private versus public services

The present Conservative commitment to bring more resources into health care through the development of the private sector is tied to ideological questions about the appropriate role of government and the effectiveness of a market system. Private health insurance coverage has reportedly increased and a growing number of firms and union agreements offer such insurance as part of the pay package, although a distinct private sector which ignores public services altogether does not yet exist in Great Britain. Moreover, private health insurance does not cover substantial populations of old people, the mentally ill and the mentally retarded, who have been recognized as priority groups by both political parties. It seems unlikely that private care can ever replace the NHS without an adequate solution to the problem of how the market system contradicts the egalitarian principles which have characterized British health services since 1948.

Equality in resources allocation

In 1979 the Royal Commission on the National Health Service reported that two of the main objectives of the NHS were equality of entitlement and equality of access to health services. Since 1948 services were to be comprehensive and available to everyone. Regardless of these objectives, the distribution of health resources from region to region and within regions remained unequal between 1948 and 1974, since regions requested and received different amounts of money in a traditional pattern which developed over time; that is, a greater proportion of resources went to the urban areas with prestigious teaching hospitals. Various proposals were put forward in the 1970s for financial allocations for services based on the population served, differences in morbidity as indications of need, the state of hospital buildings and other capital, and the special needs of teaching and research. Equality of funding per capita does not necessarily mean equality of entitlement or access, however, since two health authorities may be given equivalent amounts of money per capita while they differ greatly in efficiency, effectiveness, existing facilities and the amount of ill health and demand for care.

In 1976 a Resource Allocation Working Party (RAWP) recommended a formula for allocating money to geographical areas aimed at equal opportunity for access to health care for people at equal risk (DHSS 1976). This was based on age and sex, standardized mortality ratios (considered a proxy for need in terms of sickness or morbidity rates) and differential bed use for age, sex and selected medical conditions. This attempt at equalization, however, did not include any measure of the actual quality of care already being provided by the areas. RAWP represents a limitation, set by government, on the amount of spending available for health services in a given region. Once the amount is negotiated, planning becomes a process of rationalization.

Rationalization

The allocation of limited resources requires planning decisions on how to mobilize the most effective services and how to close the services of least use and value. The closure of hospitals and medical schools, or any substantial changes in the use of NHS facilities, requires consultation and debate which is often heated and lengthy. The questions arise as to who should participate in the debate and when the decision can be made. Limited resources also means that rational and systematic priorities are required if funds are to be used most effectively. In 1976 a consultative document, 'Priorities for Health and Personal Social Services in England', established priorities for the so-called Cinderella services: those mainly used by the elderly, mentally ill, handicapped and children. To give priority to these implies reduced or zero growth in acute hospital services and the debate continues on how far and how fast the services can and will change to meet the priority targets.

Administration

The combined effects of reorganization and the concurrent issues of resource allocation, rationalization, consumer participation and local decision-making have made improvement in managerial techniques imperative. District management teams and the development of a planning system have implied substantial changes in the role of NHS managers. From the outside there has been much criticism of 'too much bureaucracy' and 'one tier too many'. The Royal Commission (1979) cited the decline in the quality of hospital administration and suggested that the status of institutional managers be upgraded. Consensus management, the hallmark of multidisciplinary management teams, requires skill in handling extensive pressure group conflicts; educating and being educated by physicians, other professionals, the public and politicians to understand the competing needs of different groups within the NHS; managing great quantities of information, some of which is highly technical; and creating changes with lessening resources. Questions continue on to how many administrators are needed, what kind of training is best for them and what kind of responsibilities they should have.

The debate on the NHS and the issues of organization and financing are occurring in the context of dramatic and fundamental changes in the roles and nature of health care itself. Since the nineteenth century, it has been recognized that much ill health is attributable to poverty and poor environmental conditions. Strategies to break the links between low social class or poverty and health will undoubtedly involve social changes more fundamental than health services reorganization. There are also calls for more individual responsibility for health and health care, in terms of individual health behaviour such as exercise or elimination of cigarette smoking and self-care and self-help groups which do not depend on health professionals. Some have argued simply that prevention must be cheaper than cure, while others argue that health professionals do not have the ability to eradicate ill health (see Chapter 14).

The relationship between health and health care is without doubt more complex than previously recognized. The NHS and all other health care systems are slowly beginning to develop new methods of promoting health and caring for the sick. Health services as they exist at present can no longer realistically be expected to be the only means of eliminating ill health. Better understanding of the causes of health will alter public and professional expectations of what traditional health services can achieve. The changing values and attitudes will also inevitably change British health services and the administrative structure of the NHS will contribute to the accommodation of these changes through review and reorganization.

References

ABEL-SMITH, B. (1964) *The Hospitals 1800–1948*. London: Heineman Educational.

BEVERIDGE, W. (1942) *Social Insurance and Allied Services*, Cmd 6502. London: HMSO.

BRITISH MEDICAL JOURNAL (1883) Annual Meeting of the Poor Law Medical Officers' Association, 2nd August 1883. (Dr Norman Kerr speaking.) *Br. med. J.*, **ii**, 337.

BRUCE, M. (1972) *The Coming of the Welfare State*. London: Batsford.

CHADWICK, E. (1842) *Report on the Sanitary Conditions of the Labouring Population*. England: Local Reports.

CRAIGHILL, G. (1899) The administration of outdoor relief. *Proceedings of the Central and District Poor Law Conferences held from April 1898 to February 1889*. London: R. S. King & Son.

DEPARTMENT OF HEALTH AND SOCIAL SECURITY (1970) *Priorities for Health and Personal Social Services in England*. A consultative document. London: HMSO.

DEPARTMENT OF HEALTH AND SOCIAL SECURITY (1976) *Sharing Resources for Health in England*. London: HMSO.

Health and Welfare: The Development of Community Care (1973) Cmnd London: HMSO.

LEVITT, R. (1977) *The Reorganized National Health Service*, 2nd ed. London: Croom Helm.

MINISTRY OF HEALTH (1920) *Consultative Document of Medical and Allied Services, Interim Report of the Future Provision of Medical and Allied Services*. London: HMSO.

MINISTRY OF HEALTH (1956) *Report of the Committee of Enquiry into the Cost of the National Health Service*, Cmnd 9662. London: HMSO.

MINISTRY OF HEALTH AND SCOTTISH HOME AND HEALTH DEPARTMENT (1966) *Report of the Committee on Senior Nursing Staff Structure*. London: HMSO.

MINISTRY OF HEALTH (1962) *A Hospital Plan for England and Wales*. (Cmnd 1604). London: HMSO.

NAVARRO, V. (1978) *Class struggle. The State and Medicine*. p 9. Martin Robertson London.

ROYAL COMMISSION ON THE NATIONAL HEALTH SERVICE (1979) Cmnd 7615. London: HMSO.

STEVENS, R. A. (1980) *National Health Service in England in 1980*. Policy Discussion Paper Philadelphia: Leonard Davis Institute of Health Economics, University of Penn.

TUDOR HART, J. (1973) Bevan and the doctors. *Lancet*, **2**, 1196.

17

Health Professions

David Blane

Over three-quarters of a million people work for the National Health Service, making it one of the largest employers in Britain (Table 38). These workers can be divided into two groups on the basis of whether their skills are specific to health services. The slightly smaller group, which includes electricians, engineers, managers, caterers, launderers, clerks, receptionists, domestics, porters, secretaries and telephonists, can, at least in theory, find equivalent work in other industries. The second group contains nurses, physiotherapists, doctors, speech therapists, pharmacists, radiographers, dentists, occupational therapists and opticians; they are mostly restricted to working in health services because of the specific nature of their training and skills.

Professions

Occupations in this second group are often called professions, implying that they have certain distinguishing features in common which differentiate them from other occupations. The most obvious of these would seem to be direct involvement in the treatment of patients; but, given that many occupations outside the health services are also called professions (for example, lawyers, accountants, teachers, clergymen, social workers, surveyors and civil engineers), this would be too limited. In very simple terms, all professions can be seen as providing personal services to clients. Although the health service involves more professions than any other industry, it by no means has a monopoly of them.

Table 38.   *Number of staff working in the different grades in the NHS (England 1977)*

Hospitals	
Medical	28 397
Dental	895
Nurses and midwives	305 669
Professional and technical	52 798
Works and maintenance	23 059
Administrative and clerical	88 819
Ambulance	17 383
Ancillary	171 465
Community	
General medical practitioners	22 327
General dental practitioners	11 784
Opthalmic and dispensing opticians	6096
Social workers*	24 400
Home helps*	44 900
Day nursery staff*	6400
Residential care staff*	59 600
Nursers and midwives	34 144

*Involved in community care but employed by the local authorities.
From DHSS (1978).

Most sociological attempts to identify which characteristics professions have in common agree on several 'core' features (Freidson 1970). Firstly, professions possess a body of specialized knowledge. This knowledge is often taught in a university and is passed on to trainee professionals in institutions controlled by members of the profession. A profession also produces and assesses new knowledge in its field. In short, a profession's knowledge involves theory and research as well as practical skills.

Secondly, professions have usually succeeded in obtaining a monopoly of practice in their field of work. This is partly the result of a state register, access to which can only be obtained by passing the relevant examinations. It is also in part the result of employers employing only those whose names are on the register.

Thirdly, only fellow members of the profession are considered competent to assess a professional's work, on the grounds that only they have access to the profession's specialized knowledge. Thus, where professionals are employed in an institution, such as a hospital, the person with direct responsibility for their work is usually a member of the same profession.

Finally, professions have a public ideology of service to their clients; once they have accepted a client, or in hospital a patient, they claim to put the client's interests before their own. They claim, therefore, not to exploit their clients' ignorance or their dependence on the profession's specialized knowledge. In addition, one could add that, in practice, professionals tend to be drawn from the middle class and to share middle class values. When the profession is predominantly male it is also comparatively well paid with secure and interesting work (see Chapter 12).

Thus, professions occupy the highly skilled sector of the labour force involved in the provision of personal services. They have a state- and employer-backed monopoly of their field of work and their relative freedom from control by clients, fellow workers and employers gives them considerable autonomy in organizing, defining the nature of and developing their work.

An example of how the medical profession has established its monopoly and autonomy is the establishment in 1858 of the General Medical Council in England. The Council's functions have derived from its original objective: 'it is expedient that persons requiring medical aid should be enabled to distinguish qualified from unqualified practitioners' (General Medical Council 1980). In setting out to protect the public and to uphold the reputation of the profession, the Council keeps and publishes a register of duly qualified doctors, gives advice on medical ethics, ensures that the educational standard of registrants, and thus the profession, is maintained and takes disciplinary action against registrants who have become unfit to practise. The Council operates as a professional monopoly, therefore, by restricting group membership, eliminating external competition, and controlling education.

Professions are not unique in having these powers, nor would-be-professions in wanting them. A profession's monopoly and autonomy may confer greater powers on its members than a trade union's closed shop and control of the job, but the difference is only one of degree. What really distinguishes the profession from the skilled or unskilled occupation is the respectable, established nature of the former's powers, which are based in state legislation and accepted as legitimate by employers, those who control the media and the main political parties.

Differences between professions

It is evident that not all professions involved in hospital work have equal power or prestige. The Registrar General's classification of occupations reflects these inequalities by allocating some ('the leading') professions to social class I, and others ('the lesser') professions to social class II. Of the professions in the health services, doctors, dentists, opticians and pharmacists are allocated to social class I; while nurses, physiotherapists, speech therapists, radiographers, dieticians, and occupational therapists fall into social class II.

All these professions have a state register of those qualified in their field of work and the NHS is an employer which mostly respects these monopolies. The 'leading professions' differ from the 'lesser professions', however, on other criteria. Entry to the leading professions involves a lengthy university training, while training for the lesser professions usually takes place 'on the job'. The former have their own specialized knowledge, to which they continually contribute by research, while the latter's knowledge is largely derived from that of the leading professions. While all these professions have a certain autonomy in deciding how their work should best be done and in judgeing how well it has been done, the lesser professions gain access to their clients only through the instructions of the leading professions and, indeed, were established on the assumption that they were there to assist the leading professions. In addition, at any given level in the profession's hierarchy, members of leading professions are better paid than those of the lesser professions and while the former are predominantly men, the latter are mainly women (see Chapter 12).

Inequalities exist even among the leading professions. In the health services, for example, the medical profession is more powerful than its dental, pharmaceutical and ophthalmic equivalents. One difference which distinguishes the medical from the other three professions is the level of certainty and effectiveness of their knowledge (Jamous & Peloille 1970). Medical knowledge about the conditions which are brought to the professional is still very uncertain and it is impossible therefore to predict precisely the outcome of many treatments. In contrast dental, pharmaceutical and ophthalmic knowledge, although more restricted, is much more complete and hence the outcome of their procedures is more predictable. The relative indeterminancy of medical knowledge and the low predictability in the outcome of medical practices make it more difficult for those outside to judge the competence of individual members of the medical profession. This both supports the profession's claim to autonomy, that is to self-appraisal rather than appraisal by others, and creates the need for the sort of public standing which will ensure public trust.

A second difference between the medical profession and the other three leading professions in the health services concerns their numbers and political weight. This is itself a reflection of the fact that the medical profession has gained authority over most of the human body, while the dental profession's authority is limited to teeth and gums, the optician's to the eyes, and the pharmacist's to the preparation and dispensing of drugs.

There is little use in attempting to decide whether a particular occupation is a profession on the basis of criteria such as monopoly, autonomy and the abstractness and indeterminancy of its knowledge. It is more useful to consider occupations in the knowledge-based personal service sector as being spaced along a continuum of 'profession-ness', with established professions such as medicine and law approaching the ideal-type profession at one extreme of the continuum. Conceived of in this way, it is possible to define the process of professionalization by which an occupation attempts to improve its pay and prestige by acquiring characteristics of the ideal-type profession such as lengthier training, qualifying examinations, a state register and freedom from supervision by all but colleagues. The experience of occupations currently in the process of becoming 'professions', however, suggests that the advantages of being a profession do not automatically follow when the characteristics of the ideal-type profession are acquired. For example, the pay and self-autonomy differentials between doctors and nurses remain despite longer nursing training, the growth of university courses in nursing and more nurses developing nursing knowledge through research. In other words, it seems that the relationship between the advantages and the characteristics of professions still needs to be explained. Some professions, for example medical laboratory scientific officers, hospital pharmacists and speech therapists, have dealt with this by turning to trade unions to improve their pay and conditions, leaving their professional organizations to deal with educational matters such as qualification standards and registration requirements.

Effects of professions

For an employer a professional qualification, like any licensing system, has the advantage of a guaranteed-minimum standardized product and this remains the case whether the employer is the client of a self-employed professional or the personnel department of an institution. Such a guarantee becomes especially important where the employer, through lack of relevant knowledge, is unable to assess the prospective employee's competence. For example, few non-medical people feel competent to assess a doctor's ability, but the fact that the doctor's name appears on the General Medical Council's register guarantees that the doctor possesses a certain minimum medical knowledge.

In medicine, the state licensing system has been partly responsible for the great reduction in untrained and nominally trained medical practitioners. One effect of this is that professions succeed in transferring control over certain areas of life from lay into specialist hands. Clients are consequently relatively powerless in the face of the professionals they have chosen (see Chapter 14 on the social control exercized by the medical profession). This powerlessness increases as the profession's knowledge becomes more specialized and beyond the reach of most laymen. It is this which makes the profession's ethics and claims to be trustworthy so important.

Transferring a particular aspect of social life into the hands of a profession has other results. The profession becomes responsible for the production of new knowledge in its field. This allows it to emphasize the value of knowledge which coincides with the practical and material interests of its members and to attach comparatively little importance to aspects of knowledge which do not. It also tends to make the profession resistant to outside contributions to its knowledge. To use the example of medicine, the doctor's job has traditionally been the treatment of sick people and that is how most members of the medical profession make their living. The medical profession, therefore, emphasizes the 'sciences' of diagnosis and treatment, while by comparison ignoring those of aetiology and prevention. For example, some medical schools do not have a department of epidemiology and the Health Education Council's budget, largely for preventive work, amounts to considerably less than 0.1% of health service expenditure. The resistance to contributions to knowledge from outside the profession is well illustrated by the medical profession's prolonged dismissal of Pasteur's practical demonstration of the germ theory of infective disease and may be being repeated again in the case of acupuncture. Such resistance tends to be greatest when the knowledge comes from a rival group of medical practitioners, such as osteopaths (Wardwell 1979).

A profession also controls the training of its new members. The fact that professional training is much sought after and is by definition lengthy gives the senior members of a profession the power to mould the new generation of that profession, usually in their own image (Becker et al. 1961). The process starts with the selection of the appropriate few from the many applicants; continues in the form of personal contact between the trainees and senior members of the profession; and tails off but never ends in the form of promotion and the distribution of honours and rewards, a process which always contains an element of subjective judgement and patronage. Evidence to the Royal Commission on Medical Education (1968) illustrated this process in the case of entrance to medical school. Successful applicants in the 1960s — and there is no evidence to suggest much change since — tended to have medically qualified fathers, come from families in social classes I and II and to have been to fee-paying schools. Later in the medical career structure the same process partly explains the under-representation of women doctors and foreign doctors in the consultant grade

(Bewley & Bewley 1975). This prolonged process of selection and socialization makes professions stable and conservative institutions and gives the senior members great power over the rest of the profession.

Along with control over the training process goes some control over the numbers being trained. This allows a profession to go some way towards matching the supply of professionals to the effective demand for the profession's services, a process which has obvious implications for its members' incomes. For example, the debate over the right number of medical school places, and thus how many new doctors should be produced, centres on the number of medical jobs which are likely to be available in the future rather than the population's future need for medical care (Royal Commission on the National Health Service 1979).

The fact that professions have such strong internal organization means that members' main loyalty tends to be given to their profession, making professions somewhat inward-looking. Where members of different professions work together at a common task, this can have the effect of rigid demarcation lines being drawn to separate the tasks of one profession from those of another. Examples from the health services include: doctors not personally giving their patients simple physiotherapy even when their patients' need for it is not being met because of a shortage of physiotherapists; experienced ward sisters telling inexperienced junior doctors how to treat a patient's disease, and the junior doctor then ordering this treatment which the ward sister carried out; dentists involved in facial repair for car accident victims have to go through the whole medical training before they can move from teeth and gums to jaw bones and skin. More serious perhaps is the way in which some attempts to create health teams drawing on those involved in the provision of primary medical care tend to founder, with the members drawing back into their traditional professional roles and inter-professional relationships (Beales 1978). Another example concerns the way in which the integration of health and personal social services, upon which the community care programme for the chronic sick depends, is sometimes undermined by the failure of doctors employed by the NHS and social workers employed by local authorities to reconcile different approaches and to agree a common policy.

In summary, the most powerful professions have acquired

great control over their work, and over the supply side of the market for their work and hence their incomes. While ·they probably share the desire for those powers with workers in most other occupations, they are distinguished by their success in achieving them and by the respectable nature of this success. Many other occupations which similarly provide expert services to personal clients have tried to gain these powers by emulating the obvious characteristics of the leading professions, such as longer more theoretical training, university courses, research, and a state register. In practice, however, the acquisition of such professional characteristics no longer produces powers equivalent to those of the leading professions.

Perhaps the best way to understand professionalization is as an occupational strategy which succeeded in the conditions existing in nineteenth-century Britain, that is rapid industrialization producing a growing middle class able to afford a wider range of personal services, but which is less likely to succeed today when an elaborate and usually highly stratified division of labour between occupations prevents radical innovation (Johnson 1972). If this is the case, then contemporary attempts at professionalization, such as those taking place in the health service, are likely to result in the disadvantages of a professionalized work-force without the advantage of the stability which comes with better pay and conditions of work.

References

BEALES, J. (1978) *Sick Health Centres and How to Make Them Better.* Tunbridge Wells: Pitman Medical.

BECKER, H., GREER, B., HUGHES, E. & STRAUSS, A. (1961) *Boys in White: a Study of Student Culture in Medical School.* Chicago: University of Chicago Press.

BEWLEY, B. & BEWLEY, T. (1975) Hospital doctors, career structure and the misuse of medical womanpower. *Lancet,* 2, 270–72.

DEPARTMENT OF HEALTH AND SOCIAL SECURITY (1978) *Health and Personal Social Services Statistics for England.* London: HMSO.

FREIDSON, E. (1970) *Profession of Medicine.* New York: Dodds, Mead.

GENERAL MEDICAL COUNCIL (1980) *Constitution and Functions.* London: GMC.

JAMOUS, H. & PELOILLE, B. (1970) Changes in the French university hospital system. In: *Professions and Professionalization,* ed. J. Jackson. Cambridge: Cambridge University Press.

JOHNSON, T. (1972) *Professions and Power.* London: Macmillan.

ROYAL COMMISSION ON MEDICAL EDUCATION (1968) London: HMSO.
ROYAL COMMISSION ON THE NATIONAL HEALTH SERVICE (1979) London: HMSO.
WARDWELL, W. (1979) Limited and marginal practitioners. In: *Handbook of Medical Sociology*, ed. H. Freeman, S. Levine & L. Reeder. New York: Prentice-Hall.

Measurement and Evaluation in Health

18

Measurement of Health

Donald L. Patrick

The next two chapters on the measurement and evaluation of health and health care, cover topics and issues which do not only concern social scientists and health care workers. Physical scientists, administrators and laymen measure and evaluate in the laboratory, in business affairs and in every-day life. Expertise on how to measure and what to evaluate is also not limited to sociologists and other social scientists. Social scientists as measurers and evaluators, however, have a distinct contribution to make to the debate which takes place among researchers on what data should be collected and how they should be gathered.

The major contribution of social science to measurement and evaluation is the variety of approaches it uses to obtain and evaluate data on the 'real world'. On the one hand, methods sometimes identified as 'positivist' are used to gather observations and assign numerical quantities to them. On the other hand, observations on the motives, meanings, emotions or subjective aspects of individuals are reported in the notational system of every-day language. Observations on the doctor–patient relationship, for example, may be drawn from survey questionnaires administered to doctors and patients or from participant observation of consultations where actual conversations are recorded. In fact, combinations of both approaches have been discussed in almost every chapter of this textbook. The different values, goals, concepts and methods of social scientists can therefore assist medicine in searching for and constructing the processes and events which shape health and the delivery of health care.

The importance of measurement

Measurement is most important in practical affairs when decisions are taken based on observations. Measuring devices for providing observations, such as a thermometer or a ruler, are common in the natural sciences where tools for precise physical and chemical measurement are highly developed and applied on an everyday basis. Decisions are taken on the basis of relatively exact measurement. In the social sciences, exact measures are not common, most often because a single property can be measured in innumerable ways. Decisions, therefore, must rely on human yardsticks and measurement in the social sciences is concerned with providing these yardsticks.

Major developments in science, sometimes called scientific revolutions, often occur when some theory is tested or refuted by observation and measurement. For example, Newton's law of inertia was based on the quantitative concepts of distance and time. Atomic theory became viable in the nineteenth century when the weight of an atom was measured. William Harvey demonstrated that the heart was a pump by a simple and crude calculation of the volume of blood that flows through the arteries. Edwin Chadwick, in 1842, provided a manifesto for the public health movement by publishing data on the association between sanitary conditions of the labouring population and their mortality. Quantitative measures, therefore, have played a crucial role in the corroboration and falsification of scientific hypotheses.

Measurement is not, however, synonymous with quantification. Without some theory which can be invoked to explain measures and relationships between measures, quantification is meaningless. Asking 'how many times?' or 'how much?' of something can never answer the question 'what is it in the first place?'. For example, counting the number of people in different social classes and observing how social class is related to mortality and morbidity cannot explain what it is about social inequality which produces the inverse relationship between social class and ill health which has often been observed (see Chapter 9). Theories concerning risk factors such as increased life stress, poor diet, inadequate medical care and increased alcohol and smoking consumption must be invoked to explain these observations. Quantification has a powerful mystique, however, because of its scientific history, and this mystique can lead to an exaggerated regard for the significance of measures merely because they are quantitative. All scientific enquiry must have regard for what is being measured and for what can be done with the measure once it is available.

Types of scales

A precise definition of measurement is 'the assignment of numbers to aspects of objects or events according to a rule of some kind' (Stevens 1946). The rules scientists commonly employ for assigning numbers are defined by types of scales: nominal, ordinal, interval and ratio. The type of measurement scale employed determines how a measure can be analysed by numerical methods, that is, which mathematical operations can be performed on the measure.

The *nominal* scale is essentially no more than a non-overlapping classification with numbers or labels assigned to the various classes to connote relevant differences in kind. Any number or label can be assigned provided the same number is not assigned to two different classes. *The International Classification of Diseases* is an example of a frequently used nominal scale in medicine. Much social science research takes place with nominal scales such as sex, occupation and the various typologies developed for personalities and societies.

In *ordinal* scales, the numbers assigned to the classes correspond to the order of magnitude of the property scaled. The five social classes used by the British Registrar General constitute an ordinal scale in the sense that they are used to signify the greater or lesser social standing of the occupations assigned to each class. In medicine, ranked scales of events — for example, 'mild', 'moderate' or 'severe' — are commonly employed ordinal scales. These statements connote order but not how much more severe 'moderate' is than 'mild'.

An *interval* scale has all the properties of nominal and ordinal scales (distinctiveness, order) as well as the property of operationally defined distances between the scale steps. Centigrade and fahrenheit are the most common examples, in which the units between adjacent degrees are equal. Because the starting points of these scales are arbitrary (there is no absolute zero as in Kelvin temperature), it is incorrect to say that 40° (C or F) is twice as hot as 20°. Interval scales that are not also ratio scales are rare in medicine and in social sciences, except for demography. Even standardized psychological tests — such as some aptitude and achievement tests with numerical scores for right answers — are pseudo-interval, since the interval between scores is completely arbitrary, being dependent on the particular questions in the test.

Ratio scales permit one to say that something exists in x times the amount of something else. This property of a scale is made possible by an absolute zero, as well as equal intervals, in the quantity being measured. Ratio scales are common in the physical sciences (e.g. length and mass) and find practical application in measures of height, weight and amounts of money. The pulse and measures of visual and auditory acuity are ratio scales commonly used in medicine. Other examples of ratio scales used in health research include family size, number of days to get an appointment with a general practitioner and travel time to the surgery or hospital.

Measurement scales are important in medical practice because measures play such a large part in decisions about 'normal' and 'abnormal' and about which and how much 'abnormality' patients or populations have. The information that can be derived from a measure — differences in category, order and magnitude or absolute differences — depends on the type of scale and it is important to keep in mind level of measurement when interpreting or comparing measures taken on patients or groups of patients. It is also important to recognize that measurement connotes values such as sameness, more or less and better or worse; measurement scales tell us how to interpret the values assigned in the measurement process. Scale type does not help, however, in determining whether or not a measure is reliable or valid.

Reliability and validity

Reliability is the correspondence obtained when a measure is applied repeatedly. A score or measure is reliable to the extent that it is repeatable. *Observer* reliabilities refer to the extent of agreement between two or more observers or the same observer at different times, for instance when two or more clinicians judge the degree of impairment in an injured person or one clinician makes a judgement on different days. *Test measurement* reliabilities tell us about the correspondence between two versions of the same measure, such as a briefer or longer version of a personality inventory. Reliability is mainly concerned with the assessment of chance or random error. If there is a high degree of random error in some observation, then that same observation could not be expected upon repeated applications of the same test or upon repeated observations by clinicians.

Time introduces an interesting paradox with respect to reliability. If what one observes is highly variable by nature, like blood pressure, how can one tell whether differences in repeated measurements are caused by a change in the observed phenomena or by unreliable observation? In other words, what proportion of the measured variation is 'true' variation? In medicine, the quest for 'true' variation has led to experiments with simultaneous observation of a given phenomenon by multiple observers, e.g. multiple stethoscopy. In such experiments the observer becomes an integral part of the measuring process and it becomes difficult to separate the unreliability of the measuring instrument (e.g. the stethoscope) from that of the observer.

Validity is a complex idea which presents great problems to the researcher whatever the measure used. In simple terms, validity refers to the extent to which a measure really measures what it purports to measure. For example, is a sphygmomanometer reading a good measure of the haemodynamic condition, 'blood pressure'? Is the prestige attached to an occupation a valid measure of 'social class'?

There are a number of different ways of demonstrating validity. *Criterion* validity, often the most prized evidence of validity, refers to the degree of association between the measure under examination and a criterion measure which is already regarded as 'more' valid. Income might be regarded as a valid measure of social class by some investigators and thus it might be used as a criterion for the validation of occupational ranks. A measure of attitudes toward smoking might be validated by correlating the measure with actual behaviour, that is, assessing how well the measure predicts smoking behaviour.

Other kinds of validity include content, construct and consensual validity. *Content* validity refers to whether or not a measure adequately represents the concept which it is supposed to measure. Do intelligence tests, for example, cover the universe of areas where intelligence comes into play? *Construct* validity involves specifying the constructs which account for variation in a proposed measure as well as the hypothesized relationships between them. For example, intelligence might be measured by an intelligence test and by school performance, and neither measure considered superior or more valid. If the researcher hypothesized that the test and school performance were logically related, then a test of construct validity is possible by examining the correlation between these two measures. The important feature of construct validity is the prior specification of hypotheses concerning the relations between measures. Construct validity is important in medicine because often no clear criterion exists for measures of symptoms, pain or function reported by patients and convergent evidence is required from two or more measures. *Consensual* validity describes the degree of consensus among investigators about the construct validity of a measure. For example, occupational ranking is used as a measure of social class precisely because so many different investigators accept it as the best available indicator.

Reliability is a necessary, but not a sufficient, condition for the validity of a measure which is repeated on different populations. In other words, it is not possible to have a *valid* measure that is not also *reliable*. One can have a *reliable* measure, however, without it being necessarily *valid*; for example, height and weight may be measured reliably, but may not be considered valid measures of nutritional status or health status. Blood cholesterol level may be a reliable measure, while the validity question arises when one asks whether blood cholesterol is a valid assessment of the likelihood of developing coronary heart disease.

In medicine and the social sciences, research is often conducted without direct measures of what we wish to measure and we have to content ourselves with some indicator or index which we argue proximates to that phenomenon. For instance, to measure life stress we must settle for an interview, a paper-and-pencil test or a composite of instrument-produced results. The only means of validation may be a comparison between the results produced by different instruments. It may take many years before any single measure achieves consensual validity.

The measurement of health

Much research in medicine and the social sciences is concerned with the measurement of health. Definitions of 'health' are, however, as numerous as the number of people and groups who have attempted to define it. The World Health Organization (WHO) has proposed that 'health is a state of complete physical, mental and social well-being and not merely the absence of disease or infirmity'. Since health cannot be observed directly, the selection of appropriate indicators or the construction of an index becomes an important consideration.

Five classes of indicators of health status have been proposed most frequently: mortality, morbidity, discomfort, dissatisfaction and disability (Patrick & Elinson 1979). Each type of indicator has its strengths and weaknesses as a measure of health, depending on the purpose of measurement and consequent consideration of reliability and validity.

Mortality

Paradoxically, death rates or mortality statistics are most readily available and accurately determined for populations where they are least valuable in assessing a population's health. The WHO has sponsored the collection of mortality statistics throughout the world, but in those countries where death rates are still high, accuracy of measurement is thwarted by incomplete records, an uncertain population base and other weaknesses in the chain of events between the diagnosis of a cause of death and reporting in routine publications (diagnosis→certification→coding →processing→interpretation). When death rates are relatively low, they tend not to be very serviceable indicators in the assessment of outcome of health resource expenditure or health services. For example, in any given year in countries with low death rates, 99% of the population remains alive in markedly varying degrees of health. The decline in infectious disease, the increase in non-fatal, chronic conditions and the development of medical treatment to prolong life (e.g. renal dialysis and insulin therapy) have all made mortality data less useful for assessing health if mortality is regarded as a proxy for incidence. Even so, death rates can be valuable indicators for special population subgroups that have higher than average mortality, for example people living in poverty areas, ethnic minorities or infants.

Routine mortality data have been used to monitor the state of public health for over a century in Britain (Farr 1840). International comparisons are often drawn on the basis of infant

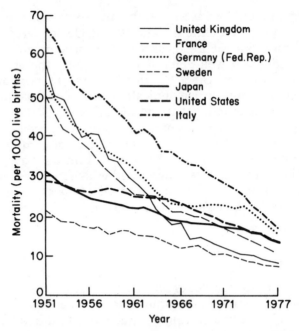

Fig. 7   International comparisons of infant mortality rates. (*Government Statistic Service* (*1980*) *Social Trends*, *p. 133*. *London: HMSO*)

or perinatal mortality rates because these are thought to reflect broad social conditions, as well as the availability of maternal and infant services. Fig. 7 shows the rate of deaths of infants under one year of age per 1000 live births in seven developed countries. In 1951, the variation in infant mortality between these countries was much greater than in 1977, making it currently a less useful indicator for the particular countries shown here. In contrast to the narrow band of rates for developed countries, the current infant mortality rates for developing nations seldom dip below 50 and reach as high as 89.2 in Egypt, 95.2 in Paraguay and 118 in the Maldives (WHO 1980). Although mortality data may be misleading or inadequate, they will continue to be used precisely because they are the only data readily accessible for the examination of trends over time and for comparison between regions with widely different social conditions and health resources.

Morbidity

Clinical judgements rendered by health professionals after examination of 'all the evidence' form the basis for many if not most morbidity studies. Clinical evidence of disease can include tissue changes, records produced by measuring equipment (e.g. radiograph or electrocardiograph) and reports of symptoms objectively observable or not directly or readily observable. Skills for determining the presence of disease are usually most developed in medical scientists or clinicians, although recent efforts are being made to encourage self-detection and judgement of 'the evidence' by laymen because it is they who experience the symptoms.

Officially obtained morbidity data on the population of Britain cover cancer registration, conditions treated in general practice, diagnosis at hospital discharge, infectious disease reporting, conditions entitling workers to certified sickness benefits and medical examination results (Alderson & Dowie 1979). Material derived from interviews or examination of population samples covers a restricted range of health difficulties with consequent low content validity as a general health measure. Other problems with morbidity data include sampling errors, bias from failure to respond or incomplete responses and data processing errors. Despite these problems, morbidity data comprise the single largest source of data on the perceived health needs of the population and they are generally considered to have high construct, predictive, criterion and consensual validity.

Discomfort

The concept of 'discomfort' can be defined in terms of self-reported feelings of pain, aches, anxiety, tiredness or sadness. These feelings may be part of, or precursors to, a diagnosable disease or identifiable injury. Sometimes there is no clear relationship between anatomical or pathological diagnoses (morbidity measure) and reports of discomfort. For example, back pain is a common presenting symptom in general practice and estimates of the percentage of back pain due to prolapsed intervertebral discs range from 80.2 to 4.4% (Barton et al. 1976; Cyriax 1978). Thus pain may have a low construct, criterion or predictive validity as an indicator of disc disease, but may indicate other causes or sources for the discomfort. Most often, indicators of discomfort are used in the study of specific illness conditions and general population surveys of discomfort are unavailable.

Dissatisfaction

Dissatisfaction can be thought of in two ways: lack of satisfaction with one's state of health, regardless of the care received, or unfavourable feelings about the health and social services offered to the consumer to meet self-perceived needs. Studies of consumer opinion have used reports of satisfaction as evaluations of the quality of care, as outcome variables, and as indicators of which aspects of a service need to be changed to improve patient response (Locker & Dunt 1978). Little is known about the procedures, criteria and standards consumers employ in evaluations of health care and there is no consensus on how indicators of consumer satisfaction should be reconciled with professional opinion in the formulation and implementation of health policy. There is nevertheless a general feeling among professional workers that it is a dimension which cannot be ignored in medical care.

Disability

A myriad of uses and definitions of 'disability' and 'dysfunction' have arisen from the increasing number of studies which have attempted to measure these indicators of health status. Attempts to refine the techniques used to assess the physical capacities of disabled persons and to create comprehensive classifications have shown that disablement may be thought of as occurring anywhere on a continuum which extends from an individual physical event on the one hand through to a socially defined condition on the other. Fig. 8 shows that impairment, disability and handicap are separate but related consequences of the disease process.

   The WHO has recently published a trial classification of impairment, disability and handicap to supplement the International Classification of Diseases (ICD) (WHO 1980a). This classification system defines *impairment* as any loss or abnormality of psychological, physiological or anatomical structure or function; *disability* as any restriction or lack of

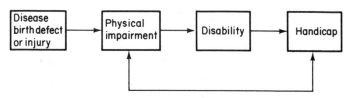

Fig. 8   The terminology of physical disablement. (*World Health Organization* (*1980*) *International Classification of Impairments, Disabilities and Handicaps. Geneva*)

ability (resulting from an impairment) to perform an activity in the manner or within the range considered normal for a human being; and *handicap* as a disadvantage for a given individual, resulting from impairment or disability, that limits or prevents the fulfillment of a role that is normal (depending on age, sex and social and cultural factors) for that individual. As measures of these constructs become available, the set of hypothesized relations in Fig. 8 can be examined, thus permitting a test of construct validity for a measure of disability. Because measures of disability are frequently derived from self-reports, concerns about their reliability are often expressed. Findings reported in the literature would indicate, however, that reliable and valid self-administered or self-reported measures of physical health are available (Brook et al. 1979).

In recent years the use of single indicators as global measures of health has been criticised on the grounds of their low validity. Attempts have been made to create composite measures or health indexes. A health index combines multiple single indicators of health according to a specified weighting system. Thus, measures of mortality and morbidity may be combined to reflect the health status of the population. Although rapid progress is being made on these indexes, application is usually confined to specific populations or geographical areas and international comparisons are not yet available.

Measurement, method and meaning

It is one thing to satisfy the criteria of good measurement and quite another to decide *what* to measure. The question of what to measure is answered only by a theory which provides a conceptualization of observable phenomena, suggests a strategy for empirical investigation or attempts to explain particular phenomena. Theory assists in the selection of measures and in thinking about the results of the measurement operations. Measures, in themselves, cannot substitute for ideas.

Measures of health — regardless of their level of precision — may have severe limitations depending on their uses. For example, counting how many people there are with a disease or disability will never illuminate the processes by which persons become impaired, disabled or handicapped. Patients' definitions of their present situations depend upon their anticipation of the future, their perceptions of need as influenced by their interaction with organizations and services, and their past. A classification for administrative purposes may not, therefore, have much to say about the meaning of disease or disablement to an individual (Blaxter 1976). On the other hand, descriptions of disabled persons, however insightful, cannot shed light on the amount and kind of services needed by the population of disabled persons. To improve the quality and scope of the services to be provided, both quantitative and qualitative information is required and different methods, quantitative and qualitative, must be employed.

The observer or the measurer plays a crucial role by selecting or creating theory and by translating theory into measurement. Different investigators may have widely varying ideas about a problem and about the methods and measures appropriate to its solution. Measurement theory in itself cannot provide the basis for choosing between these alternative approaches. The objectives of the measurement process will help in making the choice, but the decision is not a matter of objective evidence. Decisions are based on values and the decision to adopt one approach over another is a matter of subjective judgement. Similarly, the meaning of a particular measure is subjective in that alternative explanations for the same results are often possible. Measurement, then, is only the means to an end, and it is up to us to choose which ends to seek.

References

ALDERSON, M. & DOWIE, R. (1979) *Health Surveys and Related Studies.* Oxford: Pergamon Press.

BARTON, J., HAIGHT, R., MARSLAND, D. & TEMPLE, T. (1976) Low back pain in the primary care setting. *J. Family Pract.*, **3**, 363–6.

BLAXTER, M. (1976) *The Meaning of Disability*. London: Heinemann Educational.

BROOK, R., WARE, J., DAVIES-AVERY, A., STEWART, A., DONALD, C., ROGERS, W., WILLIAMS, K. & JOHNTSON, S. (1979) Overview of adult health status measures fielded in Rand's health insurance study. *Med. Care*, Suppl. **17**, 1–131.

CYRIAX, J. (1978) *Textbook of Orthopaedic Medicine, Vol. I. Diagnosis of Soft Tissue Lesions*. London: Baillière Tindall.

ELINSON, J. & SIEGMANN, A. (1979) *Socio-medical Health Indicators*. Farmingdale, N.Y.: Baywood.

FARR, W. (1840) Letter to the Registrar General. In *First Annual Report of the Registrar General of Births, Deaths, and Marriages in England*. London: HMSO.

LOCKER, D. & DUNT, D. (1978) Theoretical and methodological issues in sociological studies of consumer satisfaction with medical care. *Soc. Sci. Med.*, **12**, 283–92.

PATRICK, D. & ELINSON, J. (1979) Methods of socio-medical research. In *Handbook of Medical Sociology*, ed. H. Freeman, S. Levine & L. Reeder, 3rd ed. Englewood Cliffs, N.J.: Prentice Hall.

STEVENS, S. (1946) On the theory of scales of measurement. *Science, N.Y.*, **103**, 677–80.

WORLD HEALTH ORGANIZATION (1980a) *International Classification of Impairments, Disabilities and Handicaps*. Geneva.

WORLD HEALTH ORGANIZATION (1980b) *World Health Statistics Annual*. Geneva.

19

Evaluation of Health Care

Donald L. Patrick

In this chapter basic concepts and developments in the evaluation of effectiveness and efficiency in health care are examined. Evaluation of health and medical care has existed in some form for centuries, sometimes by sanctions for non-efficacious treatment. A physician in 3000 B.C. in Egypt, for example, was subject to the loss of a hand if a patient unnecessarily lost an eye. The definition of 'unnecessary' was just as important then as it is today in assessing the quality of medical care. Before the various approaches to defining and measuring what is or is not necessary can be considered, however, a rationale for evaluation research must be found.

Why evaluate health services?

There are five major reasons why evaluation of health care has developed so rapidly in recent decades. First is the *increasing size and complexity of modern health services*. In Britain, the National Health Service has become a mammoth organization with several administrative tiers and a complex set of activities. As Chapter 16 on the NHS has indicated, periodic attempts have been made to reorganize it. Increasing complexity has spurred the search for answers to how services can be better organized and conducted. In other countries, increasing central government participation in health services financing and new delivery systems have prompted the study of the organization and political processes within which services are delivered.

A second force encouraging evaluation is the *growth of expenditure on health services*. As shown in Table 39, health care

Table 39.   *Health care expenditure* as a percentage of gross national product*

	1950	1960	1965	1970	1975
United Kingdom	3.9	3.8	3.9	4.3	5.5
France	3.4	4.7	5.8	6.4	7.9
West Germany	—	—	—	6.4	9.4
Sweden	3.4	4.7	5.6	7.4	8.5
Netherlands	—	4.5	5.3	6.3	8.1
USA	4.5	5.3	6.2	7.6	8.6
Canada	4.0	5.6	6.1	7.1	7.1
Australia	—	5.0	5.2	5.5	7.0

*Public and private, capital and current.
  From Maxwell (1980).

expenditure in the UK rose from 3.9% of the gross national product (GNP) in 1950 to 5.5% in 1975 (Maxwell 1980). Although expenditure is still lower than that in other developed countries, Britain may be reaching the limits of growth in the percentage of the GNP that health services can consume. Politicians of all political parties think that it is no longer feasible to continue pumping a greater proportion of resources into the health care system without increased accountability. They seek 'optimum' results in the form of the benefit and the cost to the population of a particular type of activity. They ask whether increased benefit will be obtained if additional resources are made available.

Nowhere are the budget pressures felt more than in the continued *growth of medical science and technology*, a third major factor prompting evaluation. New diagnostic tools, such as computed tomographic (CAT) scanning, and therapeutic methodologies, such as coronary bypass surgery, renal dialysis and heart transplantation, have led decision-makers to ask questions about the appropriateness, cost-effectiveness and limits of new technologies. Because an increasing number of technical innovations are being developed, it seems imperative that the NHS and other national bodies develop means of evaluation which take into account the likely impacts of these technologies before they are disseminated widely (Stocking & Morrison 1978). Does new technology replace the old, complement it or lead to new uses of what already exists? What are the ethical considerations involved in using the new technologies for what ends?

A fourth impetus to evaluation is *increased public accountability*. Consumer representation in the NHS and in other health care systems, however unsteady its development has been, is now a major force in the debate about how health services should be delivered. The legal climate in some countries has meant that medical malpractice exercises an increasingly important influence on the doctor–patient relationship. Developments in health education, including the rapid expansion of self-care and self-help, have led to consumer evaluations or requests for evidence of effectiveness.

The fifth and last major reason for the development of evaluation is that *tools to measure* the effects of particular actions on the health of the population have become available for application to evaluation. Most notably, the randomized clinical trial has been applied to health care and alternative designs are being developed for evaluations where randomization and experiment are not possible. It would be a mistake, however, to suggest that the development of more sophisticated methodological tools and designs alone will prompt better evaluations or, in fact, lead to better services, since the main questions of evaluation are not technological ones. Why and how to evaluate are political questions, with several competing viewpoints. Organizations, administrators, funding bodies, consumers and the evaluators themselves all have different perspectives on what health services are for and why evaluation should take place.

Evaluation research: what are health services for?

Evaluation, as the word implies, concerns *values* and the evaluation process begins and ends as a political process of determining the worth of the treatment or service under consideration. Judgement and decision-making, then, are *evaluation*. The application of scientific method to the decision process of judgeing worth is *evaluation research*. It is not only the use of scientific approaches to isolating and studying the causes of particular outcomes or effects, but also the use of the results to decide if, how and why health services work.

Deciding whether or not there is reason enough to modify the delivery of health services starts with asking the question, 'what are health services for?' The initial stage of the evaluation process is perhaps the most difficult stage of all: the specification of objectives. The setting of objectives (the programme planning stage) entails asking the right questions at the outset and there is no more important task for service providers, administrators, policy-makers and evaluators than to specify objectives in as clear, precise and measurable terms as possible. Most often, the objectives of health services are numerous and varied and few are spelled out in any great detail. For example, it is easy to agree that health services have preventive, caring and curing objectives so that they should produce in its users feelings of physical, mental or social well-being. It is considerably more difficult to state objectives that indicate what specific action is to be taken, for what purpose the action is intended, what end-results are to be achieved and what time should elapse before the end-results can be expected.

The technical problems involved in specifying objectives can be illustrated by considering how one might initiate the evaluation of a new primary care health centre staffed with a multi-disciplinary team of doctors, nurses, social workers, community health workers and supporting personnel. The evaluation might be concerned with the best working arrangements for the staff or with the outcome of the services provided by the centre. At the programme planning stage, the administrator, the senior physician and nurse representatives of a consumer group, and the evaluator, might be concerned with setting objectives. Two immediate problems would almost certainly confront this planning group.

The first problem would arise when it became clear that more than one view-point was represented within the group. The question *'what* objectives?' naturally leads to the question *'whose* objectives?'. The dilemma of making choices is often difficult and unpleasant and until recently the power, authority and responsibility for setting objectives has been largely the province of the medical profession and, to a lesser extent, of the administrator. The public was not involved directly in establishing the goals of health services; nor were other health service employees. A change in the climate of public opinion is occurring, however, and consumers of services as well as nurses and other health workers are requesting more say in the determination of objectives. For evaluation to be initiated some form of group consensus has to be achieved. In the example, the planning group might continue to list objectives and assign priorities to them until an acceptable consensus was reached.

Consensus is reached most often when objectives are ordered, the second major challenge in the programme planning stage. Service objectives may be ordered from 'immediate' to 'ultimate', the immediate or lower-order objectives being concerned with implementation and the ultimate or higher-order objectives with the outcome of the service. In evaluating staffing arrangements at the health centre in the example, the immediate objectives might be to select members of the team and appoint a leader, to establish an appointment system and to set up all the arrangements for seeing patients at the centre. Intermediate objectives might be to increase staff performance and satisfaction, to find the best case-load for the team, to increase the services provided or to decrease referrals to hospital. Ultimate or higher-order objectives in this case might be to reduce morbidity in the patient population, to reduce cigarette smoking among clientele (and staff), especially before and after pregnancy and to reduce demand on hospital services. Measures of how the programme is established and run are the independent variables in evaluation research and evaluation of *structure* and *process* is concerned with measures such as the number of patients who attended a clinic, staff–patient ratios or facilities available. Study of the impact, the dependent variables in the research, is concerned with how much effect the service has produced and is sometimes termed *outcome* evaluation.

The setting of objectives at the programme-planning stage influences both the organization of resources to carry out the service (the implementation stage) and the assessment of performance (the outcome or impact stage). The entire process of evaluation is pictured in Fig. 9 as a pyramid rising from the lower-order to the higher-order objectives (Shortell & Richardson 1978).

As illustrated by the health centre example, the multiplicity of objectives at each stage of the evaluation process requires different perspectives. One can evaluate a medical or health

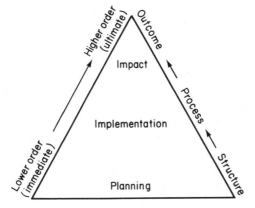

Fig. 9   The evaluation process. (*After Shortell & Richardson 1978*)

service from at least five different perspectives:

1. Effort.
2. Effectiveness/performance.
3. Adequacy of performance.
4. Efficiency.
5. Process.

Effort refers to the amount of energy expended in the action or treatment, such as the number of hours involved, the costs, and all activities of the service providers. *Effectiveness* is the result achieved with a given effort, for example the reduction in cigarette smoking of patients at the health centre with the introduction of a health education programme. *Adequacy of performance* involves comparing the level of effectiveness achieved with the level of possible or desirable achievement. For instance, the primary care centre may be 10% more effective in reducing hospital referral rates than another group practice in the same geographical area. *Efficiency* concerns the optimum use of personnel and materials in achieving results. Whether or not education, screening, diagnosis, treatment or rehabilitation can be carried out with different staffing arrangements, or fewer staff altogether, is one example of the evaluation of efficiency. *Process* evaluation is involved with assessing how and why an intervention or programme does or does not work. For instance, a health education campaign might work because it makes patients at the centre afraid of the health consequences of smoking. Would it work without the manipulation of fear? The question of why an intervention or health programme works is concerned mainly with the underlying theory of the programme and the objectives.

Clearly, all the issues involved in the evaluation process, most particularly the specification of objectives, raise difficult political and ethical problems. These problems exist whether or not the evaluation concerns specific medical procedures or broader aspects of the caring services. There are certain basic concepts and techniques, however, which aid the design and execution of all health care evaluations. These concepts and techniques primarily concern the role of observation and experiment in the evaluation.

Observation and experiment in evaluation design

The oldest and probably the most common type of evidence that a treatment has produced the desired effect is observation or opinion based on observation. For example, one might observe that the death rate for a particular condition goes up with an increase in the number of surgical operations for that condition. One can not assume, however, that fewer operations will lower the death rate for the condition without attempting to discover what would happen if patients did not receive the operation, that is without making a quantitative assessment of the surgical procedures. The possibility of bias in observational studies is high and observational evidence will not always suffice, particularly for outcome evaluations.

The cornerstone of experimental evaluation is the random allocation of patients to treatment and control groups. By randomizing one increases the likelihood that treatment and control groups are alike, so that at a later stage alternative explanations for the effect of a service intervention can be largely ruled out. An example of a randomized controlled trial is that conducted into the effects of discharging patients from hospital either 48 hours or six to seven days after operations for inguinal hernia and varicose veins (Adler et al. 1978). Patients undergoing surgery for these two conditions were randomly assigned to one of the two lengths of postoperative stay. As shown in Table 40, no statistically significant differences were

Table 40.   *Complications recorded up to seven days after operation in randomized controlled trial of length of stay for inguinal hernia and varicose vein patients*

Type of complication	Long-stay ($n=49$)	Short-stay ($n=56$)	Total ($n=105$)
Inguinal hernia patients			
Wound infection	2	2	4
Chest infection	2*	2*	4
Haematoma	—	1	1
Stitch abscess	—	1*	1
Scoline apnoea	1*	—	1
Oedema of scrotum/penis	—	1	1
Total	5	7	12

$=0.095, 0.7<P<0.8$

	Long-stay ($n=58$)	Short-stay ($n=61$)	Total ($n=119$)
Varicose vein patients			
Major			
Wound infection	—	2	2
Haematoma	—	1*	1
Thrombophlebitis	—	1	1
Minor			
Rash: 'Plaster reaction'	—	2	2
Persistent oozing wound, no infection	—	1	1
Upper respiratory infection	—	1	1
Total	0	8	8

*Noted in hospital in first 48 hours.
  $P=0.065$ major complications.
  $P=0.003$ all complications.
  From Adler et al. (1978).

found in major postoperative complications between the two lengths of stay for either condition. Long-stay and short-stay patients in full-time occupation were also found to have similar convalescence periods. Most important, this experiment in medical care was shown in itself to have changed clinical practice in that a significant reduction in mean length of stay was recorded in the study area between 1970 (the year before the start of the study) and 1975 (two complete years after the study) (Adler 1978).

While the true experiment, according to scientific criteria, may be preferable to simple observation, it is not always possible or necessary. Randomization may not be ethical in human experimentation. For example, experiments have never been conducted on dietetic therapy for phenylketonuria or surgery for carcinoma of the lung. An experiment would involve denying the treatment procedure to half the patients and this has always been considered unethical. In deciding whether or not a trial is ethical, the patients' interests must be considered and weighed against the value of the evidence to be obtained from the experiment.

Sometimes, although not often, controls are not needed for conducting a trial. In the age before antibiotics, some diseases invariably and rapidly led to death and there was no need for controls to establish a change in the fatality rate (Bradford-Hill 1967). The famous trial involving streptomycin and tuberculous meningitis needed no control group. Given accurate identification of a case, the success of treatment could be measured against the past 100% fatality rate.

Such conditions of certainty in evaluating the success of a treatment are seldom attainable in evaluations of modern clinical procedures or service delivery arrangements. The randomized controlled trial has been the design of choice, although such trials are more often conducted on specific procedures than on the broader caring functions of health care. Even with the randomized controlled trial, however, observing and evaluating treatment success can be a difficult problem.

For example, a randomized controlled trial was carried out to compare the clinical outcome in patients treated for varicose veins by routine surgery and by injection/compression sclerotherapy. Three years after treatment, there was no significant difference between the results of the two forms of treatment (Chant et al. 1972). The patients preferred injection/compression sclerotherapy, however, and a cost analysis concluded that it would benefit the patient, the health service and also the community if the majority of patients were treated as out-patients with injection/compression sclerotherapy (Piachaud & Weddell 1972). The more successful treatment, it would appear, had been identified by experimental evaluation. Five years after the original evaluation, however, the patients were followed up to see if any further treatment had been given to them. The probability of having had no further treatment was significantly greater for those who had been treated surgically (Beresford et al. 1978). It was concluded with hindsight, then, that the long-term clinical outcome was of overriding importance in the choice of treatment. Observing and evaluating treatment success may involve unintended or unanticipated consequences. Anticipating such consequences is a challenge to all those involved in the process of evaluation.

Because randomization or experimental design is not always possible or plausible, a number of evaluation designs are being developed which do not require random allocation of cases to treatment and control groups. These are called 'quasi-experimental designs', because an attempt is made to approximate some of the advantages of a true experimental design even though randomization is not possible (Campbell & Stanley 1966). These designs may also be useful when randomization breaks down during an experiment. One commonly used quasi-experimental design is the time-series, where multiple measures of effect are observed both before and after the introduction of a programme. For example, in 1967 the British government introduced a new policy that allowed police to administer a breathalyzer test, a procedure to measure the presence and amount of alcohol in the blood, at the scene of an accident. The law came into effect in October 1967. By plotting the vehicular accident rate by weeks before and after the new legislation became effective, it was possible to observe that a decline in accidents clearly occurred after the legislation (Ross et al. 1970). While there are considerable difficulties in measuring reliability and validity in evaluations using quasi-experimental designs such as time-series, their development will produce new opportunities for systematic evaluation of health care interventions that might not be evaluated otherwise.

From evidence to policy

For a service evaluation to be useful, it must produce information that can be used in decision-making by public officials and administrators. Thus, evaluation studies have to be timed to fit into the decision-maker's schedule. Decisions about programmes are, and sometimes must be, made before an evaluation study can be undertaken. Vested interests and organizational inertia may set in as programmes are established, resulting in diminishing opportunity for assessing the impact of the programme. Thus, evaluation early in the life of a programme may be necessary if evaluation is to occur at all.

The results of evaluation have to be presented simply and in terms which are specific to the issues of importance in public debate. Technical data and findings presented with a myriad of assumptions and contingencies are not easily understood by decision-makers or administrators. Some experiments have been successful in influencing decisions. Evaluations of screening procedures, for example, have resulted in decisions not to screen whole target populations. Randomized controlled trials of the length of time spent in hospital for coronary care have resulted in lower lengths of stay and an increase in home care.

The results of evaluation studies may be well-timed and well-presented and still have little immediate effect on policy. For example, Lind studied the value of 'lime' for relieving the effects of scurvy on sailors by trying six treatments on two sailors each; he found that the citrus fruit made an astounding difference to survival. This evaluation result had important implications for policy because scurvy took more lives in the British naval forces than warfare and accidents put together. It took 50 years, however, before the British Admiralty decided to introduce citrus fruit into the diet of British sailors. This 50-year lag from research to policy had profound consequences in that thousands of sailors died each year before Lind's work was recognized.

Considerable resistance to evaluation can be encountered in disputes over how evaluation results should be interpreted. If evaluation is a threatening prospect to those involved, subtle strategies and defences may be mobilized to destroy the conduct and interpretation of evaluation studies. For example, suicide-prevention centres have seldom been evaluated because workers in such centres have resisted evaluation by appealing to the public for support for their efforts. Resistance to evaluation seldom arises out of an irrational fear of methodology or the evaluations themselves; it is usually a function of uncertainty over the political or valuational aspects of the evaluation process.

The selection of evaluators and programmes to evaluate, as well as the methods used to evaluate, are not value-free. This complex network of values involves the individual evaluator, the institution in which he or she works, the sponsor of the evaluation, the population being studied and the people delivering the services. Thus it is not surprising that considerable resistance is often encountered when evaluation is suggested.

In the future, however, providers of services will increasingly be called upon to participate in evaluations of the preventing, caring and curing activities of health services. An effective partnership between clinicians, evaluators, administrators and consumers will be required if these evaluations are to influence important decisions about the objectives of health services and how these objectives are best achieved.

References

ADLER, M. (1978) Changes in local clinical practice following an experiment in medical care: evaluation of evaluation. *J. Epidem. commun. Hlth,* **32**, 143–6.

ADLER, M., WALLER, J., CREESE, A. & THORNE, S. (1978) Randomized controlled trial of early discharge for inguinal hernia and varicose veins. *J. Epidem. commun. Hlth,* **32**, 136–42.

BERESFORD, S., CHANT, A., JONES, H., PIACHAUD, D. & WEDDELL, J. (1978) Varicose veins: a comparison of surgery and injection/compression sclerotherapy: a five-year follow-up. *Lancet,* **2**, 921–4.

BRADFORD-HILL, Sir A. (1967) *Principles of Medical Statistics,* 8th ed. London: The Lancet.

CAMPBELL, D. & STANLEY, J. (1966) *Experimental and Quasi-experimental Designs for Research.* Stokie, Ill.: Rand McNally.

CHANT, A., JONES, H. & WEDDELL, J. (1972) Varicose veins: a comparison of surgery and injection/compression sclerotherapy. *Lancet,* **2**, 1188–91.

MAXWELL, R. (1980) *International Comparison of Health Needs and Services.* London: King's Fund Centre.

PIACHAUD, D. & WEDDELL, J. (1972) Cost of treating varicose veins. *Lancet,* **2**, 1191–92.

ROSS, H., CAMPBELL, D. & GLASS, G. (1970) Determining the social effects of a legal reform: the British breathalyzer crackdown of 1967. *Am. behav. Sci.,* **13**, 500.

SHORTELL, S. & RICHARDSON, W. (1978) *Health Program Evaluation*. St Louis, Missouri: C. V. Mosby.

STOCKING, B. & MORRISON, S. (1978) *The Image and the Reality: A Case-Study of the Impacts of Medical Technology*. Oxford: Nuffield Provincial Hospitals Trust.

Recommended Books

CARTWRIGHT, A. & ANDERSON, R. (1981) *General Practice Revisited.* London: Tavistock.

DEPARTMENT OF HEALTH AND SOCIAL SECURITY (1980) *Inequalities in Health.* London: HMSO.

DOYAL, L. & PENNELL, I. (1979) *Political Economy of Health.* London: Pluto.

FREIDSON, E. (1970) *Profession of Medicine.* New York, N.Y.: Dodds, Mead.

GLASER, B. & STRAUSS, A. (1968) *Time for Dying.* Chicago, Ill.: Aldine.

GOFFMAN, E. (1961) *Asylums: Essays on the Social Situation of Mental Patients and Other Inmates.* Harmondsworth: Penguin.

GOFFMAN, E. (1968) *Stigma: Notes on the Management of Spoiled Identity.* Harmondsworth: Penguin.

HONINGSBAUM, F. (1980) *Division in British Medicine: History of the Separation of General Practice from Hospital Care, 1911–1968.* London: Kogan Page.

McKEOWN, T. (1979) *The Role of Medicine: Dream, Mirage or Nemesis?* Oxford: Basil Blackwell.

MECHANIC, D. (ed.) (1980) *Readings in Medical Sociology.* New York: Free Press.

SCHEFF, T. (ed.) (1975) *Labelling Madness.* Englewood Cliffs, N.J.: Prentice-Hall.

STACEY, M. (ed.) (1976) *Sociology of the National Health Service.* Keele: Keele University Press.

SUSSER, M. W. & WATSON, W. (1971) *Sociology in Medicine,* 2nd ed. London: Oxford University Press.

TUCKETT, D. (ed.) (1976) *Introduction to Medical Sociology.* London: Tavistock.

Index